Terrific Connections

with
Authors, Illustrators, and Storytellers

Terrific Connections

with Authors, Illustrators, and Storytellers

Real Space and Virtual Links

Toni Buzzeo
Jane Kurtz

1999
Libraries Unlimited, Inc.
and Its Division Teacher Ideas Press
Englewood, Colorado

Libraries Unlimited, Inc.
and Its Division
Teacher Ideas Press
P.O. Box 6633
Englewood, CO 80155-6633
1-800-237-6124
www.lu.com/tip

Library of Congress Cataloging-in-Publication Data

Buzzeo, Toni.
    Terrific connections with authors, illustrators, and storytellers : real space and virtual links / by Toni Buzzeo, Jane Kurtz.
        xii, 185 p. 22x28 cm.
        Includes bibliographical references and index.
        ISBN 1-56308-744-8 (paper)
        1. Children's literature--Study and teaching (Elementary)--United States. 2. Authors and readers--United States. 3. Internet (Computer network) in education--United States. I. Kurtz, Jane. II. Title.
    LB1575.5.U5.B87 1999
    372.64'044--dc21   99-28468
                                                                CIP

Contents

Acknowledgments ix
Introduction xi

Part I: Live Connections with Bookpeople 1

Chapter One—Vision of a Successful Visit 3
   The Visit: A Multiple Choice Quiz 3
      Question One: The Day of the Visit 3
      Question Two: Last Minute Time Changes 4
      Question Three: Last Minute Preparations 5
      Question Four: Lunch 6
      Question Five: Last Minute Changes 6
      Question Six: Teacher Involvement 7
      Question Seven: Payment 7
      Scoring the Quiz 8
   An Over-the-Top Visit..9
      Community Preparations 9
      Hospitality..9
      Student Preparation...9
      The Author's Wish List 10
   References...12

Chapter Two—Real-Space Visits with Sizzle 13
   What Ideal Visits Look Like...13
   Working Around Limitations 15
   Heartwarming Stories 19
   When a Whole School Is Involved 20
   The Single Classroom Experience..21
   Isn't a Good Visit a Lot of Work?...22
   The Payoff 23
   Just What's So Special About Bookpeople? 24
      Inspiring Role Models 24
      Dreamers Who Reached Their Goals 25
      Wonderful Performers 25
      People Who Know Fascinating Things 26
   Have Courage—and Plan Carefully 27
   References 28

Chapter Three—Choosing the Right Bookperson 31
   Do You Want Glamour?...31
   Do You Want Someone Who Lives Nearby?...32
   What Size Group Is Ideal?...32
   Do You Have Logistical Limitations?...32
   Is Performance an Important Factor? 33
   How Experienced Is the Bookperson with Children?.................................33
   Other Strengths and Capabilities to Consider...34
      What Are the Ages You Want to Reach? 34

Chapter Three—Choosing the Right Bookperson (*Cont.*)
Fitting in with the School Mission...38
   Emphasizing Certain Themes or Sensitivities 38
   Emphasizing a Topic or Subject Area 39
   Writing Inspiration and Instruction 40
   The Storyteller Visit 43
   The Special Touch of Illustrators 48
References 49

Chapter Four—The Book Connection 51
Reading the Bookperson's Work 51
   Preparing the Students 52
   Frustrations to Avoid 54
   How a Librarian Can Help 55
   Nuts 'n' Bolts for the Visit Organizer 61
Reading Supplemental Books 62
   Preparing the Students 62
   How a Librarian Can Help 64
   Nuts 'n' Bolts for Librarians: Resource Management 67
   Nuts 'n' Bolts for Teachers: Checklists 67
References 67

Chapter Five—Creative Curriculum Connections 69
The Reading Connection 69
The Writing Connection 70
   Imagination Warm-ups 71
   The Writing Process 73
   Writing in Class 74
Other Subject-Area Connections 76
   Science 77
   Math 78
   Social Studies/History/Geography 79
   Art 80
Rererences 83

Chapter Six—Other Opportunities to Meet Bookpeople 87
The Public Library 87
The Young Authors Conference 88
   What a Successful Young Authors Conference Looks Like 88
   Young Authors Conferences Handle Glitches, Too 89
   Where the Bookperson Is Primarily Inspiration 90
   Where the Bookperson Is a Writing Resource 90
   Working with Older Students 92
   Benefits of a Young Authors Conference 93
Piggybacking School Visits with Conferences 93
Piggybacking with Bookstore Appearances 95
And One Last Possibility 97
References 97

Part II: Alternative Connections with Bookpeople 99

Chapter Seven—Mail Connections 101
Personal Mail 101
   Fan Mail 101
   Fan E-Mail 104

Classroom E-Mail 107
    Preparation for a Real-Space Visit 107
    E-Mail in Lieu of a Visit 108
    E-Mail Critiques 110
    E-Mail for Continued Conversation 111
    Ongoing E-Mail 111
Formal E-Mail Programs 113
    Authors Mentoring Authors Online: A Writers Workshop 113
    Once Upon a Computer 117
E-Mail Interviews 118
References 121

Chapter Eight—Real-Time Connections 123
Virtual Visits 123
    Advantages for All 123
    Making Contact with the Bookperson 124
    Virtual Variety: Types of Visits 124
    Caveats 125
Real-Time Chats at Managed Sites 125
    The Random House Children's Author Chat Series 125
    A Girl's World Online Clubhouse 126
The Read In! 127
    Objectives for The Read In! 128
    Student Outcomes and Goals for The Read In! 128
    Activities for The Read In! 129
    The Author Perspective 129
    The Librarian Perspective 130
    The Administrator Perspective 130
References 131

Chapter Nine—Alternate Connections 133
Sources of Contacts on the Web 133
    Lists on the Web 133
    Publisher Sites 135
Author/Illustrator Personal Web Pages 135
    Jane Kurtz 136
    Jackie French Koller 137
    Deborah Hopkinson 137
    Anna Grossnickle Hines 138
    Cynthia Leitich Smith 138
Managed Internet Sites for Author Interaction 140
    Scholastic Network 140
    Houghton Mifflin Education Place 141
    Additional Web Sites 141
Interactive Television Broadcasts 141
    Owen Valley Middle School 141
    Kennedy Center Performing Arts Series 142
    Planet Think 142
References 145

Chapter 10—A Potpourri of Resources and Props 147

    Use the Bookperson's Books Well 147

        Benefits of an Autographing Session 147

        How to Set Up an Autographing Session 148

    Props for Presentations 149

    Author Cards 151

    Curriculum Guides 152

    Realia 155

    Music 157

    Read and Feeds 158

    References 159

    References 161

    Suggested Readings 171

    Bookperson Index 173

    Title Index 175

    Subject Index 179

Acknowledgments

We would like to acknowledge all the wonderful authors, illustrators, storytellers, teachers, and librarians who contributed their accumulated experiences and wisdom to help create this book. Special thanks to Asako Yoshida, University of North Dakota reference librarian, who gave invaluable help with bibliographic references. Extra special thanks to our online writing group, the POD. Finally, we must thank our families for putting up with the hours and hours we spent at our respective computers.

Introduction

When it comes to adding zing to classrooms and libraries, perhaps there is no power like the power possessed by bookpeople. Authors craft the stories that grab our students, the stories that sometimes hug and console young readers, sometimes intrigue or puzzle them, and sometimes shake them inside out. Illustrators draw the pictures that make students giggle and gasp. Authors and illustrators also create the informational books that turn students into wide-eyed investigators, bursting with curiosity, tingling with the thrills of learning. Storytellers weave webs that enmesh children and whisk them off to other realms where they become one with the characters and situations enacted. What resources! Recognizing those resources, schools and libraries all over the country have been exploring ways to tap into their power.

"I encourage my fourth graders to think of themselves as literary scholars," says Monica Edinger, a teacher at The Dalton School in New York, "going deeper into the books they study with my guidance, often learning more about the authors and what other critics have said about the books they are studying. Occasionally, opportunities even present themselves to make the experience more personal." One of Edinger's best opportunities was with Gail Carson Levine, author of *Ella Enchanted*. She began reading the book aloud several weeks before beginning her Cinderella unit in the fall of 1997. Edinger says:

"We were totally enchanted by the cleverness of the writing and by Ella herself, a most wonderful character. As we came to the final chapters my students all cheered at the penultimate scene! I then suggested that we write Gail because of our magical experience with the book, and because I thought that, as a new author, she might quite enjoy a thoughtful letter from a classroom of fans. Indeed she did and wrote back a lovely letter offering to visit when my students had completed their own Cinderella stories. We kept alert to the book's place on many "best of 1997" lists, and when it received the Newbery Honor sent her a handmade congratulations card. Her appearance in our classroom was a very exciting and special event, much anticipated. She was lovely, and the children were thrilled to present their work to her."

Author/illustrator Joanne Stanbridge says that the "coolest" visit she has done so far was to be the guest at a library Mother-Daughter Book Club. Mothers and daughters meet about once a month to discuss a children's book which they've all read. Both times when Jo was the guest, the public librarians had helped choose books in which mother-daughter relationships figured prominently. Stanbridge says:

"What I loved was that it was so informal and so candid. I didn't do a formal presentation, although I had some things prepared, just in case—some biographical things, especially about how I felt when I was a girl and also some pictures of the Prime Minister's Residence and the Dionne Quintuplets, which I passed around as we discussed my novel *The Leftover Kid*. In both cases, the sessions were very interactive. I asked the girls to tell me the things they liked and didn't like about my book, and they did! It was also a great way for me to go fishing for raw material, to find out what kinds of books they liked or hated, what kinds of things interested them, and which things bored or confused them. I noticed that the girls and their mothers tended to equate "liking the book" with "liking the characters," and that was very interesting to me. We didn't talk much about style or craft or what it's like to write a book, but we did talk a lot about the characters, almost as if we were sitting around talking about people we knew. It was warm and funny and sometimes moving. I loved doing it."

During the boom years of children's literature in the 1980s, hundreds and hundreds of talented, funny, earnest, creative new authors joined the ranks of the published. They live in or near to every state, every region, every small community. Though famous authors juggle many demands on their time—too many to accommodate all of them—authors or illustrators who are just beginning their careers are often eager to connect with their readers.

It's such a terrific idea: connecting bookpeople with students. So why the horror stories from the trenches: the silent teachers' lounge where the author eats lunch with nobody saying a word, the conference where the kids lock the visiting author out of the auditorium, the library where someone begins vacuuming during the middle of an illustrator's presentation?

One author laughs ruefully as she tells of getting a batch of letters from students whose assignment was to "tell the author what you liked and what you didn't like about her books." It led to letters like this: "I loved your book. I couldn't put it down. I had to find out what happened next. I read it in two days the first time, then in one day straight through the second time. Now I'm reading it for the third time." Then the next paragraph said something like, "I think what your book needs is more action."

An author who read at her local library for "Read Across America" says, "My part was terribly attended, plus there was no librarian present to help with kid control and there were some unruly kids. The librarians were manning the desk, and helping patrons, and I was on my own with eight kids, two of whom were screaming and interrupting and who had parents right there, doing nothing."

An author/illustrator tells of a recent school visit during which the children seemed oddly passive during his very animated—and funny—presentation. When he mentioned the unusual reaction to the teacher as he prepared for his next session, she said, "I guess we forgot to mention they don't speak English."

A fourth author tells of a visit to a classroom in which, as things turned out, a dance class was scheduled for the same time as the author. The author sat quietly and watched the dances for an hour.

Finally, an author tells of three days in a school where, when she finished, the librarian said, "Oh, by the way, we found out we can't pay you, so here is a bag of cookies to show our appreciation."

We hope you are shaking your head no . . . no, that would never be my school or library. But even when a bookperson connection is far from a disaster, it can still fall short of the joyous celebration of reading and writing it could have been. Here, we bring you the success stories of the schools and book creators who have turned connections into a high art and whose efforts can inspire your own creative thinking.

As Monica Edinger's story helps to illustrate, in these days of phone, fax, Web surfing, and E-mail, a school doesn't even have to bring an author or illustrator onto the premises in order to make a wonderful connection. There is a "virtual world" that we all inhabit in our electronic age!

Many authors and illustrators have personal Web pages with hot links that allow readers to write personal fan mail or ask questions. We'll show you here how to locate the Web pages of authors and illustrators you'd like to contact.

Additionally, many children's authors and illustrators are willing to engage in a variety of custom-designed E-mail projects. Washington State author Mary Whittington tells of being in touch with third graders at Campbell Hall, the parochial school she attended as a child in the mid-1950s. In lieu of a live visit, which would have been too costly for the librarian who contacted her, Whittington offered to make a videotape and communicate via E-mail with any students who wanted to ask questions. Student questions have ranged from "How did you come up with your books?" to "Do you know my dad?"

Publishers are also providing virtual access to their authors more and more often. Authors and illustrators are engaged in real-time chats and teaching writing on the Internet through services such as Scholastic Network and are visiting thousands of students at once through classroom interactive television sponsored by companies such as Planet Think: The Interactive Learning Network.

Even children's specialty online booksellers are providing access to children's authors. For example, using a bulletin-board approach, online bookstores allowed customers to post questions to children's author Kathleen Duey. She then was able to respond to the questions in batches. Duey found this approach to be very simple and uninhibiting for herself and her fans. Amazon.com, the world's largest online bookstore, posts interviews with any author who wishes to participate. In addition, there are hot links to the authors' E-mail and sometimes to their homepages.

Never before have children's bookpeople been so easily accessed by libraries and schools. Whether in person, by E-mail, in live electronic chatrooms, or through interactive television, children's authors and children are finding each other every day, enriching each other's lives.

Part I

Live Connections with Bookpeople

Every author, illustrator, or storyteller who has gone on the road knows how exhausting visits can be—how they take away from creative work time and family time. Every public librarian, library media specialist, or teacher who has ever organized a day with a bookperson knows the hours that go into every single visit.

But then there are the results. "It must be really fun to be an author," a second grade student wrote after a visit from Jane. "I wish I could stay in school forever. I can't wait intell we're in third grade becos your new books are coming out." On another visit, a student slipped Jane a note that said, "Please, I want to remember you forever."

Alas, not every visit is material that can be stitched up into forever memories. A visit could even end up as one of the horror stories recounted in chapter 1. Why spend precious money and time, Jane and Toni want to know, and not make the experience a special one? Why can't every bookperson visit be as exciting a reading and writing celebration as this end-of-the-year experience described by author Kay Winters:

"What an experience! On the first day of school, the principal had pledged that if the students read more than a million minutes during the year, he would wear a gorilla suit and spend part of the day on the roof. A fire truck drove up with the principal in his ape suit. The ladder went up; he climbed to the rooftop while the sixth grade trumpet band played 'Hail to the Chief.' Then he gave a pep talk about reading. They had 'Drop Everything and Read' and then I did an assembly. The excitement was tremendous."

All right: some administrators will not go for the gorilla suit, but every visit can be a celebration and a success. Part I of our book illustrates how the best ones blossom.

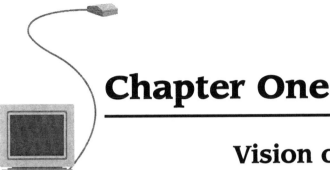

Chapter One

Vision of a Successful Visit

Imagine that your school is hosting a schoolwide author visit. Someone contacted the author well in advance and agreed to a date, a fee, and a schedule. You and your students are anxious for the opportunity to meet the author in person. The winter morning dawns sunny and bright. No weather problems will interfere. This day should proceed entirely as planned!

THE VISIT: A MULTIPLE CHOICE QUIZ

Question One: The Day of the Visit

As you approach your school building this January morning, you notice a banner over the main entrance that reads: "Welcome Children's Author." Your response is,

A. "This is it! Our author bulletin board is complete, the kids have prepared their questions, and their illustrated version of the author's upcoming book is ready to present to her during the session."

B. "Great! My students feel so connected to this author's books."

C. "Oops. Have I read all of the author's books to my students?"

D. "What author?"

 Option B

"I visited a private school and spoke to three groups of fourth and fifth graders. Their teachers had read parts of my books to them and had them think of questions. They were delightful, and I had a wonderful time with them. It was the best school visit I have ever had."

—Children's author

Option D

"Imagine showing up at a school, entering the office, and signing in, then informing the secretary who you are, only to be greeted with, 'So?'

" 'I'm here to do an assembly at your school.'

" 'Well, no one said anything to *me* about it.' At which point she goes back to doing whatever she was doing before. I try mentioning the name of the contact person, saying so-and-so made the arrangements, and the secretary fairly scoffs, 'Oh . . . that explains it.' "

—Storyteller

Question Two: Last Minute Time Changes

As you walk down the corridor, loaded with two heavy tote bags and a slipping shoulder bag, a colleague greets you. "Change in plans. The public library insists that the only time this week we can bring the kids over to do that research project is today. Ten o'clock. I'll send Judy [the library media specialist] a note to meet both of our classes at the front door."

You are thinking about how this will change the shape of the day. If you go to the public library, you'll need to reschedule your time with the author, so you,

A. call the public librarian and cancel the research visit;

B. find Judy, your school library media specialist, and discuss the appropriate group to swap with;

C. talk to your best friend, a kindergarten teacher, and decide to have your class listen to the author with the kindergarten group;

D. rush up to the classroom and jot yourself a note, which gets misplaced.

 Option B (gone awry)

"I arranged for an author to visit our public library. I contacted one of the local teachers, made sure she had extra copies of the books for her class, 'talked up' the visit, and checked back to see that the kids were being prepared. The talk was to include overheads of rough drafts from the books, props, and lots of interaction with the kids, and *I* could hardly wait to hear it.

"But when the class arrived, I didn't recognize the teacher. I said, 'Oh, are you substituting for Ms. X?'

"She said, 'No, Ms. X's class had to go down to the gym for flu shots, so she sent us instead.'

"It wasn't a substitute *teacher*. It was a substitute *class*! And they didn't even know why they were at the library. They spent the whole presentation talking and wriggling—they were only silent when the author asked them a question, and in *those* moments the place sounded like a chapel."

—Children's librarian

Option C

"I annually make an author visit to a school . . . on their district's Author for a Day program. I said I would do four classes, preferably fourth and fifth grades. . . . By phone, three weeks before the presentation, they mentioned they might also wish [to have] me for kindergarten. I said, 'Sure; however, please let me know in advance so that I can bring appropriate materials.' No word.

"Upon my arrival, they had assigned six classes—including kindergarten. . . . Since my presentations do not include slides and involve me interacting greatly with the students and walking around the room, and since kindergarten is not the most calm of classes (and I usually sit on the floor with them), and since I had brought materials more suited to the upper grades, and since it was the last presentation of the day, it was not an experience I wish to repeat!"

—Children's author

Question Three: Last Minute Preparations

The bell rings and your students rush into the classroom in their happy confusion. After you take attendance, you use reading time—the first morning block—to prepare your kids for their visit with the author. In this final preparation you

A. help them put finishing touches on their fish-print T-shirts and fish necklaces, a tie-in to the author's catfish tall tale;

B. complete the matrix you've been working on that compares the author's version of a Peruvian folktale with versions from other countries;

C. check to see whether the teacher next door has any of the five remaining books you still haven't read to your class;

D. tell the kids that there is an author visiting today, though you can't recall her name or any of her titles.

 Option C

"The issue of teacher preparation is also one of great interest to me. Often, when one travels from class to class, one sees how good the teacher really is by the extent to which [that teacher] prepares the class for an author visit. Otherwise, what is the point of having me or other authors paid to do this? Without the preparation (knowing about the books, the author, and how it can relate to the subject matter studied by the class), the visit loses much of its value."

—Children's author

 Option D

"I've had a couple [of school visits] where the only good thing that could've come out of them would have been for Scotty to beam me right up."

—Children's author

Question Four: Lunch

As your class finishes their research session at the public library, you promise the library media specialist, who is staying behind to plan Thursday's session with the public librarian, that you will hook up with the author back at school. You drop your kids off with the lunch aide and then rush down to the library media center to

A. pick up the author for a walk to a lovely nearby deli where you and the library media specialist will treat her to lunch;

B. join your colleagues in a potluck lunch with the author;

C. chat, skipping lunch and wondering if the author is doing the same;

D. forget the author in your rush to handle an emergency.

 Option C (with a twist)

"I remember a lunchroom that had a huge Welcome Children's Author banner, but I sat there in almost total silence for a 30-minute break while the teachers chatted with each other and completely ignored me."

—Children's author

 Option D

"The librarian was out of the building when I'd been told she'd be my guide. . . . 'You're on your own'; thus the old 'Where is the bathroom?' 'Where is the lunch room?' 'Where is this next room where I'm speaking?' routine. And no one had thought about my lunch."

—Children's author

Question Five: Last Minute Changes

At the end of the lunch hour, you are still puzzled about when your kids will visit with the author. In order to resolve this problem, you

A. double-check with the library media specialist about the time slot you traded for;

B. ask the author whether she will be comfortable having a larger group during her last session of the day;

C. join the afternoon kindergarten session halfway through;

D. march your kids down to the library media center after the last session is complete and demand an extra session for your class, as it wasn't your fault they missed their original session in the first place.

 Option C

"I always specify a reading for grades five and six, and another for grades seven and eight but have often arrived to a full gym that also contains 'our grades two, three, and four who are very bright.'"

—Children's author

Option D

"One time I went to a school that created a schedule where I visited every classroom [16] for a talk and no time in between, nor any time for lunch. I was *very* new then and didn't specify number of talks or anything."

—Children's author

Question Six: Teacher Involvement

You've finally settled on a time for your class to visit with the author. The kids are excited, and you are looking forward to the session yourself. When you arrive in the library with your class, you

    A. join them on the floor, or in a nearby chair, to share their experience;

    B. find them a place near the front and sit off to the side with students who will need extra supervision;

    C. send your class down ahead of you and then join the other teachers to chat and correct papers in the back of the room;

    D. drop your kids off at the door and head down to the teachers' lounge—you haven't had a break all day!

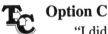 **Option C**

"I did a reading last week where the teacher did stay in the library but leafed through a magazine throughout my talk while occasionally raising her head and saying, 'Up front. Be quiet and pay attention.' Monkey see, monkey do?"

—Children's author

 Option D

"How about the school system that got a Title I grant, brought me in for three days, and used me as a babysitter. I walked into class—the teachers walked out. That stint included one classroom with three eighth grades stuffed into it (kids were actually making out in the back of the room), a room where the teacher (on the way out the door) introduced me as 'the story-teller,' and a first-grade ESL class made up entirely of Cambodian kids who didn't understand English. . . . Needless to say, those three days taught me a lot about booking school visits."

—Children's author

Question Seven: Payment

You've dismissed your kids and handled the last homework questions of the day. Before you leave, you head down to the library to

    A. present the author with a check from the PTA, help pack up her materials, and take her to a friend's house for tea, cookies, and relaxation before her author signing;

    B. present her with the check from the PTA and offer last-minute assistance in carrying her bags and presentation materials out to her car;

C. tell the author that the district needs her to fill out a form before payment can be issued and give her directions to the central office;

D. say, "Oh, by the way, we found out we can't pay you for today, but we'd like to thank you for your generosity."

 Option C

"They ask me is there anything I need. 'Did you read the material I sent you?'

" 'What material?'

" 'I send out a checklist to help you have things ready before I get here.'

" 'Oh, I never got anything.'

" 'Did you get the invoice?'

" 'Yes, we got that.'

" 'Is the payment ready today as the invoice requests?'

" 'No, the district needs you to fill out a form before payment can be issued.'

" 'That is why we send out the invoice in plenty of time.' "

—Storyteller

 Option D

"After three days I spent in one school, the librarian said, 'Oh, by the way, we found out we can't pay you, so here is a bag of cookies to show our appreciation.' "

—Children's author

Scoring the Quiz

By now you have realized that the first option is always the best, with the second option a close runner-up. The third option is barely adequate, and the fourth—well, even if we were to answer candidly, it is a rare teacher who would have circled the fourth option seven times. Most of us don't fall into the "awful" category as we prepare for an author visit. However, we can all benefit from learning how to move beyond "fine" into the top two categories, "super" and "over the top."

 Successful Storyteller Visit

"My favorite school visits are ones in which the staff and kids have read my books and have immersed themselves in the dreamworld of the book. Now we have an ocean we can all swim in. When you have read the same book, you have shared the same dream. Good starting place."

—Robin Moore, storyteller

Successful Author Visit

"I love going to schools where the kids are familiar with my books, where they're engaged in their own writing projects, where the teachers are excited about reading and writing and participate in the questions and answers, where the principal is an active participant in the whole process, where the parents are invited to attend my sessions—those school visits help get my own 'writing motor' revved up. They remind me about why I write for kids. They keep me honest. They inspire me, and I hope, inspire the kids too!"

—Kathi Appelt, children's author

AN OVER-THE-TOP VISIT

The school day that proceeds as planned is a rarity. Add to the many complications of a normal school day the visit of an author, illustrator, or storyteller, and the chances for complications to arise increase tenfold. However, with careful planning and a schoolwide commitment to making the visit top priority, no matter what else might unfold, a bookperson visit can look like the following.

Community Preparations

Parents and other community members have been working behind the scenes for weeks, gathering classroom art to decorate the walls of the library, creating life-size papier-mâché models with classes of students, and teaching pen-and-ink drawing to students who will wash their drawings with watercolors. Members of the library committee have prepared an author flyer to introduce each family to the visitor and her work. A group is planning the table covering and display designs for the author signing. Others make runs to the public library and its branches to borrow multiple copies of the books needed to enhance the school's collection.

The school building is vibrant with evidence of these advance preparations. Painted banners hang on display. Three-dimensional structures stand in hallways. Bulletin boards sport two- and three-dimensional student artwork. Cameras are on hand; multiple copies of books speed between classrooms. Videos that will increase student understanding of topics covered in the author's books make their final rounds; student gifts for the visitor wait in classrooms. Like a December family holiday, this day has been the focus of effort, attention, and mounting excitement for weeks throughout the school community. Finally, when the visitor walks through the door, the celebration begins.

Hospitality

The visitor is met by a single person (often the library media specialist) who is assigned to the bookperson for the entire day. The library media specialist carries in the bookperson's presentation materials, introduces her to the office staff and principal, shows her where the restroom is, finds a safe place for her to stow her personal belongings, and goes over the schedule with the visitor one final time.

The visitor's needs come first. She is given frequent and leisurely breaks between sessions, her water cup is always kept full, and her presentation materials and equipment are reorganized for her between sessions. She is treated to a relaxing lunch, either at school or at a nearby restaurant. She is paid in full on the day of her visit.

Student Preparation

All of the students who meet with the bookperson are familiar with her background and her work. They have read, or heard read to them, each of her titles; have read or heard books related to hers in a variety of ways; and have engaged in art, writing, and content-area projects to extend their understanding of her work. They come to the sessions with questions to ask and excitement to learn more from the visitor's experiences and knowledge. Teachers are as excited and eager as their students, having spent many weeks focusing on the approaching event.

Every visit can and should be this successful and rewarding for you, for your patrons or students, and for the bookperson who is visiting. (For an inside view of what bookpeople want during a visit, see **The Author's Wish List**, below.) As we said in the introduction, when it comes to adding zing to libraries, schools, classrooms, and curriculum, bookpeople have it all.

The Author's Wish List

Compiled by The POD, an online group of children's writers

☑ Scheduling

- Contact the author to *confirm* the author visit!

- Never ask the author to do additional sessions after details of the visit have been agreed upon.

- If the author has 15 minutes between sessions, do not let students use that time to get their books signed. The author *needs* those 15 minutes to catch his or her breath, race to the restroom, get a drink, and sit down for a minute. Speaking to large groups of kids demands high energy, and the author can't do it nonstop without a break.

- If you expect an author to do extra things, such as "read something to the entire student body" or "tell us how reading has changed your life," *tell* her or him before the visit so that she or he can be prepared.

☑ Preparing the Students

- Students must be familiar with the author's books. If possible, prepare students by reading all of the author's work with or to them. Otherwise, select several books to share, beginning well in advance of the visit.

- The best school visits occur when preparations infuse the curriculum. Read Toni's article, "The Finely Tuned Author Visit," in *Book Links* for ideas.

☑ Physical Arrangements

- Prepare to introduce the author in a fun and lively way. The librarian or teacher who does this job is basically the warm-up band to get the kids fired up.

- If the author is speaking in a large room—such as an auditorium or gym—you *must* provide a microphone for the students' questions. It's impossible to hear students unless they are in the first few rows. (An alternative to a student microphone is to provide the author with a lapel mike and room to move to the person who is speaking.)

- If possible, have the students wear name tags. It is a tremendous help to the author both during the presentation and while signing.

- Do not leave students alone with the visiting author. Authors are not hired to be babysitters. Likewise, if a teacher or librarian sees students disrupting, he or she should not be afraid to interrupt the session to remedy the situation. It is not the author's job to teach manners.

☑ Creature Comforts

- Provide someone, either an adult or an older student, to act as the author's host for the day. The host should greet the author, make introductions to teachers and staff, and guide the author from place to place.

- Provide ongoing hot tea with lemon or cold water for the author's voice.

- Make time for a midmorning snack and for restroom breaks.

- Allow enough time to get from one class to the next.

- Plan for a real lunch rather than cafeteria food.

- Don't plan evening activities that run late if the author is visiting your schools for a week. The author needs the evening to rest and regroup for the next day.

☑ Book Sales and Signings

- Do not assume that an author will bring books to sell at a school visit. Many authors do not sell their own books and feel very uncomfortable being put into the position of doing so. Check with the author in advance.

- If the author does not sell her or his own books, order books on the day the author confirms. You can never order books too early. The biggest mistake schools make is waiting too long to order.

- Double-check with booksellers or jobbers providing books to be sure that all titles are available.

- Provide a reasonably comfortable *adult-size* chair and table for the signing.

- Do not allow students to ask the author to sign slips of paper or body parts. Most authors will provide signed bookmarks—or provide a master sheet so the school can make them. That way, each child can take home something signed by the author whether the child buys a book.

- If it's a young authors conference and the students have written their own books, let them know that the author cannot sign hundreds of their books as well as her or his own.

- Schedule an hour or more during which the author is in the library without a group. During this time, each class in turn can send students with books to sign. This gives the students the opportunity to visit with the author while their books are being signed, and it solves the problem of too many restless kids waiting for their turn.

- Provide an adult to help at the signing table. It's hard for the author to keep an eye on all the visual aids brought while the kids are picking them up and looking at them unattended.

- There will always be students who want to buy books after the author's visit. Most authors will leave a few signed bookplates for that purpose, so make sure books are still available for sale after the event.

☑ Payment

- Pay the author's stated fee and do not try to negotiate a lesser fee. Author visits are exhausting and the fee is well earned.

- If you need the author's social security number or an invoice before a school-district-issued check can be processed, tell the author in advance so that the check can be ready the day of the visit.

- Don't make the author ask to be paid. This is awkward. Know that the author expects to be paid at the end of the day. There is nothing worse for the author than having to say, "Um, well, do you have my check?"

☑ Accommodations and Transportation

- It is generally not a good idea to ask an author to stay in a private home. Many authors find it impossible to relax in someone else's home. They often feel they must be entertaining when they'd really rather not talk to anyone after talking all day. However, it is appropriate to verify that this is the author's preference.

- If you have arranged for someone to pick up the author, be sure the driver arrives on time. The author will need time to catch his or her breath and set up materials before beginning presentations for the day.

- Provide someone to transport the author, when necessary, between morning and afternoon schools so that she or he arrives on time.

 # REFERENCES

Buzzeo, Toni. "The Finely Tuned Author Visit." *Book Links* 7 (March 1998): 10–15.

Chapter Two

Real-Space Visits with Sizzle

In the summer of 1998, the staff at *Parade* magazine asked Pulitzer Prize-winning historian Daniel J. Boorstin, "What binds us together as a nation?" To their surprise, he answered that it was the "unrelenting quest for knowledge and learning and a passion for books and reading." In the July 12 issue of the magazine, Boorstin then wrote, "We are a nation of readers, and our freedom to read and enthusiasm for reading keep our nation alive and thriving."

As many schools and libraries can attest, few things have more power to stir a passion for books than a chance to connect with a person who is passionate about stories and who has chosen to dedicate a big chunk of life to that passion. Some schools also know that story passion can begin bubbling long before the bookperson appears on the scene through teachers and librarians, parents and principals, enthusiastic readings and creative projects.

WHAT IDEAL VISITS LOOK LIKE

Author Roland Smith describes what a visit is like to such a school. "Banners inside and outside. Hallways turned into rain forests. Dioramas and pictures illustrating scenes from my books. Songs (this was really great). Letters. E-mail. I could go on and on—and I can't tell you how much I appreciate their efforts. I know it's a lot of work."

Author Spotlight: Roland Smith

Before becoming a full-time writer, Roland held a number of other fascinating jobs, including senior zoo keeper, curator of mammals and birds, and senior research biologist. Drawing on his experiences, he talks to school children about things such as what goes on behind the scenes at a zoo, about being part of "heroic efforts" to save the sea otters of Alaska's Prince William Sound during the *Exxon Valdez* oil spill, and about his work to help save the red wolf from extinction. He has appeared on national and local television shows such as *National Geographic*, *Audubon*, and *Discover the World of Science* and has been the photographer for several of his own books. Though known best for his nonfiction books, including *Sea Otter Rescue* and *In the Forest with Elephants*, he has also written a dramatic novel set in Kenya, *Thunder Cave*.

Mary Casanova, author of middle-grade novels *Moose Tracks*, *Riot*, and *Wolf Shadows*, notes that "When teachers treat the event as important, kids catch the fever." She describes one tiny school in North Dakota where she was "overwhelmed by their extra efforts. I was met at the door with brightly colored balloons. Hallways were painted with 'moose tracks' toward my presentation room. Students carried picket signs supporting my books (related to the labor dispute in *Riot*). Classroom doors sported reports on moose and wolves. At lunch, flowers graced the staff table, where specialty sandwiches were ordered in. At day's end, as kids headed to their yellow buses, I left smiling; my faith in the importance of books, kids, and reading [was] renewed."

Mary has also had exciting experiences in public libraries, including the one in Grand Marais, Minnesota. "It was well advertised. The librarians put a release in the paper, put flyers up around town and at the library, and planned far enough in advance to get the word out, at least a few months ahead of the event, and the library filled an auditorium (or nearly) on a beautiful summer evening. I signed books afterward. A delightful experience on the shores of Lake Superior."

In International Falls, Minnesota, Mary presented to a small group of adults and kids and signed books, giving the proceeds for a local presentation to the Friends of the Library. "When bringing in an author," she says, "libraries really boost the interest in books by making it a local celebration. For instance, as I wandered around the small towns that had hosted me, I had kids and adults stop me and say, 'Aren't you the author?' Seriously! I knew then that someone had done a good job getting a photo out to the newspaper, and I knew the presentation would be well worth my time."

Author Spotlight: Mary Casanova

Mary lives with her husband and two children on the "fringe of civilization" at the Minnesota-Canada border, where wolves howl through subzero nights, bears roam the streets, and northern lights—like ribbon candy—fill the summer skies.

One of 10 children, Mary grew up with a love of the outdoors but found reading difficult. Not until high school did she discover "the power of words" and her dream of writing. Now she tries to write for the child she was: the restless, energetic, adventure-seeking, can't-sit-still kind. Her books have helped turn many reluctant readers into readers and continue to be nominated for children's book awards around the country. Always weaving in her love of nature, Mary writes stories that matter and that kids can't put down. To learn more about Mary, check her Web site at http://www.marycasanova.com.

Author Lee Wardlaw stepped up to one school to discover that each child had been given chalk and assigned to a square of sidewalk in front of the school to do a chalk painting of a favorite Lee Wardlaw book. No sooner had she absorbed this display—hundreds of pictures—than students literally rolled out a red carpet for her. At the door, a representative from each class was waiting to shake her hand. A banner over their heads said "Welcome, Author Lee Wardlaw." Inside, a huge bulletin board was covered with Lee's book covers, photo, bio, and other displays.

At lunch, Lee says, she was joined by 10 students, in grades three through six, for sandwiches and pop. "The students had 'won' the honor of dining with me by writing an essay entitled, 'Why I Want to Have Lunch with Lee Wardlaw, the Author.' The principal said 200 kids wrote one-page essays, and she read them all! She and the librarian chose the best ones, and those were the kids who got to watch me dribble mustard down my front!" After school, one classroom was transformed into a "living museum," and parents could visit the room to see students dressed as characters from Lee's books. "The characters stood there frozen until the parents pressed a 'button.' Then [the characters] would come to life for five minutes or so, talking about who they were and what their story was. Really cool!" Lee adds that although she has had other wonderful visits, this school pulled out "all stops" in creating a literary festival around her visit.

Storyteller and author Robin Moore has presented about 5,000 school programs over the last 17 years. "Both kids and teachers," he says, "have come up with some incredibly creative ways of making my books come alive." He notes that in his best visits, students seem to feel something he sometimes feels, too—that the characters in his books are real people. Such visits remind him that the imagination can do an astonishing thing: "From a few ink marks on a page" an author can create "a living thing that was not there before." In preparation for Robin's visits, some students have written sequels or put on plays or dressed up like the characters to surprise him. "The artwork they do is always astonishing to me," he says.

WORKING AROUND LIMITATIONS

Certainly some schools have it easier than others when it comes to arranging for a bookperson visit. Yet schools have successfully worked with geographic isolation and uninterested principals; even the most plaintive and common wail of all, "we have no money," has not been a barrier to successful visits. Some schools have combined with other schools to "split" a bookperson. Some schools have funded visits through book sales (see chapter 10 for more details about book sales). Others have just approached the right author.

The Maine Chapter of the Multiple Sclerosis Society sponsors an annual read-a-thon for children and schools throughout the state. Author Maria Testa became involved through a friend with MS and became something of an "author organizer," lining up friends and colleagues who would be willing to donate their books and time to the cause. Children were rewarded based on the number of books they had read. There was a prize list for the children to choose from. Among the higher ranking prizes were autographed books by Maine authors, with books donated by publishers. Schools were rewarded based on the amount of money their students had raised through pledges. The top prizes were visits from Maine authors (who often personally donated a copy or copies of their books to the school library). Maria reports that she and fellow author Jennifer Richard Jacobson had an amazing experience traveling to an under-funded but highly enthusiastic public elementary school in Millinocket (a small mill town in northeastern Maine) and to a small, underfunded Catholic school in Bangor (a small city in central Maine and Stephen King's hometown). "These were two of the most rewarding author visits in my experience," Maria said. "I think the kids had a feeling of having *earned* the visit and that made it more special. And of course the kids were virtually all great, eager readers—the nature of the contest resulted in the winners being a pretty self-selecting group."

 Author Spotlight: Maria Testa

Maria Testa graduated from Yale Law School in 1989, and, after a couple of emotionally-charged and challenging internships, she thought about practicing law. It didn't last. Seconds later she left her home state of Rhode Island and expatriated to Dublin, Ireland, where she lived at the YWCA, consorted with all sorts of artists and other strangers, and decided she just might want to be a writer.

Maria now lives in Portland, Maine, with her husband and two sons. She has successfully avoided being a lawyer and will now only identify herself as such when pressed, or when it is convenient. She is a writer. Her children's books are *Dancing Pink Flamingos and Other Stories* (an ALA Best Book for Young Adults), *Someplace to Go*, *Nine Candles* (an IRA/CBC Children's Choice), and *Thumbs Up, Rico!*

Author Patricia Curtis Pfitsch talks about a "heartwarming" experience she had when a teacher from a very small elementary school about three hours from Patricia's house called. She had seen an article about Patricia's first novel, *Keeper of the Light*, and was wondering about her making a school visit. The problem was that the school was very poor—all they could manage for compensation was substitute teacher's pay, mileage, and school lunch, but the kids in her school had never met an author before.

"Being from a small, poor school district, myself," Patricia says, "I couldn't say no, so I said yes, and it was absolutely the best visit I'd ever had. The school was run-down—I had to use my own projector (a relic from my grandfather) for the slides, and the school lunch was . . . well, it was school lunch—except for the delicious chocolate cake one teacher had baked for the occasion! But every teacher had read the book to their class, so every kid knew the story. They'd drawn pictures, done lighthouse-related activities in all their subjects—math, science, all of them. A woman from the little weekly paper was there to interview me for an article. (This brought back memories—that's how I got my start, and this woman's dream was to write fiction, too.) Parents were there helping out with the kids and listening to my talk. The kids, because they had read the book, asked the kinds of specific questions that I had always wanted to answer about the book—Why did you do this? Why did that happen? Everyone who could afford to bought a book, and I had a great signing after the talks. I really felt like I'd won the Newbery with all the attention and respect they gave me."

 ## How to Find the Right Bookperson for You

It's definitely worth the effort to try to make a good match with a bookperson because disappointment can occur on either side during a visit.

Jane says, "Schools have contacted me after they saw articles about me or read one of my book review columns in the local paper, after someone heard me speak at a conference, or after they heard about me from another school where I spoke. Sometimes I initiate the contact because a fellow author says she's had a great visit at a certain school or because I want to speak in a specific place. For instance, I asked my older sister who was living in Kenya to speak to the librarian at her sons' school, and that's how I ended up there in March, 1999. I've 'rustled up' school visits in and around Portland, Oregon since my parents and most of my siblings live there. Other times, I've felt so connected to a teacher or librarian through E-mail conversations that I've asked about an in-person visit."

Toni adds, "I always tell people in my workshops that the 'official' way to book authors is to call the publisher. I tell them that if they want a bookperson whom they aren't able to contact in some other way, to do that, or if they want 'someone' but not a specific person, then a publisher can sometimes be helpful, but I prefer to find my own people." Toni locates people through:

- recommendations from other professionals (in fact, a database of recommended bookpeople is being started on the MASL—Maine Association of School Libraries—Web page;

- personal contact (a friend, an acquaintance, or speaker from a conference); and

- Web contact, including SCBWI, CANSCAIP, and a number of other places (see "Sources of Contact on the Web" in chapter 9).

A fair amount of serendipity is also involved in how any bookperson ends up at a particular school. The following examples from Linda Sherouse, a library media specialist from New Hampshire, illustrate this point.

- Linda met Joy Dueland through a bookstore contact.

- She met Jim Arnosky at a Keene State College Literature Festival, in Keene, New Hampshire, where Linda's daughter, Laura "made a hit with him." Linda called one of Jim's publishers and they said she should send them a letter and the process would take some time. " I didn't have time," Linda says, "so I used information and found his home phone number. He did remember Laura and was happy to come."

- Michelle Dionetti sent information in the mail and Linda contacted her by phone.

- Linda met Gail Gibbons at a meeting and, while having a book signed, Linda asked if Gail spoke at schools. Gail was booked for that year but said she would consider a long engagement the following year. Linda used a network of local contacts to find other schools where Gail could speak.

- Cynthia DeFelice was a college friend of a local couple, and they proposed her visit to Linda and offered to feed and house Cynthia.

- Linda met Erick Ingraham at the University of Southern Maine, Gorham campus, during their summer "In Celebration of Children's Literature Conference," organized by Professor Joyce Martin. When Linda asked Erick's speaking fee, it was exactly the amount she knew she had available.

- For Lois Lowry, Linda had to send a letter to Lowry's publisher after five phone calls to find out how the publisher wanted the contact handled. When she did finally get in touch with Lois, the author felt bad about the delay and offered Linda any date in the 1998–99 school year.

- Maryjane Begin-Callanan graduated from a nearby high school and remained friends with the art teacher there. Linda says, "My 'in' with her was that we once lived on the same circle in Hampton, and she babysat my children, so one of the evenings she was here, I took her out to dinner with my daughters, now grown."

- Finally, when all Linda's plans for speakers one year were falling through, her new assistant principal from Michigan just happened to hand her the book *Proud to Be Me, Pewee Platypus* by Lisa Anderson. When Linda noticed it was autographed, she asked what kind of speaker Lisa was.

As many bookpeople can attest, even the worst school visits often have an amazing energy to them. Author Bill Crider recalls one time when he was asked to speak at an elementary school and he asked who would be at the talk. "Everyone who has something in our literary magazine," he was told. "I figured," Bill says, "maybe 25 kids. When I got to the school, I discovered that everyone in the entire school except for maybe some kid who was absent all year had something in the literary magazine. Four hundred kids? At least. Had any of them read my books? Of course not. And where was I going to talk to them? In the outdoor gym. The one without any walls. It did have a roof, however. I had one of those little mikes with an amplifier that looked like the one my kid got with his first Sears Roebuck guitar. At the beginning of my talk, a bird flew under the roof and buzzed the crowd. It got a good laugh. . . . Amazingly enough, the whole thing went pretty well."

Author Spotlight: Bill Crider

Bill Crider was abandoned in a wilderness area at birth and raised by a band of musical chipmunks. He taught himself to read and speak English by reading old paperback Tarzan novels that tourists tossed away. The chipmunks left the wilderness for a recording career and paid for Bill's education with their royalties. Their only request was that he move to a town named for their harmonica player, which explains why Bill lives in Alvin, Texas. In his spare time he writes mystery, horror, and western novels for adults plus books for younger readers, all in the hope that someone, being raised somewhere by chipmunks, will read his discarded books and learn to read and speak English. In that way, Bill feels that he will be repaying at least a tiny bit of the debt that he owes to the writers who came before him. Bill owns thousands (and thousands) of old paperback books, and he is married to the lovely Judy, without whom he would be nothing (at least to hear her tell it).

Illustrator Cathryn Falwell says, "I've learned to carry a 'first-aid kit'—tape, clips, and even a flashlight! Last year, the school I visited had a power failure in the middle of my program. I was in a windowless library with only a dim auxiliary light, but the students wanted to continue. So, with the dim light and two candles, we finished quite successfully."

Practice Makes Perfect?

The author who was asked to read in her local library for Read Across America Day in March knew there might be problems from the moment she arrived, when the library staff said, "We hope people show up. We just never know with events like these."

"Every couple of hours," she says, "they had a pair of readers. I (local author) was paired with the president of the County Commissioners. They asked prominent people to read—in order to draw a crowd—and people who loved reading, especially children. The president read what had been his favorite book to read to his children, and he was *good*! He liked the exposure even though the crowd was pitiful (but bigger for him than for me. . . . they dispersed as he finished).

"Their biggest mistake, with me anyway, was leaving me alone. It was intentional; they hadn't planned to have someone with me (or anybody). . . . but they needed that. Speakers aren't necessarily good at crowd control. I know I'm not. For example, once, when I was doing a workshop in my daughter's third-grade class, the teacher left the room for a minute, and I immediately felt the class slip away from me. It's uncanny how that authority figure makes a difference, and they needed more library aides or staff for this sort of event. The librarians were perfectly nice, and they appreciated my coming in, but two rowdy kids needed to be removed from the group.

"They had me scheduled at something like 2:30, which is nap time for toddlers and is before school lets out for older kids. That contributed to our sparse crowd. It was comical. As soon as we were done and I had visited some and then walked out the door, coming in the main doors was a huge wad of after-school kids coming to the library. I *would* have had the potential big audience if they'd scheduled me a half an hour later, or, since they knew what I was reading, they could have plugged me in during the morning when the moms and strollers and toddlers were there. I don't think they should have had anyone midday. . . . but they were trying to keep reading going all day long in the library. That was the purpose of the Read Across America, and I know I was not one of their brighter literary lights.

"It was not fun, but it was good practice for me."

HEARTWARMING STORIES

If a school visit can go well under the worst of circumstances, imagine the best. For instance, Dian Curtis Regan says that after her book, *Liver Cookies* was published in 1991, "One school had the kids do their own 'love/hate' poll similar to the one in the book to find out what food people love and what food they hate, then figure out a way to combine them. One child who never responded to *anything* really got into it, and had his first ever conversation with the librarian. Everyone fussed over the 'new food' he'd invented and illustrated, and the teachers were blown away that, for some reason, this child responded to this project when he'd never been interested in anything before."

Author Linda Crotta Brennan tells a similar story. "I was in a fifth-grade classroom, doing my usual spiel, talking about how to plan a story, and as usual, I was shooting out questions and getting lots of input from the kids. One young boy, who sat off to the side, raised his hand and gave me a marvelous description of his potential character, a shark who had quite a personality.

"In the teacher's room his special education teacher pulled me aside. She told me that was the first time in all his years at school that he had ever raised his hand in class and spoke in front of other students. . . . I can't describe the feeling that gave me. Obviously, I had no clue that he was a special needs kid when I called on him, and his ideas were some of the best I received that day." As Mary Casanova points out, a visit from a bookperson often fosters a "zeal" for reading—and "a school that builds an author visit into an 'event,' spreads the message to kids that books are important."

Author Spotlight: Linda Crotta Brennan

Linda Crotta Brennan went to the University of Rhode Island and Rhode Island College for her bachelor's and master's degrees in early childhood education. There she fell in love with New England stone fences, Italian grinders (pronounced "grindahs"), a type of sandwich, and Robert Brennan, not necessarily in that order. She and Bob now live in Rhode Island with their three teenage daughters, a noble beagle, a cranky parakeet, and other assorted creatures depending on the author's current nonfiction project. (She once grew slime mold in the kitchen.)

Linda has written for magazines such as *Cricket, Highlights for Children*, and *Ranger Rick. Flannel Kisses* was her first picture book. Her second will be *Marshmallow Kisses*. To learn more about Linda, see her Web page at http://users.ids.net/~brennan/kidwrit.htm.

As one author puts it, being "a comet trailed by hundreds of adoring young fans" is as good as any award. Another author says, "There is nothing like meeting, or hearing from, a kid who loves your work. Nothing." Author Kathleen Duey says, "I love it when kids tell me they like the books, and I love going to schools. I live for that walk down the hall with 20 kids around me, jostling to stay close, or later in the library when the quiet child walks up, hands me a tiny figurine of a porcupine or horse or bear (or a pretty pencil, or best, a poem written on a torn piece of paper) then, without a word, turns and leaves me alone with the gift."

WHEN A WHOLE SCHOOL IS INVOLVED

Language arts teacher Rebecca Hayes, who teaches in a school that makes a big deal out of author visits (described more fully in chapter 10) says "the biggest thing a school can do is to value reading, then value the work of an author who is coming, then make sure all of the kids can share in the experience." She adds, "I'm really proud of the way we promote reading in our school. Our test scores may have risen, but it's more of an attitude that reading is a way of life, an invaluable experience. It *is* the attitude about reading that really does make the difference between a superficial program and one that really impacts kids."

A Success Story: Sebeka, Minnesota

Sebeka, Minnesota, is a small town in a rural area, but the school has a big commitment to author visits. Every year, the staff meets to select a children's book author and brainstorm creative ways to prepare for a schoolwide visit. Jane says, "I knew Sebeka was going to be an unusual author visit when I gave a summer workshop in Grand Forks on how to make good connections between literature and social studies—and several teachers from Sebeka came to get to know me and my books. They established an E-mail connection and asked if they could borrow my box of Ethiopian things ahead of time. When I arrived at the motel the night before, I found a welcome basket and materials telling me more about the school and community. The next morning, when I got to the school, I immediately could see all the work that had been done. Child-drawn illustrations for *Pulling the Lion's Tail* lined one wall. Along another wall was writing by some second graders who had taken the first sentence from *Trouble* and inserted their own names instead of Tekleh's name . . . and proceeded to describe the ways that trouble somehow always found them. Older students had prepared artistic representations of mountains along another wall to go with *Fire on the Mountain*. The students' work, related to my various books, filled the walls and classrooms.

"I spoke in the library all day. Hanging behind me were banners that the art teacher and students had created: a huge continent of Africa and African animals made with 'mud painting.' That night, I told stories to families in the library. Then several classes presented a small concert of African songs that the music teacher had worked on with them. I was amazed to see the way the whole school got involved, and I talk about the Sebeka experience as one of the best author visits I've ever had."

How does a schoolwide event like this get started? Jane says, "I've been in schools where my visit was the idea of the principal, in others where it was the idea of the librarian, and in a number where the push came from one teacher or a group of teachers. If there's an exuberant person who communicates well with the rest of the staff, amazing things can happen."

 ## THE SINGLE CLASSROOM EXPERIENCE

It's possible that you are shaking your head and thinking what one teacher put into words: "Sad to say, a big excitement for book projects just doesn't exist at my school. I'm pretty much of a lone wolf howling in the wilderness." Don't despair. Believe it or not, even a single classroom can have a fantastic connection with a bookperson.

In spring 1998, Monica Edinger, fourth-grade teacher at The Dalton School in New York City, wrote to the CHILD_LIT E-mail list to describe how her classroom visit from Gail Carson Levine, author of *Ella Enchanted*, came to be. She wrote, "I began reading the book aloud several weeks before beginning my Cinderella unit last fall. I told the children there was a special reason why I was reading the book and they would have to guess what it was. At first, one or two would come up to me after a reading and whisper in my ear that it was because it was a fairy tale. But before long, more and more picked up on the Cinderella theme. The death of Ella's mother alerted some, the silly stepsisters still others. By the time we came to the giant pumpkins, all knew why I was reading the book." Monica's class initiated a correspondence with Gail Carson Levine that culminated in the classroom visit described in our introduction. After the children presented their work to the author, Monica wrote, "she answered their many questions in a way that was inspirational and memorable for my aspiring young writers."

"Wait! Wait!" you say. "My school isn't in New York City or anywhere else where lots of authors live." Don't give up too easily. Bookpeople live . . . well . . . everywhere. One may well be delighted to visit your classroom. Many are thrilled to have an audience to test new material on.

Finding Relatively Unknown Authors

The Society of Children's Book Writers and Illustrators (SCBWI) has more than 10,000 members and they come from all 50 states, Puerto Rico, the Virgin Islands, Canada, France, China, Hungary—you name it! Many of the regions put out a list of authors and illustrators available for speaking. The executive office is at 8271 Beverly Boulevard, Los Angeles, California, 90048. People there can put you in touch with the advisor for your region.

Jane says, "When I read Monica's post about Gail Carson Levine's visit, I E-mailed her to ask whether she would be interested in reading my new novel, *The Storyteller's Beads*, to her class. The book wasn't even quite published yet, and although I'd gotten wonderful comments from editors and other adult readers, I was very curious to see how children would react to the story. I loved getting Monica's students' letters—seeing what clicked with them and what they didn't understand. Knowing that my book did, indeed, interest and move young readers."

Those just starting out are often happy to have a place to practice a presentation or a story. Be creative in thinking about what you might offer in return. Perhaps your class could design some projects related to an author's book—projects the author can then suggest to other classrooms. Perhaps your class could even write a curriculum guide or comments for the bookperson's Web page. Jane has fond memories of a Grand Forks fourth-grade class whose students created their own illustrations for *Trouble* before it came out. They studied the manuscript, did research into Eritrean scenes, and decided who would illustrate each page. After the book came out, they invited Jane to tea and to sign copies of the books for students in the class. The coordinator of the project also invited a reporter from the *Grand Forks Herald* to speak to the class about publicity, and the students sent press releases about their project to the media. "I was delighted to speak to that class for no fee," Jane says. "Just to show that life can throw a curveball toward even the most creative of intentions, though, the Grand Forks flood arrived on the very day our grand event was supposed to happen. I never did get to see the students' illustrations, because the flood destroyed them. But I did make a point of still paying a visit to the students the following fall when things were more or less back to normal."

ISN'T A GOOD VISIT A LOT OF WORK?

Although there are few thrills to match the experience of having an entire school work together to turn a bookperson visit into an event, anyone who has worked in a school knows that such cooperation doesn't happen at the wave of some magical wand. Sometimes it doesn't happen at all. One author mentions a school where "the two teachers who arranged for the school visit were well intentioned, but they just didn't have the political or personal power to get everyone else involved, too. I thought, from my conversations with the organizers, that it would be an exciting day. Instead, it was one of the worst I've had." A principal comments on the hurdles that sometimes have to be leaped to get everyone working together: "The hardest part," she says, "was convincing teachers that the project was important and didn't take away from what they were teaching anyway. In fact, it enhanced what they were teaching. It helps to have an ally—the library media specialist and the library committee were my partners in the project. They helped promote the project and take some of the pressure off the teachers so they felt it was a group project." Rebecca Hayes agrees that from a teacher's point of view a successful bookperson visit takes a lot of work, especially because "the preparation is as important as the actual celebration."

School Librarian Linda Sherouse points out how challenging a bookperson visit can also be for librarians: "Once the booking is confirmed, the continual communication to iron out all the details is the most time-consuming. The lodging, meals, transportation, getting someone to cover my classes so that I can be a good host, selling books, returning the unsold books, getting contests run in advance to get people excited about the visit, the advance PR to press and peers as well as parents and students. It is a major addition to an already heavy workload."

Visits are demanding for public librarians, too. Joanne Stanbridge says, "Once in preparation for an author visit, I borrowed a film projector (and a reel of film, so I could practice setting it up) from the fire department and ended up weeping with frustration, leaning my head against the projector while it chopped up bits of "Fighting the High Rise Fire" and spat them out. When I got home that night, I actually had bits of film falling out of my hair! Another time, I was talking to Lyn Hancock on the phone, setting up an author visit. She's one of those wildlife writers who kept cougars and raccoons and I don't know what other animals in her house and then wrote nonfiction books about the experience. I was calling her long distance to the Northwest Territories, out in her cabin, when suddenly she said, 'Oh no! I have to put the phone down for a minute!' and there was this interminable silence. I thought the worst. I thought a grizzly bear had broken in or flames were consuming the cabin. By the time she came back to the phone, I was yelling, 'Lyn! Lyn! What's happening?' She said breathlessly, 'I was making a surprise birthday cake for someone, and I saw him coming up the path. I had to hide everything in the closet.' Sheesh! Twenty dollars worth of long-distance silence, and I nearly had a heart attack."

Author/Illustrator Spotlight: Joanne Stanbridge

Joanne Stanbridge is the author of a middle-grade novel called *The Leftover Kid* and the illustrator of a picture book by Bernice Gold called *My Four Lions*. She is also a librarian. Having spent 10 years in charge of the children's department at Westmount Public Library in Montreal, she recently took a one-year leave of absence in order to write a series of short science fiction novels for children. She has made "terrific connections" from both sides of the experience, both hosting author visits in the public library and visiting schools and libraries in her author/illustrator role. Joanne now lives and works in Kingston, Ontario, Canada.

Visits are often hard for the bookperson, too, who, after all, must leave home, struggle with transportation mishaps, and—even in the best of circumstances—sleep in strange beds while knowing that someone is having to pick up the pieces at home. For example, while Jane and Toni (from their respective author and library media specialist points of view) both remember Jane's visit to Longfellow School as spectacular, they also remember that Jane's flight to Boston was canceled due to a blizzard, and Jane finally arrived in Portland, Maine, many stops and many hours later, without her bag of props. A parent had to be sent to the airport for the bag the next day, while Jane valiantly carried on without so much as her toothbrush.

Author Margriet Ruurs remembers "the flight to San Jose when the plane fell out of the skies four times! Everyone was literally soaked in tonic and ice cubes; tomato juice dripped off the overhead compartments. Once we arrived at the airport, I discovered that my publisher had not made a hotel reservation. There were 10,000 delegates in town . . . no room at the inn!"

Even in the midst of the visit, "real life" goes on for everybody—bookperson, media specialist, teachers, principals—sometimes in overwhelming doses. Margriet, for instance, remembers the day she was doing readings all day in a nearby school, not long after her 16-year-old son had received his driver's license. "I told him he could drop me off and pick me up again, as long as he was very careful," she says. "I was a bit nervous about his being out and about on his own for the first time. The school librarian who introduced me to each group told the students that I had two sons and that one of them had the car for the first time today, so it was fresh on my mind."

At lunchtime, she says, she looked up from her preparations for the next presentation and "saw a big policeman in the hallway. That's when the clerk motioned to me and said, 'Oh, he's looking for you.' I thought I'd die. I just knew that my son had been in a terrible accident. Why else would a policeman be looking for me in a school? I staggered over to him and he said cheerfully, 'Oh, good. There you are. I've come to see your slide show.'"

Margriet adds, "I can't tell you how relieved I was, but also how surprised. I have never before or since had a policeman come to my presentation. This admirable man liked to enjoy things with the kids and made a point of joining them often. I was so glad to see my son drive up after school. He'd had no problems at all!"

THE PAYOFF

If visits can be so hard on everybody, why go through the agony? For one thing, says illustrator Cathryn Falwell, "kids need more heroes." She describes attending presentations by the creators of popular children's books and seeing "kids who have been force-fed Uzi-toting 'heroes' in spandex, sit in complete awe of living, breathing authors and illustrators toting books and wearing rumpled cotton." Recently, she says, she took her own children to see Lynne Reid Banks. "She brought the actual cupboard [from *Indian in the Cupboard*] with her! The delightful gasps from the audience could be heard, I'm sure, clear to the parking lot!"

Storyteller Donna Washington says, "Storytelling is not something that should be a luxury. The oral transmission of story ought to be a requirement. It is astonishing how much better a student will do on a writing assignments if he or she gets the chance to tell it out loud before the pen hits the paper. Hire the professionals in to show the way, and then tell until your tongue won't move anymore."

"My real goal," says Robin Moore, "is imagination restoration. Mythologist Joseph Campbell wrote that storytelling is the essential human act—the primary attribute which distinguishes our species from all others. We are the dreamers who dream the dream of the earth, then communicate it to others. If this is true, then storytelling is an essential part of becoming a human being and should be an important focus of modern educational programs."

Speaking from the library media specialist's view, Linda Sherouse says, "Over the years, I have found that students remember the authors or illustrators they have met. Many students who have long ago graduated speak of these people when we meet out in public." Toni says, "For children, books are magical vessels, filled, as they are, with people and places unfamiliar to them and with beautiful words and art. As elementary educators, we encourage this impression and nurture children's belief in the magic and power of stories. When a children's book creator, whether author or illustrator, comes to visit, that person is a piece of the magic come to life. It's wondrous that someone who had a part of something so special is standing before us, is returning hugs, is wearing the T-shirt or earrings the kids made for her, is laughing or singing or signing her name in a book, a piece of the magic that they will keep forever."

She adds, "Some of our Longfellow School students who have graduated to middle school come back to visit us every day. Most stop into the library to say hi and to look around. They come to talk about what they are doing nowadays and, most importantly, what they are reading. And they come to see what is on display in our library. When they see the book of an author or illustrator with whom they visited while they were students here, they melt. They oooh and aaah and exclaim to each other and remember aloud the visit. The magic is recalled and revealed. It stays with them for a long, long time."

JUST WHAT'S SO SPECIAL ABOUT BOOKPEOPLE?

Inspiring Role Models

Why do bookpeople tend to have such a powerful impact on teachers and students? One reason is that the bookpeople who wander through the world of children's books tend to have vivid memories of their own childhoods—memories they are often willing to share with students. Illustrator E. B. Lewis, who often uses school visits as a time to share his own memories of school, says that when he looks into the faces of the students he's speaking to, he sees a familiar gleam. As the oldest of five children, Lewis remembers a time when he was "it." He also remembers the shock of having a younger sibling born. Desperate to gain back some of the attention he was used to having, he was only in second grade when he mastered the role of class clown. Finally, near the end of a "particularly inspiring assembly program" when Lewis was in sixth grade in a Philadelphia public school, a speaker asked some of the students what they wanted to be when they grew up. Lewis looked at the speaker, clearly a man who commanded respect and attention, and declared, in all seriousness, "I want to be a lawyer." When the auditorium rocked with laughter, Lewis says, he knew the truth of what his father had said for many years: "Earl, they're laughing at you, not with you." He says that he made up his mind, on the spot, to show everyone that he could indeed "become 'somebody' and make outstanding contributions to society."

Because he had to work so hard to reach his own goals, Lewis has become a motivating and inspiring speaker and a great role model. He urges students, for instance, to find a mentor who believes in them the way his uncle, who spent years taking him to art lessons, believed in him. One principal notes that the students who listened to E. B. Lewis left "inspired to strive to follow their dreams and attain a level of excellence that comes with hard work, perseverance, and determination." Another says that she doesn't think her school "will ever be quite the same!"

Illustrator Spotlight: E. B. Lewis

E. B. Lewis likes it when he's referred to as a "passionate painter." He lives in a house that he spent years loving from afar, a house he passed every time he traveled from Philadelphia, where he grew up, to his grandparents' house in McKee City. He's known for the detail in his watercolor paintings, for the depth of emotion in the characters he paints, and for the careful research he has done for books placed in many settings, including Zimbabwe (*The New King*), Egypt (*Magid Fasts for Ramadan*), Tanzania (*Big Boy*), and the United States (*Down the Road* and others). He even spent his own money to travel to Ethiopia to do the art research for *Only a Pigeon*. He's also been a lifelong teacher, where he tries to stir his students to also be passionate about whatever they choose to do. In 1998, one of his picture books, *The Bat Boy and His Violin*, won a Coretta Scott King Honor Award for illustration.

If E. B. was a class clown in second grade, Jane's second-grade report card reports that she was "a joy to work with." She shares the report card with students because of the next sentence, written by the teacher at the end of the year: "We have also enjoyed her poems. They are exceptionally good for her age. Perhaps it is one of her talents." Every school, she points out, "has that often shy kid, probably an introvert, perhaps sitting in the back row and not saying much, who loves to write. I never had a chance to meet a real author when I was young. It's inspiring to think that I might be a touchstone for some other aspiring author, someone like the girl who wrote the note that said, 'Please, I want to remember you forever.' " Jane says she keeps the girl's note in her own planner "to remind myself what author visits are all about."

Dreamers Who Reached Their Goals

Another reason for the power of these visits is that bookpeople represent a profession where it's incredibly difficult to achieve one's goals. Jane notes that although she knows she can have a special role in the lives of some budding writers, she considers her influence to go beyond the aspiring young authors, "to all dreamers. I sometimes show older students a folder of my rejection letters from just one year. I tell them that big dreams often call for big failures. I tell them that next time they fail at something, or are rejected, they should tell themselves, 'I have a long ways to go before I'm as bad as that author who came to our school!' " Because of the competitive nature of the publishing world, many other bookpeople have a similar story to tell. Cathryn Falwell says, "When I show the steps in the creation of a book, I make sure to include lots of drafts, mistakes, and changes, too. I have sketches, dummies, artwork, proofs, press sheets, and other things that I drag along. I don't want kids to think that books spring from the head, Zeus-like." Author/illustrator Katie Davis notes that she wrote and illustrated "really bad" picture books for decades before she learned how to create a publishable one. Mary Casanova says, "I encourage students, from my own experience with persistence and rejection, to believe in their dreams and in themselves and to never give up."

Wonderful Performers

For the visits of some bookpeople, amazing power comes out of the fact that they are entrancing performers. A principal describes E. B. Lewis's "incredible slide show" and the way he "enthralled" students when he took them, in pictures, "down every street, to each section of Philadelphia, and showed them the inspiring sources for his watercolors. The fabric of life in the city, from vistas on the river to corners on South Street, is vividly portrayed by each of his expert brush strokes. Mr. Lewis not only captures the essence of life in his painting, but also the realities and subtleties of it as well." Author Jim Aylesworth, who was a first-grade teacher for many years, reads his books aloud with tremendous energy and rhythm; in fact, he actually sings some of them. "Great, great, great!" says one library media specialist who watched him in action with children. Storyteller Robin Moore often accompanies his stories with a Celtic harp, flute, or hunting horn and weaves demonstrations of "old-time living skills" into his programs. Author Ben Mikaelsen used to do school visits in the company of a bear.

 Better Than Television . . .

A few years ago, storyteller Donna Washington was about to perform at a young authors' night, she says, "when a little boy demanded, 'Who are you?' I told him I was the storyteller, and he said, 'I don't like storytellers. I only like books.' His mother looked embarrassed, but I told him that liking books was good. When the performance finally began, the room was packed. The little boy had to come down front to see. As the set went on, his eyes got huge and round, and he started talking to the characters in the story. He got mad at them when they did things he thought were obviously silly. He laughed as hard as anyone when he thought something was funny, and he always knew the answers when I asked the audience questions. At the end of the set, he bounded out of his chair and ran up to me. His eyes were still huge. He yanked on my pants. When I looked down, he said, 'You're better than television!' "

People Who Know Fascinating Things

Finally, successful bookpeople are often people who not only know a lot about words, pictures, and stories, but who also know a lot about many other things. When you pull a bookperson into your school or library, you pull that knowledge in, too. Roland Smith knows about things such as the inner workings of zoos and isolated elephant camps in northern Burma. Jane reports that many teachers make a point to thank her for bringing "a piece of Africa" or "a sense of the big wide world" into their classrooms. "After I went through the Grand Forks flood of 1997," she says, "it suddenly became part of my school presentations to talk about what it's like to go through a life-changing loss and choose to write about it. When I used a life-long fascination to write a young middle-grade novel set on the Oregon Trail, *I'm Sorry, Almira Ann*, I began to carry 15 years of reading about and traveling along the trail with me into every classroom and gym where I was asked to speak."

A nonfiction writer such as Susan Campbell Bartoletti, author of the award-winning nonfiction book *Growing Up in Coal Country*, also brings into the classroom all the things she learned in researching and writing her books. "My area of expertise," she says, "is discovering and using primary sources. In my school talks, I often talk about how a researcher gathers and interprets the primary resources. There's so much detective work involved, which suits compulsive A-type personalities like me. But there's more to it, for primary resources can help us understand culture and cultural diversity as we unearth voices and incidents long overlooked and consider them critically. I like to think I get the chance to 'fix' history by discovering and telling stories that haven't been told.

"I also talk about the difference between 'official' codified history that is often found in history books and personal history and memory. For example, I was fascinated as I listened to my husband's grandparents tell about the anthracite region of Pennsylvania. It amazed me to hear the grandfather's stories about working at age 11 in the coal breaker and later for 45 years in the mines, and the grandmother's stories about quitting school in first grade to help her mother and getting married at age 13.

"I wanted to learn more, so I began to read about the anthracite coal industry. I read old mining inspection records, newspapers, magazines, and books. In museum archives, I searched through dusty boxes, listened to recorded interviews, and studied old photographs. I found a lot of stories that told what it was like to be a rich owner of a coal mine or even a man who worked in the mines, but no stories that told what it was like to be a woman or a child. I had found a gap, and a writer knows that wherever there is a gap, there is a story to be told. So I placed notices in local newspapers and church bulletins and found people who invited me into their living rooms to share their personal memories and histories with me.

"Two interviews stand out as examples: Mary Fanucci and Richard Owens. When I arrived at Mary's house, she led me to the kitchen to show me her husband Bruno's mining certificate, his photographs, and newspaper articles. She began to tell me all about Bruno's work in the mines. 'But Mary,' I said, 'How about you? I want to hear stories about your life.'

"Mary became nervous and shy. 'I don't have any stories to tell,' she told me. 'I only know my husband's stories.' I pressed on, and Mary discovered she had plenty to tell: how women and children defied the coal companies and secretly collected scraps of coal from the culm banks each morning, how the breaker whistle alerted the families to tragedy at the mines, and how the Black Maria carried the broken bodies of dead mine workers home. I also heard how she and her sisters worked and played, how they scrubbed their father's and brother's mine clothes on wash days and went sleigh-riding on homemade sleds.

"Richard Owens was a 94-year-old man who had quit school as a child when his foster father had died from miner's lung. 'Somebody had to go to work,' said Richard, 'and so I did.' With pride, Richard told me about working 10- to 12-hour days in the breakers and later in the coal mines, even though it meant forestalling his dream of going to school. Some stories are difficult to tell, for truth is seldom comfortable, but the gaps must be filled, the stories told nonetheless, for truth ultimately provides the strongest comfort."

Author Spotlight: Susan Campbell Bartoletti

Susan Campbell Bartoletti has always loved telling and listening to family stories. Her coal-mining ancestors and the rich immigrant history of the Pennsylvania coal-mining region where she grew up has inspired her to write picture books, novels, and nonfiction. She taught eighth-grade English for nearly 20 years. Now she divides her time between teaching creative writing and literature courses at a local university and writing. She lives in northeastern Pennsylvania with her husband and their two children. Her books are *Growing Up in Coal Country*, *Dancing with Dziadziu*, *No Man's Land*, and *Kids on Strike*.

Cathryn Falwell says, "Since I was a graphic designer in one of my 'former lives,' I have firsthand knowledge of production and the printing process, which is helpful. I have a 'proof' that has the four process colors, each on an acetate overlay. I show the kids how these four colors combine to make all the colors they see in illustrations. It never fails—I always have at least one child in the audience say 'Do it again!' Many of the letters I receive from children claim that the 'magic' of the overlays was their favorite part of the program ('awesome' being a popular description)!" Teachers who like this art connection, she says, "have followed up in their classrooms by bringing in the Sunday comics and a large magnifying glass to check out the four-color printed dots. This could also be a great introduction to the Impressionists, who used visual mixture—a yellow dab next to a blue dab—to cause the visual illusion of green. See? There's *no end* to where you can go after hosting a school visit!"

HAVE COURAGE—AND PLAN CAREFULLY

Yes, although the work to pull off a successful visit can be daunting, the rewards can be great. Yvonne Hanley, who taught children's literature at the University of North Dakota for a number of years before she also began to spend a few days a week as a school library media specialist, knows what it's like to coordinate a very first author visit—from Jane. "I learned so much," she says. "When the school is a novice to visits, the book person should feel free to say, 'Please be sure they've read all my books, or at least these titles.' In our school, it was important to have the librarian involved, because some teachers might read one or two books to their students and not read any more. It was wonderful, as a librarian, to read all the books to every child.

"The more times I read a story, the more I heard and saw. It was fun to show the students the end pages in *Trouble* and say, 'Look at how the illustrator put a map here for us. We can tell where Tekleh went by the symbols she put there.' I had never done anything like this before, and by the end I saw so many other things that could have been done."

The more bookpeople connections you explore, the more possibilities you will see. Approach a prospective visit carefully, though. As author Ben Mikaelsen points out, for every bookperson who is disappointed or frustrated because a visit turns out to be less than it could be, there also exists a school disappointed or frustrated that a visit turned out to be less of a thrill than people had hoped it would be. It's very important to choose a bookperson well. That's what the next chapter is all about. Here's to the attitude expressed by Cathryn Falwell: "A couple of years ago, I attended a workshop presented by Marvin Terban, author of a dozen or so wordplay books for children. He is a longtime veteran of school visits and was offering tips and advice. The one charge he gave us that really struck me was this: Children might only get to see one author or illustrator in their lives. If you are that person, you are, in a sense, an ambassador for the profession. So if you can't do a super bang-up job of presenting, *don't do it*. He's right. I have taken this to heart, and I really work hard to give the best knockout presentation I can when I visit kids. I would never want one single child to walk away thinking books were boring!"

REFERENCES

Banks, Lynne Reid. *The Indian in the Cupboard*. With illustrations by Brock Cole. Garden City, NY: Doubleday, 1980.

Bartoletti, Susan Campbell. *Dancing with Dziadzu*. With illustrations by Annika Nelson. San Diego: Harcourt, 1997.

——. *Growing Up in Coal Country*. Boston: Houghton Mifflin, 1996.

——. *Kids on Strike*. Boston: Houghton Mifflin, 1999.

——. *No Man's Land*. New York: Scholastic, 1999.

Boorstin, Daniel J. "I Cannot Live Without Books." *Parade* (July 12, 1998): 12–13.

Brennan, Linda Crotta. "The Dream Violin" in *The Dream Violin*. Honesdale, PA: Boyds Mills, 1994.

——. *Flannel Kisses*. With illustrations by Mari Takabayoshi. Boston: Houghton Mifflin, 1997.

——. *Marshmallow Kisses*. With illustrations by Mari Takabayoshi. Boston: Houghton Mifflin. Forthcoming.

Casanova, Mary. *Moose Tracks*. New York: Hyperion, 1995.

——. *Riot*. New York: Hyperion, 1996.

——. *Stealing Thunder*. New York: Hyperion, 1999.

——. *Wolf Shadows*. New York: Hyperion, 1998.

Gavin, Curtis. *The Bat Boy and His Violin*. With illustrations by E. B. Lewis. New York: Simon & Schuster, 1998.

Kurtz, Jane. *Fire on the Mountain*. With illustrations by E. B. Lewis. New York: Simon & Schuster, 1994.

——. *I'm Sorry, Almira Ann*. New York: Holt, 1999.

——. *Pulling the Lion's Tail*. With illustrations by Floyd Cooper. New York: Simon & Schuster, 1995.

——. *The Storyteller's Beads*. San Diego: Harcourt, 1998.

——. *Trouble*. With illustrations by Durga Bernhard. San Diego: Harcourt, 1997.

Kurtz, Jane and Christopher. *Only a Pigeon*. With illustrations by E. B. Lewis. New York: Simon & Schuster, 1997.

Levine, Gail Carson. *Ella Enchanted*. New York: HarperCollins, 1997.

Matthews, Mary. *Magid Fasts for Ramadan*. With illustrations by E. B. Lewis. New York: Clarion, 1996.

Pfitsch, Patricia Curtis. *Keeper of the Light*. New York: Simon & Schuster, 1997.

Rappaport, Doreen. *The New King*. With illustrations by E. B. Lewis. New York: Dial, 1995.

Regan, Dian Curtis. *Liver Cookies*. New York: Scholastic, 1991.

Schertle, Alice. *Down the Road.* With illustrations by E. B. Lewis. San Diego: Harcourt, 1995.

Smith, Roland. *Journey of the Red Wolf.* New York: Viking, 1996.

——. *Thunder Cave.* New York: Hyperion, 1995.

Smith, Roland, and Michael J. Schmidt. *In the Forest with Elephants.* San Diego: Harcourt, 1998.

Testa, Maria. *Dancing Pink Flamingos and Other Stories.* Minneapolis: Lerner Publications, 1995.

——. *Nine Candles.* With illustrations by Amanda Schaffer. Minneapolis: Carolrhoda Books, 1996.

——. *Someplace to Go.* With illustrations by Karen Ritz. Morton Grove, IL: Whitman, 1996.

——. *Thumbs Up, Rico!* With illustrations by Diane Paterson. Morton Grove, IL: Whitman, 1994.

Tololwa, M. Mollel. *Big Boy.* With illustrations by E. B. Lewis. New York: Clarion, 1995.

Chapter Three

Choosing the Right Bookperson

Who is the right bookperson for you? Since arranging for a visit is a major investment of time—and, usually, money—it's worth thinking through the possibilities carefully. The impact a visit can have on a young reader's life is an even more important feature to stay aware of. These days, you have a lot of choices, and you also have a number of considerations to juggle as you think about how to create the most exciting and meaty experience you possibly can.

DO YOU WANT GLAMOUR?

One consideration is the "glamour factor." You may want someone that students, teachers, and parents will all have heard about long before the visit occurs—"You mean *that* person is visiting our school?"

The advantages of a "glamour bookperson" are fairly obvious: 1) The visit illustrates, perhaps better than any other kind, that *real people write books.* Any bookperson visit does this to some extent, but a glamourous bookperson perhaps illustrates it best of all; 2) book sales often soar when the visiting bookperson is someone well known, which can be important, not only from the standpoint of getting books into kids' hands, but also if the program relies on book sales for helping fund the visit; and 3) it's usually easier to get publicity support from newspapers and other local media if the visitor has a certain amount of fame.

The disadvantages are also fairly obvious. Glamour bookpeople can sometimes be demanding and picky. Some libraries and schools have even described certain ones as "a bit jaded." They also tend to be expensive; they can afford to be. Elizabeth Vollrath, Youth Services Librarian at Portage County Public Library in Wisconsin notes, "Our library would not be able to bring in 'big names' if we didn't piggyback with the schools or University of Wisconsin–Stevens Point, because of the cost, frankly. Each group who sponsors the author pays a part. It is excellent public relations to work together. The community sees us all as being in the education business. My community, Stevens Point, is in the central part of Wisconsin, two hours north of Madison. It is not on the beaten path, so to speak, so I feel very lucky to have a great, supportive community that will work together to bring famous authors to the area and, most importantly, to young people."

Clark Underbakke, a classroom teacher who helps organize the University of Alabama's young authors conference each year, says, "It is no secret that a 'known' author or illustrator has a much higher honorarium." He adds, "We try to have one or two 'big' names each year. But, I must admit that some of the people I have loved the very most were unknown to me and most of the people in the area." For example, he says, Shellye Gill from Alaska "rocked!" He adds, "Not everyone has the name recognition of, say, Lois Ehlert or Mem Fox. We *love* everyone, big name or not!" (For more on young authors conferences, see chapter six.)

DO YOU WANT SOMEONE WHO LIVES NEARBY?

Another thing to consider is the regional factor. You may want someone from your own geographic region for several reasons: 1) It's a wonderful thing to give students the message that book people live, not only in New York City and California, but also in your own community, communicating an important message to a young writer: You, too, can consider becoming a bookperson; 2) you can often enter into a great previsit conversation with a regional bookperson, sometimes meeting in person or talking by telephone or E-mail to discuss the visit. Jane says, "With local schools, I have sometimes even gone to the school several weeks beforehand to meet with teachers and let them know the ways that I can be helpful to them and how they can also help me"; and 3) a regional bookperson can sometimes have special reading and writing hooks. Author Mary Casanova says, "With regional visits, I find kids feel an extra kinship with my stories' north-woods settings and are quick to share their own experiences with me. I make writing books look almost easy; after all, I'm writing about places and things somewhat familiar."

Disadvantages to the regional book person are also clear. Sometimes the reaction is similar to what one teacher puts into words: "A local person I can hear anytime." Alas, a prophet really is sometimes not without honor except in her own village. Besides, sometimes schools want to use a visit to help students taste something of the world outside their front door. As Mary also notes, "When I visit out of state, my stories become something of the exotic. Either way, I have a great time relating with the students and looking for ways of making connections, whatever our geographic or cultural backgrounds. Books certainly provide a wonderful bridge."

WHAT SIZE GROUP IS IDEAL?

One very important factor to take into consideration is what size group the bookperson you have in mind prefers. Some bookpeople are performers who can be put in a gymnasium full of respectful-but-wiggling students and thrive. Others strongly prefer speaking to individual classes or small groups and will be less effective in that large gathering in the gym you had in mind. "I like to work with groups of under 50 kids," says illustrator Cathryn Falwell, "so I can get each one up front to participate during my presentation if they want to." For instance, she says, "One of my books, *Shape Space*, is about a young gymnast/dancer who opens up a big red box and pulls out a huge collection of big, colorful geometric shapes. She plays with them, builds castles and towers, creates a costume from them, and even uses them to make a dancing-partner friend. The book repeats a refrain, 'rectangle, triangle, rectangle, triangle, semicircle, semicircle, circle, square!' So I get eight volunteers to form a line up front and hand them each a large colored foam-core shape in the order of the refrain. I then read the book aloud, the kids chant the chorus when it comes along, and the shape-holders lift their shapes, cheerleader style, as theirs is named. Sometimes we add a little choreography if it's a willing group. Once I had a girl in a wheelchair as one of the shape team, and she was thrilled!"

DO YOU HAVE LOGISTICAL LIMITATIONS?

How flexible is the visitor and how flexible are *you*? Some visitors like suggestions and ideas about what seems to work for your particular school or library. Others have definite preferences about issues such as which microphone system you use. Walter the Giant Storyteller, an experienced performer whose voice is a powerful tool that he is careful to take care of, says, "The best assistance anyone, librarian, parent volunteer, or someone else, can give me is to follow all my instructions, answer all my questions, and then get out of my way. There are only two kinds of school performances that are 'better' than others: One, where they are really specific about what they want from me and have done a good job of communicating that so I can hone my performance to fit their needs, and two, where they have no idea what they want but can follow directions so that the microphone is there, the water is there, the staff knows the schedule, and so on. Sadly, both of these are rare, but the former is by far the rarest."

It's very helpful if you know your own school or library and have some sense of how it clicks (or doesn't). For instance, your own sound system may determine how you set things up. Library media specialist Linda Sherouse points out, "Sound transmission is one of the greatest challenges we face. We have an antiquated system, and our small lapel mike has not worked in a long time. Because of this, we need to have many presentations to smaller groups to have the students get the most out of the visit."

Walter says, "I try immensely to defer to the system that is in place at any given school, tailoring my performance length and/or content to their 'usual' way of doing things. If you, the librarian, have speakers come and do presentations at your school several times a year, then I want the kids to feel at home, that I am part of an assembly system that they understand the rules of. Behavior is a big deal in lots of schools, and knowing what is expected of them helps the kids to behave in an orderly fashion. But if you do not have speakers on a regular basis and have no set system in place for this type of assembly, then I can be disruptive." He adds, "I am very good at starting and ending a performance so that I take control of the crowd and then give it back, but if the school has no system in place, or an ineffectual leader, taking and giving something that is hard to define is difficult and distracts from my performance effectiveness. So I guess what I am saying is, it works best for me if everyone knows what is expected."

IS PERFORMANCE AN IMPORTANT FACTOR?

As you look at what you want from a visit, be aware that the "performance factor" can be something important to consider. Ask yourself just how important it is to you to have an outstanding performance. Some people prefer small, intimate connections; in fact, many bookpeople tend to be somewhat introverted. Other bookpeople specialize in the performance end of things. Author Roland Smith speaks for many children's authors when he says, "Even though I really like doing school visits, I don't write books so I can do school visits. I do school visits because I'm a writer. I know people who write books so they can do school visits." Gary Harbo, an example of this second type of bookperson, does an enormous number of school visits, reaching 25,000 elementary school children a year, according to his Web page (http://www.garyharbo.com).

Though Gary once specialized in wildlife paintings, his own children coaxed him into drawing cartoons, and he has now produced at least five books in two versions, one for two to six year olds and the other for seven to eleven year olds. Harbo's books, which he publishes through his own Minnesota-based company, Kutie Kari Books, Inc., raise reservations for some library media specialists. One says that Gary's books "show evidence of his being a beginning writer. But he's growing as a writer. And it's his skill as an illustrator that makes his visit worthwhile." Even beyond his skill as an illustrator, many librarians point out, is his ability to connect with his audience. "Both Gary's personality and the activity he did with the students really captured the audience at our young authors conference," says library media specialist Yvonne Hanley. "The children loved him, and every child left with a drawing."

HOW EXPERIENCED IS THE BOOKPERSON WITH CHILDREN?

A bookperson need not be a sparkling performer to have a wonderful school or library visit, given the right expectations and setup. An even more important factor to consider, something that can make a huge difference to the success of the visit, is how much experience the bookperson has with youngsters. Just because a person writes or illustrates books for children does not mean that person spends much time around children, or even likes them, as many a librarian or teacher has discovered to his or her dismay. Jane says, "Over and over, I hear schools say, 'Oh, your teaching experience really shines through. You know how to tailor what you're saying and showing, so that kids can really understand and relate.' I've realized that my years in the classroom really help a lot when it comes to school author visits."

Virginia Bohndorf, library media specialist at Piper Elementary School in Kansas City, agrees. "It absolutely makes a difference as to whether or not the author has been around kids. All of the following are aspects: ability to speak to the group without being condescending, proximity to control behavior problems, relating incidents to known quantities in kids' lives, varying the type of presentation as opposed to all verbal. Many adults have material that is of interest to kids, but they just don't know how to communicate with them."

OTHER STRENGTHS AND CAPABILITIES TO CONSIDER

What Are the Ages You Want to Reach?

Another thing to consider is what age levels you want to reach. Some bookpeople have different presentations for different age groups. For instance, Katie Davis, author and illustrator of *Who Hops?* and *I Hate to Go to Bed!* visits both elementary and pre-K classes and tailors her shows to the age group. For the younger children, she reads her latest book and follows the reading with an interactive drawing and storytelling session. She creates a story and illustrates it, combining the animals in the book and the expressions she asks the children to make. "The children don't just watch the show," she says, "they're a part of it, and they get to learn how to do simple drawings of emotions." For older students, she's created a slide show that illustrates how a book is made. "It shows mistakes I made along the way," she says, "the kinds of art I did as a child, and how many times I had to rework the books before they got to a publishable level."

Illustrator Spotlight: Katie Davis

"Parson School of Design, Pratt Institute of Art, Rhode Island School of Design. . . . I have walked by all these schools of fine art. I have attended none of them.

"I've always been creative but never thought of myself as an artist. I could write, though, so after graduating from Boston University, I went into public relations and advertising. After getting fired six or seven times, I figured I should be working for myself. Plus, I hated wearing pantyhose.

"I've been writing and illustrating picture books—really bad ones—for decades. I got a little better when, in 1996, I attended the Society of Children's Writers and Illustrators national conference. I took every word from every speech as a pearl. I learned a *lot*, and then I got to work.

"The idea for my first book, *Who Hops?*, came from playing with my children. They were freaking out in their car seats, so I tried to divert their attention. After asking if frogs, rabbits, and kangaroos hop, my kids lost interest, so in desperation I flummoxed them with, 'Do cows hop?' They laughed every time, so I thought, 'Hey, this could be a book!'

"Now I have four books at various stages of publication. Sometimes people act as though a silly, fun book isn't a 'real' book! Sheesh! If those people only heard my editor and me going over each line like the humor police! 'Is that funny enough?' 'I think it's funny, don't you think it's funny? Listen how funny this is . . . '

"I also get to do personal appearances and meet the people who read my books, and I feel very lucky to have a job that I love so much. You can visit me at my Web page at http://www.katiedavis.com."

Mary Casanova says, "School presentations require lots of flexibility; sometimes I talk with high school students about censorship, sometimes I speak to junior high students about plot development, often I speak with upper elementary about the stories behind my stories, and more and more—now that I have picture books coming out as well as novels—I find myself sharing with K–2 students. Whatever the age group, I like to share about myself and my books and to develop a rapport with the students that will foster an increased interest in reading, and hopefully in writing as well."

"With younger children," says Cathryn Falwell, "I focus on concepts and include the basics of how a book is made. For older children, I focus on the creative process and the development of ideas and go into more detail on the steps of making a book. I like to have more material than I actually need. Then I can tailor the presentation to the specific group as I go along."

A Successful Visit with Young Children

Toni points out that a visit to very young students—preschool through primary—has to have its own special elements to make it work. For example, Cathryn says, "With young children, I like to go back to where we began. I bring out the character from *Shape Space* and tell the kids I need them to help build a factory out of shapes. We discuss what this factory should make, and I lead them to agree on ice cream (teachers know this trick, of course). I start by putting a red rectangle on the display board. Each child can then come up and choose a shape from a collection of sticky cutouts I have on acetate. They add it to our display board and we build our factory. Then we make sure our imagination hats are still in place, and we say, 'One, two, three, ice cream!' I'm sure you'll be surprised to hear that when I peel back the original rectangle, three ice cream cones appear! What is really amazing to me is that, in spite of the sophisticated high-tech special effects that kids today are immersed in, this simple little game never fails to wow them, even the 10 and 11 year olds. I find it refreshing to know that magic lives in the hearts of children."

One time, Cathryn says, she presented a program to a group of kindergarten children in a public library in Hartford, Connecticut. "It was the first time I had read *Dragon Tooth* to a group, and I had the freshly finished artwork with me, since I was sending it out to the publisher the next day. The character in the book has a very wobbly tooth, which precipitates her dragon creation. I looked up from reading to find 20 little kids, all wiggling their teeth! The teacher told me she planned to follow this up with a discussion of teeth and visits to the dentist!"

Author/Illustrator Spotlight: Cathryn Falwell

Cathryn Falwell thinks of herself as an illustrator who sometimes puts words around her pictures. She was born in Kansas and spent her early childhood in Missouri, Wisconsin, and Minnesota before moving to Connecticut. A printmaking major, she received a B.F.A. in art from the University of Connecticut's School of Fine Arts in 1975.

Cathryn was a teacher and a freelance graphic designer in New Hampshire for several years. Returning to Connecticut, she worked as an art director and designer for an award-winning graphic design firm. In 1983, she established her own design business in Hartford.

After her second child was born, she decided to pursue the children's book field, something she had wanted to do since second grade. Her first book was published in 1991; the 18th will be out in 1999. In addition to receiving several awards, Cathryn's books have appeared on PBS's *Reading Rainbow* and *Barney*. Some of her new books are *Feast for 10*, *Word Wizard*, and *Christmas for 10*.

In August 1996, Cathryn moved to Maine with her husband, Peter Mirkin, and their sons Alex and Nick. They live in a small town on five wooded acres with a pond.

Illustrator and author Charlotte Agell, says Toni, was ideal as a visitor to young children "because everything was so sensual. It mattered what Charlotte wore and how she moved and that she played with the kids and danced and drew." Charlotte herself talks about what it's like to have a visit with very young children. "I come prepared to meet a lot of wigglers," she says. "I like to have the students sit very near me, if possible. I draw big pictures on the easel right away (to grab their attention) and bring my magic wand (and *use it*—to transform them into editors, for example). I also make sure to work in activities that require a little movement." For instance, Charlotte might have them act out a part of one of her books or walk around the classroom to look at illustrations. "If the group is too big for that sort of thing," she adds, "we at least roll our shoulders and shake our hands while counting loudly to 10 in all the languages we can think of or make up on the spot."

 ### A Glimpse of a Visit from Charlotte Agell

Catherine Ferguson, library educational technician at Longfellow School in Portland, Maine, describes what makes Charlotte's visits so effective for young children. "When Charlotte arrives, she is a visual delight. She wears comfortable shoes and a dress made from fabric with child appeal, soft and full. Charlotte is 'dancing feet' and sparkling eyes with the smile and exuberance of a child. Excitement is all around as the children arrive. Youthful energy fills the air and Charlotte begins. She is magic . . . she is Wendy and we are in Never Never Land.

"All eyes follow Charlotte as she celebrates children. The highlight of her presentation comes when she shares *Dancing Feet*, clapping with each word in energetic fashion. She touches and lifts our hearts as she connects with the child in us all. We never want to leave. As our day with Charlotte comes to an end, we all feel enriched. We knew her only from the books she had written. We now know how her books came to be written. Charlotte Agell knows children and we now know Charlotte Agell."

 ### Author/Illustrator Spotlight: Charlotte Agell

Charlotte Agell is the author/illustrator of *The Sailor's Book*, *Dancing Feet*, *I Swam with a Seal*, *To the Island*, a quartet of seasonal picture books published by Tilbury House, and the forthcoming *Up the Mountain*. Reviewers have called her books "ebullient" and "good for talking, dancing and acting out."

Originally from Sweden, she also grew up in Montreal and Hong Kong. She came to Maine, a place she'd only heard about in stories, in 1977, and has lived there very happily ever since, with her husband, Peter Simmons, and now two children, Anna and Jon.

A Successful Visit with Older Children

Visits to students in middle school and high school can be tricky, too. Jane says, "The only visit I ever walked away from feeling like a failure was one where I spoke to a whole auditorium full of junior-high students. At that time, I didn't use color transparencies in my presentation yet, and I did use lots of interaction with the students. Every time a student asked a question, I would see a little ripple of neck craning and giggling and talking. The students who were brave enough to ask the questions, in particular, seemed to need to make sure their questions were an acceptable level of coolness for their peers." In classroom settings, Jane says she has enjoyed talking with older students. "I tend to emphasize different things than with the elementary students," she says. "My many rejections, for instance, which I know budding athletes and drama students can often relate to, or the economics of being an author."

Some bookpeople seem specially tuned to the world of older students and can make connections even with the toughest of crowds. Walter the Giant Storyteller says that he doesn't get to speak with middle- and high-school students as often as he would like. In Grand Forks, he did have a chance—at Community High School, the alternative high school for students who are having trouble with classes in the regular high schools. Later, the library media specialist there, Judy Hager, wrote to say, "Walter was fantastic! All my students enjoyed him. His appearance at Community was highly successful. It was basically a stone-faced audience, but later they did evaluations on his presentation and they really really liked him. The teachers were quite enthusiastic, and I heard afterward from other sources skeptical to the idea that not only did the students enjoy him but they seemed to get something out of his presentation, and the staff themselves enjoyed him."

 ### Working with Young Adults in the Public Library

Author Nancy Werlin says, "I have twice given creative writing workshops for teens in public libraries. One was a three-hour session in a small suburban library in Peabody, Massachusetts. It was publicized in newspapers and with flyers, and approximately 12 kids ranging from fifth to eighth grade came. We talked about plot and characterization and brainstormed together on the board to create three characters and a plot for a story. Then we took some time to each write a one-page story and ended by having everyone read his or her story aloud.

"The second workshop was a one-week, three-hours per morning creative writing workshop at the Boston Public Library. This workshop was specifically for teens; the library sets aside funding to do it every summer, and each summer invites a different YA writer to run the class. Here, more time could be spent talking as a group about the features that go into a good story or novel, and we were able to do daily exercises on a variety of topics, including beginnings, dialog, quick characterizations, setting a mood, working out a plot, and of course, pulling it all together.

"In the longer program, I could spend some time each evening reading the work of the students and suggesting some writers that I thought each one might like to read along with commenting on what they were accomplishing. Even in four days, we were also able to develop a little community, in which topics like the importance of approaching your own and others' work respectfully could be covered. My students were fascinated with what I could tell them about the daily life of a writer, the difficulties of making a living, or the wonder of finally discovering the key to a story that had taken five revisions to find. On my end, it was exhilarating to notice how these kids would bloom creatively with the close and serious attention to their work, their ideas. At the end, we exchanged E-mail addresses, and many of the kids check in with me from time to time—and I with them."

⌨ FITTING IN WITH THE SCHOOL MISSION

Emphasizing Certain Themes or Sensitivities

Some schools use a bookperson visit as a way to reinforce certain values or themes that they have chosen to focus on for the year—or for every year. Linda Sherouse, library media specialist, talks about a bookperson visit from Lisa Anderson. Although Lisa was "a virtual unknown," Linda says, the school brought her in during a two-day Focus on Diversity celebration. "She spoke to all grade levels and was perhaps the *most* dynamic speaker ever! She has multiple sclerosis and cerebral palsy, wears leg braces, and uses a walker and a wheelchair. She had the students in all of the grades in the palm of her hand, and after finishing speaking to grades seven and eight, she had an adoring crowd of young ladies gathered around her wanting to ask her more questions!"

 Bridges to Other Cultures

Jane says, "Even in California, which I think of as a very cosmopolitan state, I had teachers coming up to me after my presentation and saying, 'Thank you for bringing the world into my classroom. My students need to see life outside of their own small county.' A librarian in Kansas said, 'Ethiopia will always be a real, and a special, place to these students because of everything we did before and during your visit.' "

Haemi Balgassi, whose books relate to her Korean-American heritage, often shows elementary students how to write their own names in Korean. Even the shyest kids, to her initial surprise, tend to come forward. Sometimes students ask her to sign their books in Korean. "During one of my programs," she says, "two boys, fifth graders, I think, decided to use the time to showcase their comedic talents. They clowned around, annoying other students around them, not to mention their librarian and me. Well, at the end of the program, when it was their turn to have their books signed, I asked for their names. One of the boys replied, 'I'm Dumb.' Pointing to the other boy, he said, 'He's Dumber.' When he saw that he wasn't going to get a reaction from me, he hurriedly said, 'I'm Mike.' As I was writing in the book, Mike leaned over to watch me, biting his lip. 'Uh, you did write *Mike*, didn't you? You didn't write *Dumb*, did you?' I gave him a wide grin, handed his book back to him, and said, 'Well, you'll never know, will you?' Ah, the look on his face! I still smile thinking about it. And yes, I did sign it to 'Mike,' of course!"

Author Spotlight: Haemi Balgassi

Smithsonian Magazine named Haemi Balgassi's first picture chapter book, *Peacebound Trains*, one of the best children's books of 1996, as did the *San Francisco Chronicle* and *American Booksellers Magazine*. *School Library Journal* praised the story as being "gracefully written and told with great emotion," and *The New York Times Book Review* called the narrative "powerful." The author based the story on her mother and grandmother's real-life experiences during the Korean War.

Haemi Balgassi's first novel, *Tae's Sonata*, was inspired in part by her own childhood. *American Booksellers Magazine* called the novel "a jewel of a book," and honored it as a 1997 "Pick of the Lists." *Bulletin for the Center of Children's Books* praised the novel, saying, "Strong characterizations and believable emotions make this stand out from other early young adult fare."

Both *Peacebound Trains* and *Tae's Sonata* were honored as Notable Children's Books in the Field of Social Studies by the National Council for the Social Studies and Children's Book Council. Haemi Balgassi lives with her husband and two daughters in Westfield, Massachusetts. To learn more about her, check her Web page: http://home.sprynet.com/sprynet/balgassi.

Emphasizing a Topic or Subject Area

Perhaps some kind of subject area is extra meaningful for your school. A bookperson who publishes nonfiction—a sometimes overlooked area of publishing—can have special insights into the research process, into how to create lively prose, or into a particular subject that is a priority for a particular school. Author Roland Smith, who writes nonfiction and "realistic" fiction, points out that "teachers and librarians can do a lot with the material if they choose. Environmental issues, wildlife, endangered habitats, diverse cultures are just a few of the subjects they could and have tied into curriculum." Linda Sherouse says, "I try to find speakers that connect to our curriculum, to the books that are in the literature-based reading series, or that are authors of curriculum-related trade books read in the classroom. One huge factor is student popularity of the books written or illustrated by the visitor!" (She also notes, "Availability and money are two factors that hamper my attempts to always make one of these connections.")

Author Ellen Jackson says, "I had a wonderful time at the Santa Barbara Public Library reading *The Book of Slime* to the kids. In the book there's a recipe for 'slime pie.' We made the pie, and everyone had a piece while I read the book and talked about slimy animals, specifically slugs and snails. Afterward, we had a snail race. All the snails were put in the center of a piece of cardboard inside a circle. The first snail to cross over the perimeter of the circle was the winner. We had a great time!

"When I read *Brown Cow, Green Grass, Yellow Mellow Sun* at the library, the kids sat in a circle and each took a turn shaking a jar containing whipping cream until it turned into butter—because the book describes how the sun makes the grass grow, how the cow eats the grass and gives milk, and how the milk becomes butter."

Susan Campbell Bartoletti, author of *Growing Up in Coal Country*, says, "I've always been impressed with how teachers have made connections with my books. I have been in schools where teams of teachers have applied Howard Gardner's theory of multiple intelligences and created curricula in all seven areas: logical/mathematics, verbal/linguistics, musical/rhythmical, body/kinesthetic, interpersonal, intrapersonal, and spatial."

A middle-school teacher herself for many years, Susan has also been impressed with the way teachers have worked to "incorporate primary resources into their classroom activities. Teachers have used contemporary (c. 1900) help-wanted ads and other newspaper advertisements and articles to create math lessons and give students a sense of time and place for a discussion of the issues of gender, ethnicity, and class. It's interesting to see how the help-wanted ads were divided into jobs for 'girls' and 'boys' and what sort of employment opportunities existed for children. It's also interesting to see the discrimination that immigrants faced. It was common, for instance, for a newspaper article to report the subject's ethnic identity: for instance, a headline might read, 'Two Italians Found Guilty.'

"Teachers have also used my book as a springboard into helping students discover their own local and family history. Students have also researched the coal disasters and strikes mentioned in the book and created ballads. Some students also continued their 'disaster' and strike research and looked at their own local history.

"Students have collected their own oral histories. One of my favorite assignments is to have students interview the oldest person they can find and find out that person's earliest memory. Another interesting interview is to find out people's first jobs. They love discovering their teacher's and principal's first job."

Writing Inspiration and Instruction

Definitely give some thought to what kind of visit fits best with your writing mission in any given school year, and tell the visiting author if you particularly want the visit to focus on the writing process. Author Jennifer Richard Jacobson says, "For grades two through four, I do a presentation on patterns of threes in storytelling. I point out that in many stories, particularly picture books, the character tries and fails, tries and fails, tries and succeeds. I teach them the melodrama 'Pay the Rent,' encouraging boos and sighs. Then I tell them that although I think it is a clever thing that you can do with a piece of paper, it's not that great of a story. Together, we rewrite the story using the pattern of threes and having the heroine solve her own problem. I talk of how a character's persistence is often rewarded, and I talk of the writer's need for persistence through all stages of writing. At this point, I often show them the process *A Net of Stars* went through in its 21 submissions."

 Author Spotlight: Jennifer Richard Jacobson

Jennifer says, "One September, I announced to the first-grade class I was teaching that I wanted to write and publish a children's book. All year, the students supported me in my goal by writing with me, listening to my stories, and giving feedback in writing conferences. Little did I know that it can take years to get a first book published. When my first picture book, *A Net of Stars*, finally came out, those first graders who had helped me were graduating from high school! Many came to my first book signing.

"Since then, I have published nine more books, some for parents, some for teachers, and another children's picture book called *Moon Sandwich Mom*. I have learned that one must be persistent when it comes to dreams, and this theme often makes its way into my stories. I live in Maine with my husband and two children and continue to write full time."

Jennifer's newest professional book is *The Big Book of Reproducible Graphic Organizers: 50 Great Templates to Help Kids Get More Out of Reading, Writing, Social Studies, & More.*

The Novelist

A novelist can be a great choice for reaching students who read mostly novels—or for schools wanting to illustrate just how a professional writer works. Mary Casanova says, "Kids like to know where I get the ideas for my novels, so I tell them. By sharing the stories behind my stories, they get a clearer idea of how they can turn their own life experiences into story material. Besides sharing lively and sometimes humorous anecdotes, I also weave excerpts of my books for examples of techniques they can use in their own writing. And I always tell them about the huge box of drafts I accumulated in the writing of my first novel, *Moose Tracks*. I show them a few sample pages of my revisions, and they quickly get the idea that rewriting is indeed part of the writing process. Teachers love to have this idea reinforced!"

Author Franny Billingsley points out what a strong influence an author can have on students' images of themselves as writers. When she speaks and does writing activities with students she tries hard to say "something positive to *every* comment or shared piece of writing, even if it's dead off from what I was driving at. I think the more kids are able to participate in the process, the more they're able to 'own' their education—and the more they can take home with them what I'm talking about. So the cycle of, say, figuring out what kind of kid Nuria [from Franny's first novel, *Well Wished*] is from what she carries with her (*they* figure it out; I never tell them), to their framing of their own characters a bit with imagining props for those characters, to sharing what they've created aloud and hearing me comment on it—the understanding of it sort of gets into their bones."

The Poet

Author Anastasia Suen began doing author visits by offering 30- to 45-minute sessions, depending on the age of the students. "We started with a theme that I discussed with the teacher or librarian. I selected poems based on the theme and showed three to seven selections on the overhead. That way, everyone could see the words. We talked about rhythm and rhyme and repetition, the three Rs of poetry, and then we wrote an original poem based on the same theme. We go through the whole writing process, step by step."

Anastasia adds that she discovered "the hard way," what would work and what wouldn't. For her, what works is to choose a narrow theme ("spring," for example), "show poems that give examples, talk about poetry writing techniques in general, and then give the kids permission *not* to rhyme." She has students each fold a piece of paper in half and "brainstorm right off the top of their heads. I count to five and I want them to give me five topics related to the theme." She then stops everyone ("pencils up!") and asks them to circle their favorite.

"Now," she says, "I ask for five to ten words about that topic, and I count to 10 this time before I stop them. (Otherwise, I have kids after 45 minutes who 'can't decide.' I learned to use the 'freewriting' technique and make it like a race, so we get jump-started!) After they have words and a topic, I let them write without any interruptions. We often use a thesaurus, and I walk around and give advice where needed. They all want me to look at their poems."

Many authors who write picture books are poets at heart. After all, the texts of many picture books have much in common with poetry: strong images, rhythm, telling details, an economy of words. Picture book authors have the added advantage of being able to talk about the illustration process, an extra dimension to bookmaking.

The Magazine Writer

Don't overlook local authors who may not have published a book but have published magazine stories. Anastasia began doing her poetry writing workshops in schools long before she had any books come out, she says. She started speaking in schools when her work had only been published in magazines. even after her books began to be accepted by publishers, "well, they still had to be illustrated, so I just kept teaching while I waited." Before she had her own children, she says, she had been a teacher and already knew that she "enjoyed visiting the classroom. I come in and play for a while!"

Clearly, Anastasia was a valuable resource for the classroom even before any of her books came out, though she admits, "There does seem to be a view that 'real' authors write books. Sad but true."

Other authors, though, have reported that while students were impressed with their books, they were even more impressed with stories the author had written that appeared in such publications as *Highlights*, a magazine many students are familiar with from home or doctors' offices. Anastasia points out that writing for magazines actually takes a somewhat different set of skills than book writing—skills that are important for students to practice. "The tricky thing about writing for magazines," she says, "is to write about a topic and narrow the article to a single, specific slant. If you write about birds, for instance, you can't write about every bird. You only have so many words! The writer has to take a big topic and narrow it down *and* make it interesting to the reader."

In talking to students about magazine writing, as with poetry, Anastasia stresses the importance of being specific. "Generic is blah," she says. "I tell them to use their senses, to see it, feel it, taste it. . . . The writing is much sharper that way. The more specific you are, the better the writing. Details are very important." She says that teachers tell her the writing tips "help the students with their TAAS (Texas Assessment of Academic Skills) tests, our statewide testing program here in Texas. Writing tight is harder than just writing. It makes you think. What a concept! You have to think when you write!"

 Author Spotlight: Anastasia Suen

Anastasia says, "My mother played the radio from sunup to sundown when I was a child, and we went to the library every week. Music and words, words and music. I began writing poetry when I was 11.

"The ideas for my poems and books came from my family. My father worked at Cape Canaveral in the early NASA days. *Man on the Moon* recounts the Apollo 11 mission. My grandfather worked for the railroad. *Window Music* takes the reader on a train ride. My other grandfather built the P-51 Mustang airplane. *Air Show* showcases the history of flight. I wrote *Baby Born*, a celebration of a baby's first year, using my daughter's baby calendar. The idea for *Delivery*, an upcoming book about how things get delivered, came to me on the freeway when I was driving to visit my brother.

"As a credentialed teacher, I have worked in the classroom with children of all ages. Now I work behind the scenes to help make the books you use at school. Sometimes I write the books you use in the classroom. Sometimes I select the poems that you see in your school books. I love exploring new ideas. How about you?"

To learn more about Anastasia, look at her Web page http://www.flash.net/~asuen.

Taking a Peek at Writers' Work Habits

It can be very helpful for young writers to see that not every writer works in the same way. Anastasia Suen points out that each person's method "depends on who you are as a writer. Are you a discovery writer? Do you find out what you have to say after it comes out of your pen, or appears on your screen? Then you need the approach a lot of authors call BIC—butt in chair—no two ways about it. If you don't sit down, you simply don't write. On the other hand, some writers outline, plan, and think a book out before they put pen to paper (or hands to keyboard, as the case may be). 'Think writers' (my term) think first, and then they write. BIC doesn't help us think, it makes us crazy. We think while we are busy with something else. One isn't better than the other. As long as you end up with a finished story, what difference does it make? You have to do what works for you.

"I write fast, but at the same time, I write very slowly. I seem to have so many things going at once, and yet when I had three weeks in a row without school visits in March, I went stir-crazy. I know BIC is strongly recommended, but . . . it makes me crazy. I can't stay home and sit in that chair. I write in bed first thing in the morning—5 minutes, 10 minutes, 20, before I really wake up, and I write in my head when I walk everyday. I have to walk or run everyday, or I go crazy. That's when I plot out my books, when I work on lines. One of my author friends recently said she liked the tightness, the restrictions of writing within a certain form. I love it! I know how many pages I have and what the turns need, and I plan it all in my head before I write. Then I sit down and write very fast. I found that out the hard way, too. (Is there any other way?) I have to write it right now when I'm interested in it, or forget it! So, I can have a book in my files—in my head—for years and then write a new version, zoom, in a few hours, in a few days. If it doesn't feel right, I file it away for another time, which could be years later. Then I work on something else. I write everyday, but I don't sit in that chair for a long time everyday. I write for 'wigglers' because I am one!"

The Storyteller Visit

Janice M. Del Negro, editor of the *Bulletin of the Center for Children's Book* and a storyteller herself, notes that public libraries use storytellers more than they use any other kind of performer and that some lucky libraries even have librarians on their staff who do storytelling too. Schools are also increasingly making good use of storytellers. Janice says, "When a librarian or teacher invites a storyteller into the library or classroom, they are weaving the threads of community. Storytelling creates a community of listeners from a group divided by age, gender, race, and economics. The act of story-listening is a communal activity that can provide a group of diverse individual listeners with a common culture, a unity from the diversity of many."

Great Storyteller Visits

Storyteller Michael Parent identifies a few things that have made a big difference in his most successful storyteller visits: repeat visits, time for some smaller sessions, personal contact with students, students who have been read to, and students who are themselves writing stories. "Don't hesitate to have the same teller back if the kids really connect," he advises. "Don't think about variety as the ultimate thing."

Sometimes, Michael emphasizes, a truly excellent connection with a bookperson takes a while to build. His very best visit came out of a series of visits to a small country school in Palmyra, Virginia, which, back in the late 1970s or early 1980s, began to invite Michael to visit year after year, holding bake sales and other fundraising events to finance his presentations. "The principal, Wayne Guenther, was very committed to bringing this cultural experience to the kids," Michael says. Many years later, when Wayne Guenther was principal of Central Elementary School in Palmyra, he arranged for another visit from Michael.

At this point, Michael had published *Of Kings and Fools: Stories from the French Tradition in North America*, as well as other books and tapes. The visit was set up so everyone heard Michael in two big assemblies. Then Michael spent 12 minutes in every classroom where students were writing stories. He talked about storytelling and also about becoming a writer, and students asked questions.

The next year, Michael says, was the *great* visit. In this visit, two assemblies were held where Michael told stories. Next, 10 or 15 students who had written the best stories in the school read them aloud from the stage to their assembled classmates. Later in the day, Michael offered four sessions, 40 minutes each, with these student writers. He read them stories from his self-published book, *Growing Up Is a Full-time Job* and asked for general comments. "The children thus had the opportunity to be critics or feedback-givers," he says. Then he asked specific questions to be sure he had made various aspects of the story clear enough. Afterward, he says, "Kids came up to encourage me, saying things like, 'You did a good job with those stories.' "

David Alexander, a storyteller who has made school visits all over the world, says that one of his best school visits was at Santa Fe Trail Elementary in Kansas City, Kansas. "I spent four days telling stories and working with the upper grades teaching them about how to tell stories. Each student learned a three-minute story, and about 10 learned the stories well enough to share them in front of the entire school on the last day of the residency." He points out that such an ambitious program wouldn't have worked without a great deal of advance planning from administration and staff. "Teachers were prepared with an advance overview of the residency, the librarian read several of my books aloud during student visits, and a detailed schedule was worked out ahead of the visit to provide maximum efficiency for the upper grades to work on their stories ahead of the assembly." Even with all this planning, he notes, it was also necessary for both teachers and students to have a "flexible attitude," and to allow "for adjustment to the inevitable last minute glitches."

Storyteller Spotlight: David Alexander

"Stories are the manner in which I communicate—conversing, teaching, and performing in front of classrooms and audiences both in the United States and overseas. Since giving up a 27-year career as an educator in 1996, I have been a full time storyteller, author, and publisher. About half my teaching career was in the United States, and the rest was in international schools in Ethiopia, Pakistan, and Indonesia. I think sometimes that I am a story, and I hope there will be someone who comes along one day and will decide to be the keeper of it, for it is the only way I can live after death."

Factors to Consider in Choosing a Storyteller

As with other bookpeople, storytellers have a wide variety of possible strengths and focuses to choose from. Storyteller Donna Washington says, "Since I am a writer, as well as a storyteller and creative dramatist, I do both residencies and performances. In performance, I tell stories. Clients may choose what kinds of stories, within reason. As long as I am given enough time, I can work with whatever it is you need: Ancient Chinese, Egypt, Japanese, Irish, African . . . you name it.

"As a drama teacher, I like to focus on how simple stories can be taken off of a page and put onto the stage, or at least acted out in the classroom. I use games and exercises that help students build self-confidence and have fun while being exposed to elements from our rich cultural heritage.

"In writing residencies, I like to help students find ways of looking at their lives to find the fun. Whether we are creating fractured fairy tales or doing personal narrative or descriptive writing, we start with what we know and move on to what we can imagine."

Storyteller Spotlight: Donna Washington

Armed with a bachelor's of science in speech from Northwestern University, Donna Washington has been loose in the world since 1989. In that time, she has written and performed four one-woman shows, adapted folktales into two full-length stage productions for "Upstage Downstage," and performed as a storyteller at venues all over America and in Asia and Europe. She has also worked as an actress with "Upstage Downstage," The Trinity Theater Ensemble, and the Chicago Children's Theatre Company. Donna makes appearances in schools, libraries, young authors conventions, and literacy drives around the country. Her voice narrates a series of wordless picture books by Children's Press and two videotapes by Warren Coleman Communications. Her first privately produced audiocasette, *Live and Learn: The Exploding Frogs and Other Stories* can be ordered through QBOT5@aol.com. Her books include *The Story of Kwanzaa* and *A Pride of African Tales*.

More Options for Storyteller Visits

Storyteller Kathy Jarombek, a former children's librarian who does freelance storytelling in schools, says that she does several different types of visits, but that by far the most common type "is where I am there as an entertainer. This is true of all public libraries and many, perhaps 75 percent, of my school visits. The children's librarian or the cultural enrichment chair of the PTA calls and asks me to do a half-hour or 45-minute program. I then work out the details of my performance with my contact person: whether a microphone is needed, the configuration of the room where I'll be telling, the age of the kids, and all." In these visits, Kathy says, not much is required of the teacher or librarian except to stay involved, "not correcting papers or talking with another teacher in the back of the room." Once, a teacher left a second-grade classroom where Kathy was telling stories, and a student promptly developed a bloody nose! "Sometimes," Kathy says, "I feel that these performances are sort of superficial—one week a magician, the next week a storyteller!—but sometimes I'm reminded again of the power of storytelling and the connection between teller and audience. A few years ago, I was shopping in the A&P when a young woman, probably in her early 20s, came up and asked if I was the storyteller. When I said yes, she said that I had come to her middle school to tell stories when she was in seventh grade. She then started recounting the plot of 'Mary Culhane and the Dead Man'!"

A second type of visit is where a teacher, usually of fifth-grade students or older, asks Kathy "to come into her classroom to tell folktales and then talk about the different types of folktales and the ways in which these tales transmitted cultural wisdom from generation to generation." This type of visit is most effective, Kathy says, if the teacher has read various folktales with the students ahead of time. "Last year, a middle school teacher called me to come into her class for this purpose and then said, 'Oh, and while you're here, could you do the same thing with the other fifth-grade class?' Well, the difference between the two classes was like night and day. The teacher who had hired me had spent a week with her kids reading folktales, and the kids were really focused and asked a lot of questions. The other class enjoyed the storytelling portion of the program, but, without any background, they had a much harder time concentrating when I began discussing the types of folktales and their meanings. They were willing to participate when I asked them questions but asked none of their own."

In a third type of visit, students in fourth through eighth grades have had the opportunity to use Kathy as a model, instructor, and (sometimes) a coach, while they choose and learn their own folktales to tell. "Before I visit, the kids need to know exactly what the assignment entails and what they are expected to do. The teacher needs to inform me how far along they are—have they talked yet about folktale structure? Have they chosen their stories yet? Interestingly, many teachers say the child they least expected to shines at this—the shy child, the child who never takes an interest in anything—has often done very well!"

Elements to Strengthen Storyteller Visits

Storyteller David Alexander says that by far his favorite type of involvement with a school is a long-term residency "where students and staff become more than just a brief encounter or, worse, nameless faces in the crowd." Michael Parent agrees. "Set up the visit day so that a human relationship can exist between the storyteller and the kids," he says. "When there are big assemblies, it is important that the teller also go to individual classes or a double class to talk to the kids afterward. This way, at least some of the kids can relate and maybe ask questions during an informal session." Even if a student doesn't get the chance to ask a question during these smaller sessions, he points out, that student is "still relating to the teller through someone else they know who *is* asking questions."

 The Personal Connection with Students

At the North Jakarta International School, David says, he began the first day of a residency in a preschool classroom with the aim of getting to know the students. He opened with the first line of his favorite animal story about an enormous cat: "Once upon a time there was a king!"

A four-year-old boy in a khaki school uniform popped up, strode past the other speechless children and said, "Excuse me, sir. Your voice is disturbing the children."

It was David's turn to be stunned. "Sorry," he said. "I will try to keep it down."

"Thank you very much, sir," the boy said. He returned to his place, and David returned to the story "in a quieter and gentler voice, without further incident." Afterward, one of the teachers told David that the boy's father was the South African ambassador to Indonesia. The family was recently back in South Africa and ended up in a reception line to meet Nelson Mandela. When they reached the head of state, the boy said, "My name is Sakhile Belle. You can call me Mr. Belle." Fortunately, Nelson Mandela had the sense of humor to laugh heartily. "I made it a point," David says, "to drop by Sakhile's room every day of the residency after that, just to glean more wisdom that only a four year old can dispense."

Storytellers Who Are Also Authors

Storytellers may or may not have their own books to bring as part of their visits. Some have managed to translate a story that they usually tell into a written version so compelling that a major publisher picks it up. Janice Del Negro's *Lucy Dove* is a good example—a spooky story by a masterful storyteller, wonderfully illustrated, published by a major publisher. Others produce their own books. Storyteller David Alexander was teaching in an international school in Indonesia when he decided to produce a written version of one of his stories, "To Your Good Health, Your Majesty!" illustrated by one of his artistically gifted eighth-grade students. He later decided to also produce a book called *The Little Wide Mouth Gecko*, using one of his favorite "telling" stories with illustrations by Indonesian artist Yoes Rizal, who "dressed it up in Indonesian culture."

When the storyteller is also an author, try to integrate the writing experience into the visit. Michael Parent, for instance, offers writing workshops called "Go Write Ahead." He spends an hour to an hour and 15 minutes helping students write the "bare bones" of a story that they may later read aloud or learn to tell. "It personalizes their experience," he says.

"Storytelling is the link between speaking and writing," says Donna Washington. "Storytelling takes the spoken word and shapes it into form. Writing is when you take this form and transfer it onto paper or into the computer. Storytelling can fire the imagination in a way television cannot. Even reading a picture book is not as dynamic as having someone tell you a story. Students take whatever they need from a storyteller because stories have many meanings and appeal to people in different ways."

 Storytellers in Public Libraries

Connie Rockman, who has worked as both a librarian and storyteller, has these tips for hosting a successful visit:

"Public libraries and storytelling have been interconnected for a century now. In the early days of public library children's rooms (in the late 1890s and early 1900s), children's librarians learned that storytelling was a valuable tool for directing their young patrons to reading. Public library story hours were attended by children eight to twelve years old and were often formal affairs. At the Carnegie Library in Pittsburgh, Pennsylvania, for example, librarians told stories throughout the year around a cycle of legends. One year it was King Arthur; the next year it was *The Odyssey*, etc., with certain librarians designated to learn parts of the cycle. As the century progressed, other forms of entertainment began to compete for the school-age child's attention, and story hours in libraries began to concentrate on the preschool years.

"One way to revive the interest in storytelling as an entertaining and educational part of the public library's mission to school-age children is to hire itinerant storytellers for a large-scale special event. As a librarian in Stamford, Connecticut, for 10 years, it was my pleasure to bring professional storytellers to the main library auditorium for a once-a-year extravaganza. Setting the stage, advertising, and priming the audience are the responsibilities of the host librarian. Advertise the program by visiting school classes yourself, telling a story or two, and promising more wonderful tales as you hand out flyers for the program. Ask for a public service spot on your local radio station and find a way to make the program sound enticing to parents. Try to get a photo of your storyteller in the local newspaper, especially if they have stunning publicity shots for you to use.

"Be aware of the performer's needs for a comfortable working space, type of microphone, arrangement of the room, temperature of the room, and adequate staff to 'police' the crowd for squirmers, screamers, and squigglers. One storyteller/singer told me of a child who climbed up on a stage and started to play with the strings of her guitar while the parent beamed from the sidelines. It is the host's job to take action in a similar situation. In your introduction of the performer, include some ground rules for the audience. I find that using masking tape on the carpet to mark out areas for seating helps to keep them from crowding the performer. Ban strollers and infants from the program, or ask parents at least to remove infants and toddlers who are making distracting sounds.

"It is an unfortunate fact of our society that many parents are oblivious to the havoc their 'above average' but too-young children cause in an audience. I once hosted a program for author/illustrator Rosemary Wells. She was prepared to show a school-age audience the process of creating a picture book but was faced with an audience made up of toddlers whose parents knew about the 'Max and Ruby' board books and wanted to expose their bright two and three year olds to meeting the author. The toddlers, of course, could not have cared less, and the parents couldn't understand why. Sometimes, even with the best publicity, you cannot second-guess the audience's motives for attending!

"Authors and storytellers in public libraries deserve the best audience and the best setting you can give them. Try to provide a room where there are no distractions from passing traffic, and where late-comers can be brought in without notice, and let the audience know what is expected. All of these things can go a long way to make your program a success."

The Special Touch of Illustrators

Great Illustrator Visits

Illustrators have a little something extra to offer a school or library—they draw pictures! Librarian Peggy Koppleman notes that when illustrator Nancy Carlson visited Grand Forks schools, "her presentations were very exciting for students because she drew a picture while she was talking to the students. At each school, she leaves the character she draws." Illustrator Doug Cushman draws for students as he tells a story. Sometimes, he asks one of the students to "draw a scribble." Then Doug makes a character out of it. "The kids (and teachers)," he admits, "are pretty impressed. I get a lot of 'Wow!' and 'He's good!'s. The point, however, is that you don't have to be an artist to create a character for a picture book. An idea can come from anywhere, even a scribble on a piece of paper."

Doug also has slides that show a comic book he created as a high-school student, so that students can see his own early love of illustration and how he has turned that passion into a career. "I get great reactions from the kids with it," he says, "especially when I tell them that the bulldog in the plaid jacket was my high school principal! I show my French comic book (also high school) with the little puppy barking in French. I also show them a book I did when I was in fourth or fifth grade, titled 'Space Cat.' The kids love to see how I started."

Sometimes illustrators bring interesting and different book ideas as well. When an illustrator from Minneapolis, Max Haynes, visited in Grand Forks schools, he developed a project where children created their own version of a fairy tale. He then selected his favorite pieces of the children's writing, put the story all together, and illustrated it.

Teacher Clark Underbakke tells of watching illustrator Ralph Masiello "who had the second graders in our building standing on end with his lightning-fast drawings of bugs and skulls and other objects from his ABC books with Jerry Pollatta. He also had us in near tears telling about the creation of the art for *The Flag We Love* [by Pam Munoz Ryan]. A great guy!" He adds, "I also think of the timeless beauty of Peter Parnall's delicate drawings and how they so perfectly complement Byrd Baylor's tender, powerful words. *What* a year the time they *both* came! Wow!" The memories make a wonderful pile for him, he says—"Lois Ehlert's telling us that a great deal of the original artwork from her books is stacked underneath her bed in her apartment. Can you imagine? I remember Yoshi telling us how she dyes the silk to create her phenomenal illustrations. I could talk about this event forever."

Library media specialist Yvonne Hanley agrees that illustrators work special magic. "Even before I watched an illustrator work with children in a school," she says, "I saw Stephen Kellogg and other illustrators at conferences and took *such delight* in watching them do illustrations. Illustrators can give a wonderful insight into how a story can be told visually." Now she's seen the ways illustrators can inspire children, too. "The thing is, many children think they can't write, but they can draw. And when you listen to an illustrator, even the way that illustrator speaks gives you a deeper understanding of the story and a mental picture. Kids can watch it happening. You can't watch a writer write."

Illustrators Who Are Also Authors

Author/illustrator Doug Cushman says that his presentation changes with each new book published, "but the main theme is the same—using pictures as a jumping point for writing." The pictures he can draw as he talks, he says, are important because "to get through to the audience (and I mean both kids and adults) one has to be entertaining. If an illustrator can draw right there in front of the crowd, [he or she is] halfway home." He admits, in fact, that he feels "a little naked in front of a group if I don't have a marker in my hand and a pad of paper at my back." At the same time, he emphasizes that "there has to be a point to drawing, whether it's telling a story or showing how an idea is created. I do just that in my presentations. I tell how one of my Aunt Eater stories came about using a real-life event (getting seasick—always great visuals for kids!). Then I show them some little tricks on how to create their own characters."

Doug hopes that teachers leave his presentations "thinking that the writing process can be tackled from another point of view, almost 'through the back door.' " Because he shows slides of his early work, he hopes that students leave knowing that this published illustrator is "just like them. I read comic books as a kid just like they do. My early drawings look exactly like their drawings. They see that I was no different than they are. I come across as a little more human, not some big talented adult who is more special than they are." (For more information about Doug and his visits, check his Web page: http://www.doug-cushman.com.)

REFERENCES

Agell, Charlotte. *Dancing Feet*. San Diego: Harcourt, 1994.

——. *I Swam with a Seal*. San Diego: Harcourt, 1995.

——. *The Sailor's Book*. Willowdale, Ontario: Firefly, 1991.

——. *To the Island*. New York: DK Ink, 1998.

——. *Up the Mountain*. New York: DK Ink. Forthcoming.

Alexander, David. *The Little Wide Mouth Gecko*. With illustrations by Yoes Rizal. Topeka, KS: Desktop Publishers, 1996.

Balgassi, Haemi. *Peacebound Trains*. With illustrations by Chris Soentpiet. New York: Clarion, 1996.

——. *Tae's Sonata*. New York: Clarion, 1997.

Bartoletti, Susan Campbell. *Growing Up in Coal Country*. Boston: Houghton Mifflin, 1996.

Billingsley, Franny. *Well Wished*. New York: Atheneum, 1997.

Casanova, Mary. *Moose Tracks*. New York: Hyperion, 1995.

Davis, Katie. *I Hate to Go to Bed!* San Diego: Harcourt, 1999.

——. *Who Hops?* San Diego: Harcourt, 1998.

Del Negro, Janice. *Lucy Dove*. With illustrations by Leonid Gore. New York: DK Ink, 1998.

Falwell, Cathryn. *Christmas for 10*. New York: Clarion, 1998.

——. *Dragon Tooth*. New York: Clarion, 1996.

——. *Feast for 10*. New York: Clarion, 1993.

——. *Shape Space*. New York: Clarion, 1992.

——. *Word Wizard*. New York: Clarion, 1998.

Jackson, Ellen. *The Book of Slime*. With illustrations by Jan Davey Ellis. Brookfield, CT: Millbrook, 1997.

——. *Brown Cow, Green Grass, Yellow Mellow Sun*. With illustrations by Victoria Raymond. New York: Hyperion, 1995.

Jacobson, Jennifer, and Dottie Raymer. *The Big Book of Reproducible Graphic Organizers: 50 Great Templates to Help Get More Out of Reading, Writing, Social Studies, & More*. New York: Scholastic Professional Books, 1999.

Jacobson, Jennifer Richard. *Moon Sandwich Mom*. With illustrations by Benrei Huang. Morton Grove, IL: Whitman, 1999.

——. *A Net of Stars*. With illustrations by Greg Shed. New York: Dial, 1998.

Parent, Michael, and Julien Olivier. *Of Kings and Fools: Stories from the French Tradition in North America*. Little Rock, AR: August House, 1996.

Ryan, Pam Munoz. *The Flag We Love*. With illustrations by Jerry Polatta. Watertown, MA: Charlesbridge, 1996.

Suen, Anastasia. *Air Show*. New York: Holt. Forthcoming.

——. *Baby Born*. With illustrations by Chih-Wei Chang. New York: Lee & Low, 1998.

——. *Man on the Moon*. With illustrations by Benrei Huang. New York: Viking, 1997.

——. *Window Music*. With illustrations by Wade Zahares. New York: Viking, 1998.

Washington, Donna. *A Pride of African Tales*. With illustrations by James Ransome. New York: HarperCollins, 1999.

——. *The Story of Kwanzaa*. With illustrations by Stephen Taylor. New York: HarperCollins, 1996.

Chapter Four

The Book Connection

 ### READING THE BOOKPERSON'S WORK

Perhaps it seems obvious, but we should always remember that *books* are at the heart of every good visit. A prospective author or illustrator might ask you, in a worried tone, "Will the children have read [or] listened to my books?" That, of course, is the most basic and essential level of preparation. Author Frank B. Edwards says, "I think a lot of teachers are afraid they will steal the author's thunder if they preview the stories too much, but I have never known an author who thought that was the case. There is nothing more frustrating than spending an hour-long presentation 'introducing' one's work to kids for the first time or having kids realize they are indeed familiar with some titles as the talk winds to a close. The kids and teachers may be excited over the visit, but the author has ended up only serving appetizers instead of the main course and dessert." All visiting authors and illustrators agree. Children must be familiar with their work!

Author Spotlight: Frank B. Edwards

Frank B. Edwards is an author and editor who gave up a life of adult nonfiction in 1990 to pursue his love of children's picture books full time. Working with Tucson-based illustrator/author John Bianchi, he cofounded Bungalo Books, which has produced more than 30 books to date with sales of 1.3 million copies.

His first kids' book remains his favorite: *Mortimer Mooner Stopped Taking a Bath*. He is currently working on a series of books for new readers in first grade and an illustrated series of junior-level chapter books based on classic adventure series.

He lives near Kingston, Ontario, with his school teacher wife and their three children. More information about Frank and his books is available at http://www.BungaloBooks.com.

Preparing the Students

Author and Illustrator Visits

Start your preparations with your visitor's books. Encourage students to pore over the illustrations, savor and then discuss the text, and make the stories within these books their own. Author Jacqueline Briggs Martin talks about students who, in advance of a visit, have interacted in this way with her Bizzy Bones series. "I think it does make Bizzy part of the 'furniture' of their minds." A visiting bookperson should expect that all children will have had this level of experience, that the characters and settings of the books will have moved in to furnish their minds.

Author Spotlight: Jacqueline Briggs Martin

"I have always loved the sounds of words. I grew up on a dairy farm in Maine with three brothers and two sisters and remember being fascinated by the sounds of our cows' names. Riverflat Blanche Wisconsin was one of my favorites. I received a B.A. degree from Wellesley College and an M.A. in child development from the University of Minnesota, but did not expect to write children's books.

"When our children, Sarah and Justin, were young we read picture books every day—stacks of them. It was then that I decided I would like to write books that children and parents could enjoy together. The three-book Bizzy Bones series were my first books. Since then I have published eight others, including the ALA Notable Book *Grandmother Bryant's Pocket* and a picture-book biography of a self-taught scientist, *Snowflake Bentley*, which won the 1999 Caldecott Medal.

"In addition to writing, I like to grow roses and the vegetables needed for hot salsa, chilies, tomatoes, onions, and herbs.

"I live in Iowa with my husband Richard. We have enjoyed canoeing, tent camping, and hiking since our children were young, and still do now that they are grown.

"I do have a Web site, and, though the address may change as server possibilities improve, I will always be linked to the Children's Book Council site at http://www.cbcbooks.org/navigation/autindex.htm. I hope you'll visit via that link."

Author Sara Jane Boyers says, "When the classes are familiar with my books, the sessions are great fun and educational for both the students and for me. I am so interested in what children have to say and prepare my visits in a manner in which I am sure to elicit a response. It is rare that I have an unsuccessful session with students; however, if they are unfamiliar with my work, the time goes way too fast and the benefit for them and for me is not as great as it could be." As book people say over and over, a visit without preparation not only fails to be the success that it could be, it is also often a frustrating experience for students and author alike.

Author Spotlight: Sara Jane Boyers

"OK. I'm 13, hoping to be a journalist and designer. My mother says, 'Law school.' The result is that career classes love me! I've spent nine years as a music lawyer and ten years managing performers' careers, all the while juggling a third, and never-ending, career raising children. I've gone on to career numbers four and five which finally bring it all together—designing children's books and packaging adult fiction and nonfiction.

"My goal is to inspire critical thinking, whether through art and poetry, civics, or just plain wonder. I write about my favorite subjects. Thus, I have a series of illustrated books on contemporary art and poetry: *Life Doesn't Frighten Me* (Jean-Michel Basquiat's paintings with Maya Angelou's 1978 poem) and *O Beautiful for Spacious Skies* (Wayne Thiebaud's art with "America the Beautiful" by Katharine Lee Bates). More to come!

"Listening always to my children and their friends, I have also written *Teen Power Politics: Make Yourself Heard*, which seeks their attention with in-your-face issues affecting teens. I hope to invest them in our nation via voting, media literacy, and community activism (with, of course, a little art and poetry!).

"I live by the beach with one husband, two teens, and 16 animals. When not writing or feeding the herd, I photograph, speak in schools (K–12), and collect art and toy train signals."

Storyteller Visits

In preparing for a storyteller's visit, says storyteller Michael Parent, "the primary task is to help the kids to get to know the teller's work. The librarian or coordinator should take time to read the storyteller's tales in print to the kids, listen to the teller on audiotape, or watch the teller on videotape. The secondary task is to help them to know something about the teller him [or] herself."

Echoing Michael's words is storyteller Robin Moore. "What can a librarian do to prepare? Reading aloud and storytelling. When these two activities are already a part of the school environment, the students will be much more skillful in their listening. Listening with both the heart and the head is a learned skill. Being an audience is a learned skill. So is exploring the imagination. If kids are not asked to do these things in an educational setting, they may be confused about what to do when the storyteller is speaking. They may think they are watching television instead of sitting around the ancestral fire."

Storyteller Spotlight: Michael Parent

Michael is a storyteller, writer, and workshop leader. He has performed traditional and original stories, in both English and French, in many settings throughout the United States and Europe, since 1977. He has been featured at many festivals, including the National Storytelling Festival in Jonesborough, Tennessee, the International Storytelling Colloquium in Paris, and Open Borders Quebec–U.S. Cultural Exchange Performance Festival. School assembly programs have been and continue to be one of this dynamic performer's specialties. Michael's school shows include "singalongable songs" that the children join in on, folktales during which the audience is often assigned "jobs" to do that add involvement for the listeners and flavor to the story, and an original story (usually including juggling) that addresses issues related to growing up.

Michael grew up in a bilingual Franco-American family in Maine, enjoying a childhood that inspired many of his stories. After several years spent in Charlottesville, Virginia, Michael has returned to live in his home state.

Frustrations to Avoid

The Author's View

One California author tells the story of a school using the county's arts council list to "order up" an author right out of the council catalog. The author drove an hour out into the country to a small school. Somehow, no one at the school had any idea that she was coming, nor did they have any idea who she was when she arrived. And of course, they had not read any of her books!

Another author tells the story of walking into the classroom she was to be visiting and having the teacher say, "Sorry, what is your name?" No, the kids weren't familiar with her books either.

Still another author recalls the small rural school where she spoke to students who had never had an author visit before and had not been prepared for the visit in advance. The kids got excited about the bits of her books that she was showing them and started asking the teacher, "Where can we get those books to read?" The teacher answered, "You'll have to ask the Book Mobile the next time it comes around." Imagine. This school had spent several hundred dollars, plus travel expenses, in order for the author to visit each classroom as well as talk to faculty after school, but they did not spend the effort, energy, or money necessary to have the books available for the kids to read before and after the author's visit!

The Storyteller's View

A storyteller suggests that it is essential to pay close attention to the physical setup and scheduling issues that each individual performer has found effective. "Listen to the storyteller's advice on setup and scheduling. Some of their requests may seem nitpicky or nonsensical. But rest assured, this knowledge is hard won. When you have survived a program that has been a total disaster, the mind works furiously, trying to figure out what went wrong so that you will never make that mistake again. Often, the problem had something to do with poor planning."

The Librarian's View

Authors, illustrators, and storytellers aren't the only ones frustrated when classes aren't prepared for a visit. A public librarian who cosponsors an annual author program with one of the five elementary schools in town tells of hiring an author to speak to the entire seventh grade and then offer two writing workshops to classes. Despite repeated efforts to make connections, she says, "cooperation from anyone at the school was minimal at best." There was a library media specialist in the school, but according to the public librarian, "she didn't have enough time to help me, and also, she was not assigned by the principal to be the school coordinator. I had asked for her help in getting the teacher to cooperate, but she was met with the same disinterest as I was. The school library had only one copy of the author's books, so they couldn't make a display without help from us. I finally got permission to at least bring our copies up to the school to be displayed in the media center. The teacher assigned to coordinate on behalf of the school was not at all interested."

Similarly, a school library media specialist tells of her disappointment when teachers do not use the materials she has provided them in advance of a visit. The day before a recent visit, she learned that a few teachers hadn't even read the visitor's picture books aloud to their classes, despite the fact that their colleagues had not only read the books, but they had also done wonderful projects with their students and encouraged them to prepare interview questions. In another instance, she walked into a classroom with the author/illustrator team to see the books neatly displayed on the chalk ledge as they had been for some time. However, the teacher greeted the visitors by saying, "Oh, I forgot you were coming. I didn't read anything to the students yet." This librarian no longer assumes that teachers will remember to prepare. "I've learned to check in with everyone several times before a visit to see if they have done anything with their class." On the other hand, she reports, "the vast majority of the time I've been very pleased with most of the staff who do extensive preparation for visits. These visits are the most successful for everyone—the visitor, students, and staff."

How a Librarian Can Help

You may be a teacher who has taken on the task of bringing an author, illustrator, or storyteller to your classroom or school. Or you may be a teacher who is looking forward to being a participant in a visit. Either way, it will be beneficial, if possible, for you to connect with a librarian who can help you to enhance the visit. Some schools, of course, don't have a resident school library media specialist, and some rural towns don't have a town librarian, but even in those circumstances it might be possible for you to connect with a regional library children's librarian for help. If you are a school library media specialist or a public children's librarian, you can be a tremendous resource as organizer, advisor, cosponsor, and chief cheerleader for a visit.

The School Library Media Specialist

Michael Parent says that what happens in the school library on a daily basis is the key to kids' interaction with stories. "As a nerve center for story-related activities and imagination building, though, the library provides an essential foundation for such activities as a visit from writers, poets, storytellers, and various other artists. It's the librarian," if there is one, he says, "who keeps things crackling, imagination-wise, in a school," because the best preparation that kids can have for a visiting storyteller is to be read to and told stories. Michael sees no great difference between the two in preparing kids to be *listeners* to stories.

Storyteller Robin Moore agrees. The librarian's role, he says, is "to be keeper of the flame. The ancestral campfire around which our stories have been told for thousands of years must have a place in the school. That place is the library. The librarian who understands the library as a sacred space for storytelling will be an excellent host for any storyteller."

The Public Children's Librarian

Many public librarians work in cooperation with local schools to host visits by bookpeople, supporting schools in a variety of ways. Sometimes they secure or offer funding. Sometimes they manage the organizational details. Sometimes they really manage the whole show. Regardless, both schools and public libraries benefit from these collaborations.

Public Library/School Partnerships: Kalamazoo Public Library

For the past 25 years, the Kalamazoo Public Library in Kalamazoo, Michigan, has brought bookpeople to Kalamazoo schools. Funds have come from the Michigan Council for the Arts, Michigan Council for the Humanities, Plaza Art Circle, and Upjohn Foundation, says the library's community liaison for children, Mary Rife. During some years, the library's program includes just one author/illustrator visit to the library in honor of Children's Book Week in November. Other years, the bookperson visits selected schools and offers community programs, too. In still other years, the library has brought in an author every month during the school year to speak in area schools. In fact, this is the way they celebrated their 100th anniversary of children's services in 1997, with a total of 22 authors and illustrators who visited every public school in the city. In addition, nonpublic school students were invited to attend programs in the branch libraries. The public library, the community, and the schools were all represented on the planning committee. The $33,000 program, funded with a grant from the Gilmore Foundation, a gift from the Kalamazoo County Juvenile Home, special gift funds at the library, and a small grant from the public schools, received broad community support and cooperation.

For all programs, Mary says, the library is responsible for booking the visitors, contacting the schools, making all travel and local arrangements, and managing all of the printing for the registrations sent to each teacher in the intermediate school district as well as to those on their own mailing list. Generally, she adds, they are the fiscal agent for the project and also pay the author.

In fall 1998, the Kalamazoo Public Library and the Willard Public Library in Battle Creek, Michigan, joined forces to bring author Rafe Martin to their communities. Funded by a Kellogg Foundation Expert in Residence Grant, Martin offered a program titled A Storyteller's Tale: Empowering the Imagination. Rafe began his residency in Kalamazoo with an evening reception, followed by a daylong program at the university open to adults—teachers, librarians, storytellers, college students, parents. On the weekend, he presented three storytimes at three Kalamazoo branch libraries. In Battle Creek he visited five schools and offered an evening family storytime as well at the Willard Public Library.

In speaking of school/library cooperative visit programs, Mary says, "Scheduling authors in the schools can be tricky. In Kalamazoo, we have 18 public elementary schools and 14 non-public schools. . . . Last year one school could not find a large enough room to collect their children for the presentation on one of the days that the author was here." A nonpublic school nearby came to their rescue, Mary says, by hosting four of the public school classes in addition to planning for their own students. Schools offer assistance to the public library for visiting book-people too. "On various occasions the schools have hosted one of our visitors for lunch or dinner. Occasionally they have provided artwork and expertise in designing our flyers and invitations." The children's librarian, whose library or branch serves each school, plans directly with the school library media specialist of each school involved. Mary agrees that it is a tremendous amount of work. However, she says, the ripples are wide. "Hearing the children coming in requesting books by our visitors is heartwarming. We also find that after someone has visited, their books are often on reserve. Some of our teachers have indicated that the authors were new to them and that they would now use their works. And one year, after an eight- or nine-month visiting program, both in the schools and at the libraries, a 20-year-old patron came in with each one of the bookmarks [prepared for the visiting bookpeople] and told us that he wanted to read those books as he had not had time to read them yet!"

 ## Public Library/School Partnerships: Lacey Timberland Library

At the Lacey Timberland Library in Lacey, Washington, youth services associate Nancy Schutz has twice arranged to have authors visit her public library as well as several schools in the North Thurston School District. When she invited author Ben Mikaelsen to visit a middle school, two elementary schools, and her library, he commented on the great relationship that Nancy's public library had with the local school librarians. When Nancy invited Hanneke Ippisch to visit the library, one high school, and two middle schools, her library went a step further. In addition to arranging the visit, they also cosponsored the event, paying more than their share in order to make the visit affordable to the schools. Nancy also provided transportation for Hanneke throughout her visit and served as the contact person for her. Under their current philosophy, Lacey Timberland Library "would like the authors to reach as many students as possible and that means, in many cases, arranging for them to go to the schools. We want authors to visit the library as well, but we cannot afford to absorb the entire cost and realize that it is difficult for us to 'create' an audience of young adults."

Public Library/School Partnerships: Carmel Clay Public Library

In her position as young adult services coordinator at the Carmel Clay Public Library in Carmel, Indiana, Renee Vaillancourt cooperated with the media specialists and teachers at Carmel High School on several occasions to bring authors of young adult books to town. The authors presented in classrooms during the day and then at the library in the evening. The school and the public library split the costs of the honoraria, travel, and lodging. Renee says, "I feel pretty confident in saying that both the school and the public library saw the collaboration as a win-win situation. The school probably got more for their money (sometimes they would have a presentation open to the public as well as having the author in the classrooms—the public library always only had one event), but we both benefited from having the author in town."

 ## Public Library/School Partnerships: Fort Collins Public Library

In Fort Collins, Colorado, for the past five years local Rotary Clubs have raised money to support a visit from one or two popular authors for grades four through six, reports lead librarian for children's services Lu Benke of the Fort Collins Public Library. The library cooperates with the school district to arrange assembly programs at four local schools over two days. Through the district media services director, Lu determines which schools will host the visits, and then the media services director contacts the media specialists at the individual schools to line things up, including the book ordering and signings at each school. Lu recommends the authors, ascertains their availability and cost, and makes the initial contacts. The public library also helps with publicity and serves as a base for home schoolers and private schoolers to receive information about the author visits.

Lu reports that school response has been positive and the visits successful. There have, however, been a few difficulties. "Teachers in some schools did not encourage the kids to read the authors' books or become familiar with the authors before the visits. As we observed the visits, it was obvious that the kids got the most out of the visits if they were familiar with at least one book by the author." In response, Lu is looking for ways to increase involvement of the teachers in the choice of authors and the planning process. In addition, she is working to improve participation by private and home schoolers.

One unexpected benefit of the program, says Lu, is that "the Rotary Clubs are becoming more of a major funding source, supporting reading for children in both the public libraries and the schools. The former director really nurtured this by getting the Rotarians to read the authors' books and attend the presentations and/or the lunches, and establishing a "banquet" specifically for the Rotarians and the authors to socialize. The new director is continuing this trend, and this past year the Rotarians donated $14,500 to our new branch for children's services and are hoping to donate at least that much to the main library children's services in the next two years."

 ## Public Library/School Partnerships: Clearwater Public Library

Jana Fine, youth services librarian at the Clearwater Public Library in Clearwater, Florida, has been taking authors into the public schools since the library director decided that the main floor of the library could no longer accommodate author talks with their audiences of 500 children. The library decided, instead, to take authors to the schools. Since then, when the library brings a bookperson in (with funding from their friends and foundation), they host one program at the library for the three schools within walking distance and the public, and then take the guest to two other schools for a program that day. They try to bring a visitor to each of the 10 elementary schools, three middle schools, and two high schools, in addition to the private schools. "I have very good working relationships with the information specialists in the elementary, middle, and high schools in our city," Jana says, "visiting almost all of them at least once a year, and working to encourage cooperative programming." The library hosts eight to ten bookpeople per year and has had more than 50 visitors over a 14-year period.

 ## Public Library/School Partnerships: Schenectady County Public Library

Children's librarian Serena Butch at the Schenectady County Public Library in Schenectady, New York, has also worked with school librarians for author visits. In all cases, she says, there was a school media specialist to work with. "We usually worked out an arrangement where the author would do a public library program after speaking at a school. Usually there was a financial incentive—that is, the author's travel fees or even speaking fees would be reduced by sharing the cost between us." The shared visits were very well received, Serena says. "Not only were they a good opportunity to work with our school counterparts, but they provided a different audience for the author. While the school visits are fairly structured, may be curriculum related, and are tightly scheduled, the public library program was more flexible. We usually had an evening program, invited more of a family audience, and let the author speak about whatever he or she wanted. One of the best shared programs was with Cynthia

DeFelice. In the schools she talked specifically about her books, using different ones across the grade levels. For the evening program, she had a big audience of families and she basically performed as a storyteller. She was fantastic! We also did a fairly big shared visit several years ago with Steven Kellogg. We had a third partner in that case with a local children's museum. To tell you the truth, we could rarely afford an author without some outside partnerships. That is why the visits to both schools and the public library are few and far between."

TC Public Library/School Partnerships: Monroe Public Library

The Monroe Public Library in Monroe, Connecticut, does not have a room in which to hold programs, says Children's Librarian Claudia Livolsi. Therefore, the library cosponsors a program with one of the five public elementary schools each year. Claudia notes that visits in which there is cooperation between the participating school, especially from the library media specialist, and her library are much more successful than those without a close collaboration. Regardless, she says, "I [have] had many kids who attended [the author visit] tell me how much they enjoyed the programs."

Frequently, at the time of a visit, an author will hear teachers say that they haven't had a chance to read all of the author's books to the students. "We've had trouble getting our hands on them," they complain. Quite likely, they didn't involve their school library media specialist or public children's librarian!

Interlibrary loan (the system that allows libraries to borrow and share resources) is a wonderful resource in many situations, but particularly when a bookperson is coming to visit a school or community. For example, when Toni is hosting an author/illustrator visit at Longfellow Elementary School in Portland, Maine, she prepurchases two copies of each of the titles she does not hold in the Longfellow School collection. From this base, she builds a large collection of the visitor's books with the help of interlibrary loan. Two months in advance of the visit (see **Nuts 'n' Bolts for the Visit Organizer: Advance Planning for an Author/Illustrator Visit**, p. 61) she contacts each of the other library media specialists in the district and asks to borrow all of the books by the visitor held in their collections. If Mary Peverada, the public children's librarian isn't planning a simultaneous visit by the same author/illustrator, she also borrows all copies of the visitor's books from the Portland Public Library and all of its branches. This ensures that all teachers and students at Longfellow School will have access to the books as they need them. In some cases, it has been possible to supply every classroom with a library copy of each of the visitor's books!

Nuts 'n' Bolts for the Visit Organizer

Advance Planning for an Author/Illustrator Visit

Prepared by Toni Buzzeo, MA, MLIS
and the Longfellow School (Portland, Maine) Library Committee

Nine Months to One Year in Advance

___1. Select author based on recommendations.

___2. Contact author individually or through his or her publisher to determine price and availability.

___3. Seek funding approval.

___4. Set dates and times, coordinating with school calendar, author, and possible evening events (which will enhance author-signing attendance).

___5. Send a letter of agreement/contract stipulating dates and times, sessions, and costs covered (final schedule will be prepared later).

Two to Three Months in Advance

___1. Contact author to request photographs, biographical material, a copy of his or her signature, and any available curriculum or enhancement materials, such as lesson plans, galleys of upcoming work, free posters, and bookmarks.

___2. Make a list of special equipment or materials author will need during the visit.

___3. Set the schedule for the author days (submit a draft to faculty for fine-tuning).

___4. Gather the following teacher resources:

    a. Order two copies of each title for the library.

    b. Borrow copies of the author's books from area public libraries/other schools.

    c. Order copies of supplemental books that extend the author's books.

    d. Catalog all of these copies under a single material type in the online catalog.

    e. Prepare teacher packets to include copies of Web pages (if available), any lesson plans, the final schedule, an annotated bibliography of the author's works, and biographical material about the author.

    f. Order books for author signing from publishers, jobber, or bookstore.

Three Weeks to One Month in Advance

___1. Create an author brochure to go home to all families, including a photo and the signature of the author, as well as a bibliography and a special activity for families to use in preparation for the visit.

___2. Set up bulletin boards.

Two Weeks in Advance

___1. Order author check from funding source.

___2. Decorate library/classroom.

___3. Purchase or make gift for author.

___4. Obtain author supplies and equipment.

___5. Assign people to escort author, take photographs, and set up and staff author signing tables.

___6. Schedule staff luncheon with author and solicit desserts.

Reprinted from "The Finely Tuned Author Visit" by Toni Buzzeo, *Book Links*, March 1998. Permission granted from *Book Links: Connecting Books, Libraries, and Classrooms*, the American Library Association.

READING SUPPLEMENTAL BOOKS

We hope you are now fired up to Read! Read! Read! before the visit of any bookperson to your classroom or school. However, the best-prepared children are those who have gone beyond the reading of the visitor's books to the terrific connections that can, and should, be made from these books to other related books. Many of these books will play a part in the curriculum connections we will discuss in the next chapter. Others are important simply as a way of broadening the children's experience as they prepare for a visit.

Preparing the Students

For example, Kevin Hawkes has illustrated his own stories in *Then the Troll Heard the Squeak* and *His Royal Buckliness*. Much more frequently, though, he illustrates the text of other writers. How rich in discussion opportunities it is to gather other books by the authors that Kevin has illustrated to compare how that one author's work is treated by different illustrators. For instance, Kevin illustrated Michelle Dionetti's *Painting the Wind*. Another of Dionetti's picture books, *Coal Mine Peaches*, was illustrated by Anita Riggio. The reflective tone of *Coal Mine Peaches* seems to require Anita's haunting watercolors, while the exuberance of Paris and of Van Gogh's own art propels Kevin's flights of color and light in *Painting the Wind*. Students who compare the illustration requirements of the text for the two books will come to a visit with Kevin Hawkes much more prepared to appreciate his illustration style and to ask probing questions.

Author/Illustrator Spotlight: Anita Riggio

"Often, children ask me if I'd dreamed about being an author and illustrator as I was growing up. The truth is that I didn't realize picture books were made by *real* people until I was an adult.

"Today, children have the opportunity to connect people to the books they make. Hopefully, in doing so, children visualize dreams for themselves—dreams that are not only in the field of publishing.

"In my work with children, I emphasize that the *process* of bookmaking is real work—sometimes frustrating, but always rewarding. Sharing my adventures with the 'A-word,' as in, 'Please rewrite (or redraw or repaint) *again*' always brings giggles and groans of recognition. That recognition elicits insightful questions and often lively discussion—my favorite part of the presentations.

"So, did I dream of becoming a writer and illustrator of picture books when I was a child? Not exactly. I dreamed of becoming a newspaper reporter, a detective, an artist, an actress, a teacher, and a ballerina, though, and creating and talking about my books allows me to 'be' most of those things.

"I hope that sharing my work with children will teach them a bit about writing and illustrating. More importantly, I hope it offers a rope they can use to lasso their own dreams."

In the larger picture, illustration in picture books is often the first and most constant exposure to art that children receive. Librarian Laura Manthey says, "Many children will never be in an art museum, never have the opportunity to study art. But think about what they can learn to appreciate through picture books. Over six or seven years in elementary school they can be exposed to a tremendous variety of art."

Similarly, nonfiction authors often have many different illustrators. It is challenging for students to study the illustrations in each of the author's books to determine how the chosen illustrator's style matches the subject of the book. Beyond that, students exercise complex thinking skills as they look at the illustrations prepared for books other than those written by the visiting author. For example, study the similarities and subtle differences between David Frampton's illustrations for Jane Kurtz's folktale *Miro in the Kingdom of the Sun*; Carol Carrick's historical study of the whale trade, *Whaling Days*; and Miriam Chaikin's *Clouds of Glory: Jewish Legends & Stories About Bible Times*. Offering students an opportunity to compare an illustrator's responses to other texts will cause them to think further about the text at hand as well as about the interplay of text and illustration in the nonfiction-book format. The questions they ask of the author will be illuminated by this broader base of knowledge.

 Student Illustration Projects

In preparing for author visits, students at Longfellow School have twice had opportunities to bring their *own* artistic vision to a text. In both cases, it was a wonderful experience.

Prior to a visit from Jane Kurtz, Toni asked Jane to send a copy of the text of Jane's soon-to-be-released picture book, *Trouble*. All third-grade teachers read the text to their classes. These classes then worked with Bob Auclair, Longfellow School art teacher, to design an illustrated version of *Trouble* as they imagined it. During Jane's visit, the illustrated books were presented to the author and she, in turn, shared Durga Bernhard's final illustrations with them on full-screen overhead transparencies.

Before her visit to Longfellow School, author Deborah Hopkinson sent Toni the text for her forthcoming picture book about Fannie Farmer, *Fannie in the Kitchen*. Fourth-grade teachers read this text to their classes, and once again students, with their classroom teachers and Bob Auclair, designed their own illustrated copies of the book. One class studied old cookbooks from the last century, including an original copy of *The Fannie Farmer Cookbook*. Two classes even prepared their books to look like old-fashioned tied-recipe files! Students presented their books to Deborah Hopkinson, but both students and author have to wait for the publication of the book to see illustrator Nancy Carpenter's artistic vision of the story.

Author Spotlight: Deborah Hopkinson

"When I dreamed of being a writer, I imagined myself working alone in some idyllic 'room with a view,' not positioned in a gym in front of 300 noisy kids with a slide projector that won't work! Now, of course, I would not give up my connections with students and teachers for the world. I treasure the thank-you letters I've received from students responding to my picture books, *Sweet Clara and the Freedom Quilt*, *Birdie's Lighthouse*, *A Band of Angels*, and *Maria's Comet*, and I look forward to getting their reactions to my forthcoming books: *Fannie in the Kitchen* and *Under the Quilt of Night*. When I'm not writing or presenting, you'll find me working at Whitman College in Walla Walla, Washington."

Visits from storytellers may also require advance gathering of books. If the storyteller's performance is to be planned around tales from a particular region of the country or world or a particular theme, a collection of books will be helpful in preparing children for the visit. In fact, Walter the Giant Storyteller prefers that schools suggest a theme around which he will build his performance. Walter, who performs published books, then provides schools and libraries with a list of titles. He encourages libraries to have those books on hand for children to check out the day of the reading and schools to have multiple copies.

How a Librarian Can Help

The ideal situation will include a librarian as the most efficient and effective resource gatherer. A librarian can create bibliographies of books—including related books by other authors and illustrators or books related to a storyteller's performance—turning to interlibrary loan, if necessary, to find all of the books needed for the project. If you're working in a school without a library media specialist and do not have a town librarian available to you, you might try calling the nearest large city or regional library to ask for help.

The third category of supplemental books teachers and students need in order to prepare for a visit is the category where a librarian can prove to be the most useful. These are books related to the subjects or themes of the books written or illustrated by the visiting bookperson. As author Roland Smith says, "Because I write fiction and nonfiction (and the fiction is realistic), there is a lot teachers and librarians can do with the material if they choose. Environmental issues, wildlife, endangered habitats, diverse cultures are just a few of the subjects they could, and have, tied into curriculum." A collection of books and AV materials that enrich, extend, and enhance the topics of the visitor's books can be a tremendous resource.

At Longfellow School, teachers often tailor the timing of various curriculum studies to coincide with the upcoming visit. For example, a visit from Jacqueline Briggs Martin was a perfect opportunity to tie in several curriculum units in fourth grade (see *Washing the Willow Tree Loon*, p. 65). Likewise, a visit from Jane Kurtz allowed several primary classrooms to engage in a comparative folklore study (see *Fire on the Mountain*, p. 65–66). So many children's books have rich connections to the curriculum. And the ties of a visitor's books to the curriculum become even richer when you study them in relation to other books and media about the curriculum topic.

Washing the Willow Tree Loon by Jacqueline Briggs Martin

Washing the Willow Tree Loon is the sensitive story of the many human efforts to save wildlife, especially an oil-covered loon, after an oil spill in Turtle Bay. Joan Gildart, a fourth-grade teacher at Longfellow School, took the opportunity to combine the study of Maine wildlife (a segment of the Maine unit), the study of environments and ecosystems, and the study of the tragic 1996 *Julie N* oil spill in Portland Harbor with the reading of *Washing the Willow Tree Loon* in advance of Jacqueline Briggs Martin's visit. She used the following collection Toni gathered:

Berger, Melvin. *Oil Spill! Let's Read-And-Find-Out Science, Stage 2*. With illustrations by Paul Mirocha. New York: HarperCollins, 1994.

Grindley, Sally. *Peter's Place*. With illustrations by Michael Foreman. New York: Harcourt, 1996.

Klein, Tom. *Loon Magic for Kids*. Milwaukee: Gareth Stevens, 1990.

Lantier-Sampon, Patricia. *The Wonder of Loons*. Milwaukee: Gareth Stevens, 1992.

Legacy for a Loon. Prod. by Walter and Myrna Berlet. 20 min., Maine Inland Fishes and Wildlife Department, 1982, videocassette.

Martin, Jacqueline Briggs. *Washing the Willow Tree Loon*. With illustrations by Nancy Carpenter. New York: Simon & Schuster, 1995.

Pringle, Laurence P. *Oil Spills: Damage, Recovery, and Prevention* (A Save-the-Earth Book). New York: Morrow, 1993.

Quest: Investigating the World We Call Maine. "Episode #301: Oil Spill!" Prod. Kate Arno, 55 min., Maine Public Television, 1997, videocassette.

Fire on the Mountain by Jane Kurtz

In this retelling of an Ethiopian folktale, Alemayu, a dreamer, goes off to spend the whole night on a cold mountain, in response to a rich man's challenge, and it requires all of his imagination to survive. When the rich man cheats him out of the reward, Alemayu and his sister must once again use their wisdom and imagination to come up with a solution. Prior to Jane's visit, primary-grade teachers at Longfellow School compared Jane's version of this folktale with other versions, published in the books below, and then engaged in activities ranging from Double Bubble (Venn diagram) comparison to writing their own versions of the story. They used the following collection of resources that Toni gathered:

Creeden, Sharon. "The Warmth of a Fire." In *Fair Is Fair: World Folktales of Justice*. Little Rock, AR: August House, 1997.

Jaffe, Nina. *In the Month of Kislev*. With illustrations by Louise August. New York: Viking, 1992.

Yolen, Jane. "Rich Man, Poor Man." In *Favorite Folktales from Around the World*, edited by Jane Yolen. New York: Pantheon, 1988.

Birdie's Lighthouse by Deborah Hopkinson

Combining stories drawn from the diaries of four real-life lighthouse heroines, Deborah has written the fictional story of Birdie (Bertha) Holland, who moved with her family to Maine's Turtle Island lighthouse and ultimately kept the lights burning there in her father's absence during a formidable storm. Before Deborah's visit, Longfellow School intermediate students read *Birdie's Lighthouse* and other lighthouse books, studied lighthouses, and even built some lighthouses themselves from a variety of materials. Other lighthouse resources that can be used in connection with Deborah's title follow:

Fleming, Candace. *Women of the Lights*. Illustrated by James Watling. Morton Grove, IL: Whitman, 1995.

Gibbons, Gail. *Beacons of Light: Lighthouses*. New York: Morrow, 1990.

Guiberson, Brenda Z. *Lighthouses: Watchers at Sea*. New York: Holt, 1995.

Jones, Dorothy H., and Ruth S. Sargent. *Abbie Burgess: Lighthouse Heroine*. Rockport, ME: Down East, 1976.

Light Spirit: Lighthouses of the Maine Coast. Prod. by Jeff Dobbs, 50 min, Jeff Dobbs Productions, 1997, videocassette.

Pfitsch, Patricia Curtis. *Keeper of the Light*. New York: Simon & Schuster, 1997.

Roop, Peter and Connie. *Keep the Lights Burning, Abbie*. Illustrated by Peter E. Hanson. Minneapolis: Carolrhoda, 1987.

As before, it is the public librarian and/or the school library media specialist who is the best resource for suggesting related books, or for locating books that may be difficult (but seldom impossible!) to find as preparations are underway for a successful visit. The good news is that all of this preparation and hard work will ensure success. As Roland Smith says, "If [the students] aren't prepared, [the visit] will go fine, but it will be nothing like a visit where they are prepared. In a school that isn't prepared, [the children] are excited by the end of the day after I've spoken, but it's too late because I'm heading out the door." In a school where students have read the visitor's books, have studied the interplay of text and illustration, have studied curriculum content related to the visitor's book, the excitement is in the air as the visitor walks through the door in the morning. "The better prepared the students, the more engaging the visit," says author Mary Casanova. "If a school has put its effort into this kind of preparation, then the energy regarding the visit is electric."

Nuts 'n' Bolts for Librarians: Resource Management

It can seem an impossible task to manage so many special collections linked to an upcoming visit, from multiple copies of the visitor's books to the multitude of books related to each of these books. It is easiest to handle all of these books by circulating them as you do your other materials. (The Longfellow School Library Media Center is automated, and Toni temporarily attaches a bar code to each borrowed item, allowing her to set special circulation periods for these items and to utilize the reserve function.) In addition, by using removable tape, it is possible to note the connection each supplemental book has to the visitor's books. For example, when Jane visited Longfellow School, Toni placed a piece of removable tape vertically on the front cover of each book, whether a book was from her own collection or a borrowed title. On the tape, she wrote the name of the book to which it was connected. For example, on *In the Month of Kislev* she wrote "Fire on the Mountain." This was a reminder to the teachers who borrowed it, and to herself and her colleague, that this book was a variant of the story Jane told in *Fire on the Mountain* and could be used with it.

Nuts 'n' Bolts for Teachers: Checklists

One of the most important things you can do as you prepare for a visit is to share the visitor's books and the supplemental books with your students. If the visitor has a long list of titles, keeping track of them can be a task in itself. Toni recommends working from a checklist. Ask the school or public librarian to provide you with a list of books by the visitor. As you plan units to coincide with these books, you might also want a list of the associated books your librarian recommends to you. Then, use the list as a checklist. The Longfellow teachers do this and find that they are easily able to identify the books that they have not yet shared, or additional resources that will supplement their curriculum study surrounding an individual title.

REFERENCES

Angelou, Maya. *Life Doesn't Frighten Me*. With illustrations by Jean-Michel Basquiat. Edited by Sara Jane Boyers. New York: Stewart, Tabori & Chang, 1993.

Bates, Katharine Lee. *O Beautiful for Spacious Skies*. With illustrations by Wayne Thiebaud. Edited by Sara Jane Boyers. San Francisco: Chronicle, 1994.

Boyers, Sara Jane. *Teen Power Politics: Make Yourself Heard*. Brookfield, CT: Twenty-First Century, 1999.

Carrick, Carol. *Whaling Days*. With illustrations by David Frampton. New York: Clarion, 1993.

Chaikin, Miriam. *Clouds of Glory : Jewish Legends & Stories About Bible Times*. With illustrations by David Frampton. New York: Clarion, 1998.

Dionetti, Michelle. *Coal Mine Peaches*. With illustrations by Anita Riggio. New York: Orchard, 1991.

——. *Painting the Wind*. With illustrations by Kevin Hawkes. Boston: Little Brown, 1996.

Edwards, Frank B. *Mortimer Mooner Stopped Taking a Bath*. With illustrations by John Bianchi. Newburgh, Ontario: Bungalo, 1990.

Hawkes, Kevin. *His Royal Buckliness*. New York: Lothrop, Lee & Shepard, 1992.

——. *Then the Troll Heard the Squeak*. New York: Lothrop, Lee & Shepard, 1991.

Hopkinson, Deborah. *A Band of Angels*. With illustrations by Raul Colon. New York: Atheneum, 1999.

——. *Birdie's Lighthouse*. With illustrations by Kimberly Bulcken Root. New York: Atheneum, 1997.

——. *Fannie in the Kitchen*. With illustrations by Nancy Carpenter. New York: Atheneum. Forthcoming.

——. *Maria's Comet*. With illustrations by Deborah Lanino. New York: Atheneum, 1999.

——. *Sweet Clara and the Freedom Quilt*. With illustrations by James Ransome. New York: Knopf, 1993.

——. *Under the Quilt of Night*. With illustrations by James Ransome. New York: Atheneum. Forthcoming.

Kurtz, Jane. *Fire on the Mountain*. With illustrations by E. B. Lewis. New York: Simon & Schuster, 1994.

——. *Miro in the Kingdom of the Sun*. With illustrations by David Frampton. Boston: Houghton Mifflin, 1996.

——. *Trouble*. With illustrations by Durga Bernhard. New York: Harcourt, 1997.

Martin, Jacqueline Briggs. *Bizzy Bones and the Lost Quilt*. With illustrations by Stella Qrmai. New York: Lothrop, Lee & Shepard, 1988.

——. *Bizzy Bones and Moosemouse*. With illustrations by Stella Qrmai. New York: Lothrop, Lee & Shepard, 1986.

——. *Bizzy Bones and Uncle Ezra*. With illustrations by Stella Qrmai. New York: Lothrop, Lee & Shepard, 1984.

——. *Grandmother Bryant's Pocket*. With illustrations by Petra Mathers. Boston: Houghton Mifflin, 1996.

——. *Snowflake Bentley*. With illustrations by Mary Azarian. Boston: Houghton Mifflin, 1998.

——. *Washing the Willow Tree Loon*. With illustrations by Nancy Carpenter. New York: Simon & Schuster, 1995.

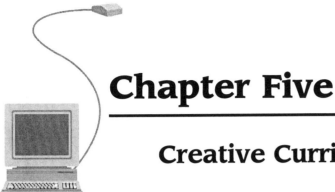

Chapter Five

Creative Curriculum Connections

A school getting ready for a super bookperson visit is a buzzing hive of connections, with threads zinging out in every direction, pulling in various subject areas and all kinds of resources—many of them determined by the work the bookperson does but also by the particular kind of response the work draws from various readers. The best activities to go with a visit, says author Jacqueline Briggs Martin, "are those that help students get 'into' the books and make them their own—and then somehow extend from the book."

Obviously, the first thing a great bookperson visit can do is help students to become more excited about reading. Simply meeting an author whose books a student is familiar with can create that excitement for many. Linda Sherouse, library media specialist, says that when she reads books to her students, she always adds "elements of information to each book, sharing about the creators, but to meet an author in person makes a far greater impression." Following are some other activities that different people have tried to make the reading connection.

THE READING CONNECTION

At one school, students greeted Dian Curtis Regan, author of the Monster of the Month books, dressed as monsters. They drew the monsters on tagboard and then put their own heads through, where the monster's head would be. Another school staged a real kissing contest and did extensive research on kissing trivia to go with her novel *The Kissing Contest*. At a high school, Dian gave her presentation from the middle of a wishing well, to go along with her novel *Princess Nevermore*.

Before Alice Mead, author of *Junebug*, came to visit Toni's school, a volunteer had each child bring a bottle to school. ("Oy vey!" Toni reports her principal as saying.) After they heard the novel *Junebug*, they wrote their personal wishes on pieces of paper and put the wishes in their bottles. "The bottles were lined up in the library all along the tops of the bookshelves," says Toni. "It was visually stunning and also an activity that kids got so invested in. It struck their fancy."

A sixth-grade class, says author Lee Wardlaw, "even put on a 30-minute play for my first book, *Me + Math = Headache*. I can't tell you what a thrill that was, hearing the audience of parents, teachers, and students laughing at the lines that I wrote!"

Patricia Curtis Pfitsch tells of visiting a school where a reading teacher had her students do "really neat things." Some students wrote diaries as if they were Faith, the protagonist in *Keeper of the Light*. The covers had things written on them—"My Diary" and "Willie Keep Out," a message to Faith's little brother. Other students, Patricia says, "wrote essays about what Faith would be like as a neighbor. Some wrote letters to friends recommending the book. Some drew posters advertising the book. Some made up crosswords with information from the book, and one kid invented a game called The Race to the Lighthouse. That kid said he chose to make a game because Faith didn't have a television and probably would have played games in the evenings. Some made food that was mentioned in the story—potato soup, coffee, baked potatoes. Some made three-dimensional illustrations of the shipwreck scene. I was *very* impressed."

"One of the best activities that anyone has ever come up with for an author visit was invented by a former aide of mine for a visit from Gail Gibbons," says Linda Sherouse. "She suggested, and we created, a treasure hunt out on the playground. The students hunted for laminated pieces of a puzzle and then had to be the first team to assemble the puzzle correctly. We also had a glass display case filled with edible gold coins and small model ships to feature her book, *Sunken Treasure*. The children could each take one chance to estimate the number of coins in the case and win them. A large 'treasure chest' sat on the floor of the library with a display of her books in it. It was a great theme, and we played it to the max!"

 ### A Giant Theme

"Sometimes a school grabs hold of the 'giant' theme and uses that as a curriculum opportunity," says Walter the Giant Storyteller, "and I arrive at the school to find posters of giants, drawings of me based on my photo or my growth chart, or just a lesson on big, bigger, biggest. Sometimes, kids have read folktales and fairy tales with giants in them, done measurements of the biggest things they could find, in anticipation of meeting a person who is bigger than any of them, or done a thorough listing of things that start with the letter *g* or things big or small. Kindergartners can get too wrapped up in the 'a giant is coming to our school' and be quite afraid to meet me, which is why I always start an assembly sitting down. This often elicits the comment, 'He's not so big—I thought he was a giant.' I give ample time and then stand up slowly, rising to my full height before a gaping crowd. Sometimes I can even get the librarian to be a sport and stand next to me as I rise, driving home the point. Great fun."

 ### Author/Storyteller Spotlight: Walter M. Mayes

Walter M. Mayes, a.k.a. Walter the Giant Storyteller, travels the country reading and performing books for children of all ages and adults from all walks of life. He is tall (six foot seven and a half inches), enthusiastic, and as the coauthor of *Valerie and Walter's Best Books for Children: A Lively, Opinionated Guide* he is recognized as an authority on children's books and believes that reading and stories must be elevated to the level of daily necessity in all our children's lives, using the rallying cry "Love, Food Shelter, Clothing . . . Books!" as his slogan. In more than 15 years of traveling he has visited 46 states, more than 2,000 schools, and spoken to well over a million children. He lives in San Francisco and is the father of Anthony, age nine, who is also quite a reader.

THE WRITING CONNECTION

The other most obvious connection is the writing connection. Writers write. Teachers can design writing activities based on the bookperson's visit. When Jacqueline Briggs Martin visits a school, older students have tried their own story about the *Finest Horse in Town*, starting with the sentence, "We don't know what really happened . . ." Students at another school even made a musical play out of *Good Times on Grandfather Mountain* and performed it at the end of the day for the entire school.

Some bookpeople particularly stress writing in their visits. Jane says, "I emphasize many of the same writing principles in my presentations that I do in my writing classes—'write what you know,' for instance (showing them how my books relate to my own childhood in Ethiopia), and 'all writing is rewriting.' Teachers sometimes say, 'You said exactly what I've been stressing . . . but it sounded more convincing coming from you.' I show all the revision comments on one page of one of my picture books. Or I make a first chapter of *The Storyteller's Beads* available to look at, before or after my visit, to show the dramatic changes it went through."

 Writing in the Public Library

Mary Casanova gave writing workshpos for adults and children in the public library in Warroad, Minnesota, for three years in a row. She charged an honorarium, plus requested lodging and mileage. "I think I negotiated downward to make it possible," she says. "Since libraries are designed to serve the public, there was no charge for attending the workshops, but I encouraged the library to offset the cost of bringing me in by selling my books, thereby bringing in more funds."

Imagination Warm-ups

Author Mary Whittington says that more and more schools are asking her to do a "hands-on, mini workshop." One she often does is on how to generate ideas, and she usually uses an exercise that "involves urging kids to make full use of their imaginations. 'Okay,' I say. 'What's the most boring surface in this room?' Often it's the floor, but we've also used walls, painted and brick, windows, chalkboards, desk surfaces, and other things. If I'm working with an assembly of more than 100 kids, I'll take suggestions from the floor, and then I make the final decision as to what the most boring surface is. In a smaller group, I ask for a show of hands."

Mary then begins questioning the students. "What if it's not a floor (wall, window, etc.)? What if it's a . . . ?" In larger groups, she keeps track of suggestions and makes the decision about what to use. "I'm the leader here," she tells students, "and the leader has the final say. If you'd prefer to use your suggestion, fine, but do it later, okay? For right now, the floor is not a floor. It's the back of a monster."

Once the general idea is set, Mary pushes for specifics. "Is this monster extremely humongous? Or are we small? Where is the monster? What is it doing? What will happen if . . . " She has to make up each of these "what if" scenarios quickly, because each session is totally different. When a story starts to form with characters (which usually takes about 10 minutes), she elaborates a bit. Then she says, "All right. Let's stop here. If you want to continue the story, better do it back in your classroom or at home. But before I go on to my next topic, think for a second. Think of this story that's starting to take off. Remember how it started? Right. We started with this boring floor. Pretty neat, huh?"

 Author Spotlight: Mary Whittington

Born in Hollywood, California, Mary K. Whittington grew up in Burbank and the San Fernando Valley during the 1940s and 1950s. The oldest of three sisters, she preferred reading to playing outside, earning the name Bookworm at an early age. She read everything, especially books that engaged her imagination, and she wanted to be a writer when she grew up.

However, as a result of working in a marine biology lab during her senior year in high school, she decided to be a biology major in college. This didn't work. Any subject involving writing did, and by the time she graduated with a degree in sociology, she had a job, teaching writing skills to university students.

In 1979, Mary moved to the Pacific Northwest, where her childhood dream of becoming a writer came true. Today, she lives on half an acre with her longtime friend, Wini, their Australian shepherd, Saki, and their cat, Carmina. Mary writes children's and young adult fantasy books and scary stories. She also talks about writing at schools and libraries, teaches music lessons, and cares for the multitudinous rosebushes in her yard.

Mary's picture books are out of print, but you can read her stories in three anthologies, *Vampires*, *The Haunted House*, and *Bruce Coville's Book of Ghosts: More Tales to Haunt You*. You can also read more about her in *Something About the Author: Autobiography Series*, Vol. 25, 1998 (Linda R. Andres, editor, Gale Research).

Author/illustrator Cathryn Falwell also stresses the power of creative thinking. "I often start out," she says, "by getting the kids to warm up their imaginations. We put on our imaginary imagination hats, turn up the controls, and then play around with some cutout black shapes I stick on a board." For instance, she puts up a triangle and asks, "What else could this be?" The students respond with various suggestions: "An ice-cream cone! Teepee! A slice of pizza! A bird beak!" Cathryn then shows how she uses cut paper to make her illustrations. "I use a repositionable spray adhesive on the things I bring along," she says. "That way, I can move them around on a foam-core board that I stand on an easel."

 ## Curriculum Connections and the Public Library

Public libraries can keep their eyes open for curriculum connections as well. In November, libraries sometimes do something special for Children's Book Week by scheduling author events. Anastasia Suen has put on her "teacher hat" for summer reading programs or National Poetry Month. "For example," she says, "one year I had the little ones create shape poems using *When a Line Bends, a Shape Begins*. I had the poems cut out, and they made art with colored origami paper shapes. We read the poems first and then did the craft. I did two sets of programs that year. The older ones wrote poetry. In each branch we put them on the wall for Poetry Month. In one branch, we wrote sports poems and then mounted each poem on a sports page that I had saved from the newspaper. The full page had the heading 'Sports' and the color photos, and the poems fit in along with the regular articles. It looked quite nice. Some of the kids also illustrated their poems. I read from Lee Bennett Hopkin's collection that time, and then we brainstormed, and they wrote. The poems were quite nice, and everyone did a different sport. At another library, we did silly poems in honor of April Fool's Day, and I read Jack Prelutsky and Shel Silverstein. I don't sell books at these visits, though they do check out all of my books after I leave!"

The Writing Process

Franny Billingsley, author of *Well Wished*, likes to illustrate the process of the novel, "starting with character and ending with character." Franny begins by showing the students what Nuria and Catty (the two main characters from *Well Wished*) carry around with them—"Nuria in her hot-pink waistpack, Catty in her sequined bag. What does the fact that Nuria carries around her rock collection, a feather, a really crumpled Kleenex tissue (used, maybe), and a jump rope say about her? What do beads, a mirror, and a beautifully folded Kleenex tissue say about Catty? The kids always nail the characters on the head, bang, bang, bang."

If the presentation includes enough time for writing exercises, Franny will then have students pick a character and give the character a name. "I talk about the importance of names and how Nuria, whom I'd initially called Sara—which I'd stolen from *A Little Princess* because I'd loved that book so much as a kid—couldn't be a Sara because the name wasn't long-ago and far-away and magical enough. How Catty's name was easy to choose because I wanted her to be sort of sly and secretive, like a cat." Then Franny has the students choose three things the character would carry around. "We read them aloud, comment on how you can really *see* this kid, or how it sounds just like my neighbor . . . "

At this point, Franny takes a "step backward." She says, "I had to make my characters be the way they are (Nuria an energetic, outdoor kid, Catty a manipulative kid who's in a wheelchair) because of where I got my idea. I got my idea in a blood bank, giving blood, while next to me was a young woman getting blood because she had a terrible disease that made her so weak she couldn't even unscrew the lid off a jar of peanut butter. And I got to thinking, what would it be like to be an active outdoor person (which I am) and be stuck in a body like that?"

Next, Franny talks about the difficulties of beginnings—"the horror of facing that white, empty page." She says to the students, "So in January of 1988 (were you even born then?) I picked up my pen and began." She reads them beginnings that work—beginnings that show a problem or a mystery—and reads them two different drafts of her own beginnings. "We talk about what I was trying to do and what did and didn't work about them. Then I read my beginning as published." (For more information on beginnings that work, see Franny's article "Searching for a Plot" in *Book Links*.)

When it comes to middles, Franny talks about "how hard it is (for me) to get my character into trouble." How was Nuria going to get into Catty's body? Franny reads *Heckedy Peg* to the students and asks them to think about how the kids get into trouble. "Ah, they get *themselves* into trouble by breaking the rules." Only after examining a lot of books to see how the middles worked, Franny tells them, did she come up with the Wishing Well concept, "where Nuria wasn't supposed to make a wish."

Last, Franny says, "I circle back round to character. I had to make Nuria into the kind of reckless, impetuous kid who'd make a wish on the well even when she was forbidden to do so." At this point, she plays a game with the students. "If Nuria were a flower, what would she be? (I'd picked dandelion—is it a weed? Is it a flower? It's colorful. Not too pretty. Grows anywhere. Amazingly, many kids guess dandelion—or daisy. Kids are remarkably intuitive.)" Catty, Franny tells them, "would be a rose—fragile, needs a hothouse, has hidden thorns."

What kind of weather would Nuria be? Franny sees if they can guess that she would be a storm, hail, monsoon, and the like. What kind of picture-book illustration? Here, she shows the students the page from *Monster Mama* where Patrick Edward is screaming, "all his red hair sticking up all over." Music? The students guess Beethoven, rap, Spice Girls, heavy metal. Franny plays the music she had picked—"wild, passionate, Gypsy violins."

If there is time, students can write their own beginnings, getting their characters in trouble or setting a mystery, and their own middles, putting the characters into as terrible trouble as possible. They can think about how they would resolve the problems. When the whole session is over, the students "have the kernel of something they could take home and finish—which one group did and I am looking at now and commenting on. Some kids end up thinking Nuria is real. We talk about her as though she is, and she has become real in their minds. They might, say, ask where she lives. I have to remind them that I made her up."

Author Spotlight: Franny Billingsley

Franny Billingsley quit practicing law in 1983 and moved to Barcelona to recover. She brought all her favorite children's books with her, intending to do nothing but read and eat *tapas*, but she got hooked on writing instead. She now lives in her hometown of Chicago with her husband and two children and works as a children's book buyer for an independent bookstore. Her books to date are *Well Wished* and *The Folk Keeper*.

Writing in Class

Anastasia Suen did a poetry writing workshop with third and fourth graders at one school where she visited. "All of the classes had read *Man on the Moon* ahead of time, which was nice, but we didn't write poetry about space. Instead, I let each teacher select a theme from her own classroom, and we created original poetry on the spot. The theme changed from room to room, as I went through the day." What she loved about this visit, Anastasia says, "was the coteaching. I love it when I am writing with the kids and everyone gets involved. In many of the classes, all three of us were writing, brainstorming, and encouraging the kids: the teacher, the poet, and the librarian. The energy that was created was incredible! The kids were *so* excited about poetry, and it showed in their work, too."

The Lincoln School Writing Residency

It's worth a check with your state arts council to see whether any authors are on the roster and available for a writing residency. Though it's hard for an author to squeeze out time for a one- or two-week period of coming into classrooms and writing with students, a local author may be available—and the education that ensues may be worth everyone's time and effort.

Jane has done several residencies. "I usually write poems with students," she says, "and I stress several principles of good writing that I am still stressing with my university students: 1) good writing is in the details; 2) good writing may take good imagination, but it also takes good observation; 3) use the five senses; 4) use comparisons to make your reader experience what you have experienced; and 5) write about what you know about and what you passionately care about."

During the Grand Forks flood of 1997, Jane was evacuated from her house for about a month and had only seen the house once, briefly, before she flew off to Atlanta to be part of a workshop at the International Reading Association national convention. "People kept saying, 'You'll write about it,' she says, "but I didn't think I would. Then Deborah Hopkinson, my roommate, said, 'What if you approached the flood the way you described doing writing with students in your residencies?' When I flew back to Grand Forks for my first day of mucking out the lower level of my house, what she'd said kept knocking at my brain. I periodically took off my yellow gloves and jotted down fragments of what the experience was really like, using those principles I always use in poetry residencies."

In fall 1998, Dr. Ann Porter, principal of the school where Jane's children had attended elementary school, asked Jane if she would do a writing residency helping Lincoln School students write about their flood experiences. (The school itself had been destroyed by the flood, but the students were together for one last year, having school in a local church.) Jane says, "I shared my own poems with them—which I knew by then would be published as the picture book, *River Friendly, River Wild*—and encouraged them to write their own poems about their flood experiences. We looked at each of those principles on a different day when I went in. We wrote and revised and created a book—we even had a night when parents could contribute their own writings."

A writing residency, Jane says, is a demanding experience, and the Lincoln School residency would not have worked without the participation of many people—teachers, principal, school secretary, parent volunteers, librarian, and library committee. Dr. Porter also admits that it was demanding but says, "Don't be afraid! Do it! Everyone will grow from the experience. This is what education is all about—giving students experiences that are real. Giving students opportunities to express themselves and the tools to do it with."

A Flood with Lots of Mud

Where I went during the flood I tasted tomatoes.

They tasted sweet and fresh like sugar.

The juice slid down my face.

The sugar on it shimmered and

When I picked it up some of the sugar went falling to my plate.

On TV I saw the flood water slither down the street,

And the fire spreading to other buildings.

I touched the mud.

It trickled down my hand like gak,

But it did not look like gak.

Before the flood, I could not find any mud in my house.

I heard helicopters.

They sounded like if you constantly hit on a drum.

It sounded like thunder,

But you could not see lightning striking out of the sky.

Before the flood, I did not hear many helicopters.

I smelled my garage.

It smelled like garbage that sat outside for a long time in the shimmering sun.

You could not smell anything before the flood.

—Mike, fourth grade

The Big Bad Flood

A while ago before the flood,
I liked to go down in my basement,
And jump off the couch on to a mattress,
And pretend I was flying.
I also liked to set up
My Fisher Price village
In my basement
And play all day.
When we got home from evacuation,
We had to clean,
Clean the basement that smelled
Like mold and old gloppy gunk.
We also had to chip off the tile
On the basement floor.
When the hammer struck,
The floor went kerploop.
The Red Cross food
Was kinda gross.
It tasted like
Old dried out things.
I looked around and
On the berms were piles
And piles
Of old flooded stuff.
I picked up some mud.
It was like
Mashed potatoes
And applesauce.
I saw my school
Get torn down.
I felt like crying,
But I did not.
I could talk
Forever and
Ever.
But I will not.

—Lucy, fifth grade

⏎ OTHER SUBJECT-AREA CONNECTIONS

But don't stop with reading and writing. Connections can also be made with every other subject area in the curriculum, and many bookpeople would love to see more connections made, turning each visit into a grand learning experience. Walter the Giant Storyteller says, "On occasion, we get a request to have me read stories with trees in them, 'as we are doing a unit on trees,' or to read stories that highlight self-esteem issues 'because our yearlong school goal is to foster self-esteem in all our students.' Only rarely do I get a class-by-class, grade-by-grade breakdown of the things that the students are studying and an accompanying request to provide stories to back up those subjects."

Storyteller Donna Washington agrees. "I always request that the school try to tie what I am doing in with the curriculum," she says. "One of the more interesting experiences I had was when a school called and said their kids were studying Australia. They wanted to know if I knew any Australian stories. I didn't, but I said I would learn some. When I got to the school, the kids were having a great time. They had kangaroos and wallabies cut out and glued to the walls. When I started telling the stories, they knew quite a few, in somewhat different versions. It was wonderful."

 The Impact a Good Connection Can Have on Student Lives

Donna Washington tells about a middle school that spent the year discussing self-esteem and then asked Donna, as well as some other speakers, to deal with that issue. "When I got there," Donna says, "I told them stories about my childhood. In my stories, I am definitely a kid. I do the exact things that they are doing and, of course, I get in trouble for those things, too. In the last story, I get away with the trouble I caused, but years later, I confess and everyone is still mad about it." Donna adds, "The principal phoned me later to tell me that the set had been a great success, and the students were comparing themselves to the stories I told. All in all, they were finding out that they were not the only people in the world who got into scrapes of their own design. I also got one very touching letter from a child who was having trouble in his home and at school. He said, 'Mrs. Washington, after I heard your stories it made me happy. When I came to school today, I was afraid I was going to do something bad. After your stories, I didn't feel like that anymore. I felt like what you said is true. The only person who can change how my day goes is me. I went home yesterday and did all of my chores and my homework without anyone asking me to. My mom couldn't believe it. I'm gonna try to do that today too.'"

Author Jennifer Richard Jacobson says, "For younger children—kindergarten and first graders—I do a storytelling presentation on being brave. I show them a picture of my neighbor (a child) and tell them some of the brave stories he told me such as hitting a bobcat between the eyes. I then tell them one of the stories of my childhood, a time when I wasn't brave, when I got stuck on a roof. I give them other bits and pieces of me, along with lots of props and things that I've learned, and I tell them that even though none of these stories are my book *A Net of Stars*, the stories have found their way into the book. Then I read *A Net of Stars*. The kids light up or literally bounce every time they recognize a way that I've used my own experiences to tell the story."

Science

After *Man on the Moon* was published, Anastasia Suen did a reading to prekindergarten and kindergarten children. Then they created "moons" by coloring in craters and rocks on the backs of paper plates and landed an *Eagle* on each moon. "To make an *Eagle* for each child, I use an actual drawing from the 1969 press kit, with permission from NASA," says Anastasia. "We land on the equator, just like the astronauts did. It's not only a science lesson but also a lesson in history!"

As part of the same visit, Anastasia showed slides to the first and second grades, including photos from the book and photos that Anastasia's family took at the Kennedy Space Center, Johnson Space Center, and the Smithsonian Air and Space Museum. "I talked about the book's illustration and then showed a slide of the real thing! The kids love it when I show photos of my kids and tell them that my son took many of the pictures."

After reading *Monster of the Month Club* and its sequels, by Dian Curtis Regan, students have prepared a healthy lunch that might be served at Harmony House Bed and Breakfast and have also made Botswana Brownies. "The activities the home schoolers do in the books can be done by regular classrooms, too," Dian points out. "That's the teacher in me coming out. In book three, there is a hydroponics experiment and in book four, an astronomy project."

The Caldecott Award-winning picture book *Snowflake Bentley* practically begs for science activities related to snowflakes. Jacqueline Briggs Martin points out that snowflakes are actually snow crystals, so growing salt or sugar crystals is a good related activity. "When I was writing the book," she adds, "I tried catching snowflakes on a dark tray the way William Bentley did. It's not easy, but it did make me more aware of individual snowflakes."

Math

In preparation for a visit by Carmen Bernier-Grand, author of *Juan Bobo*, a librarian in Fresham, Oregon, "made a picture of Juan Bobo's pig," Carmen says, "asked the students to take the pig's measurements, and gave them fabric to make outfits to send the pig to places other than church. When I went there, she had a whole bulletin board of pigs dressed in soccer clothes, ballet clothes, exercise clothes, you name it. Unfortunately, I didn't have a camera. But what I liked most was that the librarian combined my two fields: math and language arts."

Author Spotlight: Carmen T. Bernier-Grand

When Carmen T. Bernier-Grand was growing up in Puerto Rico, her teachers always told her she had a great imagination. "But I wasn't sure how I felt about that," she remembers, "because my sister used to say it meant I was a liar." So Carmen decided to earn a master's degree in mathematics. She taught at the University of Puerto Rico for seven years. Then she made a decision to pursue an advanced mathematics degree in the United States, startling her entire family. "No one wanted me to come to the U.S.," she confesses. "But I did."

Once in the United States, Carmen began to write for children, and she wrote in English, her second language. Although she abandoned the idea that having a vivid imagination meant she was a liar, she never forgot how it felt. "I don't think I grew up," she says. "I'm still there—in my childhood in Puerto Rico."

Carmen says she thinks, writes, and dreams in two languages: Spanish and English. The primary source of her inspiration, though, comes from the vivid memories of her Puerto Rican childhood. "I write about the little pieces of my life," she explains, "the relationships, the social issues, the culture."

Her first book, *Juan Bobo: Four Folktales from Puerto Rico*, won a Bulletin of the Center for Children's Books Book Ribbon. *Poet and Politician of Puerto Rico: Don Luis Muñoz Marin* was an El Nuevo Dia Book of the Year. Her newest book is *In the Shade of the Nispero Tree*.

Carmen, who lives in Portland, Oregon, with her husband and two teenaged children, believes, "Writing is a way of making a difference in the world." She hopes her books help young readers "find their own way."

Jane often visits schools where teachers have created math activities around the game often called "mancala" here in the United States (but called "gebeta" in Eritrea and in Jane's book, *Trouble*, that is set in Eritrea). "Some classes have researched the different rules for this game that is played the world over," Jane says. "Others have had students create their own gebeta boards, often out of egg cartons. Doing a little mancala research on the Web turns up an amazing number of math connections."

Author/illustrator Cathryn Falwell says, "Since the child in *Shape Space* builds a life-sized playscape with her shapes, I ask the kids about their ideas. On several occasions, I have received a pile of wonderful drawings and cut-paper collages that kids have created with shapes. This is a great way for kids to think about geometric shapes—to go beyond learning the names to actually thinking about their structure and their relationship to each other. (A triangle could be a slide! What else could it be? How many rectangles do I need to make a ladder? What if I use a long rectangle on this side? Aha! I can put these two triangles together, and they make a square!) Kindergarten teachers sometimes provide children with precut multicolored shapes. Circles can be tough for older children, also (me too!) so precuts can also be handy to add in for them."

Social Studies/History/Geography

Teachers have used the amber beads from Jane's *The Storyteller's Beads* to study and discuss the uses of beads in various societies and to research the trade routes that spread various bead materials throughout the world. A third-grade teacher in California researched various amber sites on the Web, including http://www.emporia.edu/S/www/earthsci/amber/amber.htm.

Teachers have used Dian Curtis Regan's Ghost Twins series to have students create a fictitious world (like the Kickingbird Lake resort) and sketch out a map of the area as if it were real, putting in details such as forests, lakes, towns, buildings, and roads. Students use the maps in each Ghost Twins book as a guide. Students also pick a year from history and create page one from a newspaper (like the newspaper clipping at the start of each Ghost Twins book). What would some of the stories be in, say, 1921, 1937, 1955, or 1968?

"Prior to Lisa Anderson's visit," says Linda Sherouse, "I scripted her book, *Proud to Be Me, Peewee Platypus*, into a play. I worked with a group of second graders to perform the play, and we staged it for K–3. Those students knew the story well by the time they met Lisa and her husband in the Peewee full-body costume. It's a very sensitive story about accepting the physical differences in others and feeling good about what you are capable of, and they listened carefully and discussed the lessons contained in the story with her."

Susan Campbell Bartoletti, author of *Growing Up in Coal Country*, says, "One of my favorite curriculum connections was in one school where a team of students created a coal museum. They took over part of the school and turned the halls and classrooms and even the stairwell into a coal museum, showing the various stages of the colliery and patch-village life. The students researched their respective areas and became tour guide 'experts.' In the colliery, they were breaker boys, nippers, mule drivers, spraggers, and miners. In the patch village, they were miners' wives, the choir master, company store owner, etc. It was really cool."

Students in a school in Kansas used *Only a Pigeon* and created Venn diagrams to show similarities and differences between Onduahlem's life and theirs and between life in an African city and in a rural setting.

Kris Zuidema, an elementary library media specialist in Maine School Administrative District 6, says that *Birdie's Lighthouse* by Deborah Hopkinson inspired one of the aides, Jane Brown, "to help students from various classes to build a three- to four-foot papier-mâché lighthouse complete with blinking light on top and simulated rocks around the base." Everyone, says Kris, including Deborah, "was most impressed with this large, beautiful, well-designed structure."

Because much of what we know and teach as "history" comes from primary sources people created as they were living through the experiences, a wonderful history connection can be made through diaries. Wanda Nason, a third-grade teacher at Edna Libby School in Sebago Lake, Maine, had her students make their own small diaries in preparation for Deborah's visit to go along with *Birdie's Lighthouse*. Each day, Wanda gave her students events of the day at the lighthouse, and they wrote entries in their diaries.

To prepare for Anne Sibley O'Brien's visit, another third-grade teacher at Edna Libby School, Ellen Lucy, connected with *Talking Walls* by making a large paper wall (covering one of the classroom walls) where all the children could sign their names. Inspired by *Welcoming Babies*, students wrote letters to small children to welcome them into the world. "For *Princess and the Beggar*," says Kris, "each student wrote a letter to the king to tell him how they felt about him. They illustrated their favorite part of the story and wrote a sequel. Ellen gets very involved in preparing for author/illustrator visits."

At one school, says Jacqueline Briggs Martin, "students made relief maps of the maps on the endpapers of the Bizzy Bones books. Along with learning about the books, they also learned about perspective, direction, and a bit about mapping, which made the activity a very rich one."

Children's Book Week is generally the same week as National Geography Week—"very useful for my books," says Jane. "I've visited schools where people told me afterward, 'Ethiopia will never be just another spot on the map for these children now.' Actually, I'm thrilled if Ethiopia is even a clear spot on the map for people. A friend of mine, who just started teaching college classes, asked her students to take 30 seconds and write down all the African countries they could name. One of her students asked, 'You mean cities?' The response is not surprising, given that Africa is often presented as a moderately sized country rather than as a huge and varied continent. Ethiopia alone has 80 different languages."

Art

In preparation for Deborah Hopkinson's visit to Edna Libby School, after students read *Sweet Clara and the Freedom Quilt*, the art teacher designed an activity to create colorful paper patchwork quilts. Each student created a quilt design on paper. In connection with *Birdie's Lighthouse*, some students created silhouette lighthouses with sunsets in the background. The background was created with watercolor wash painting, and the striking lighthouses were cut from black paper. Other students created "school-size milk-carton houses," says Kris, "covered with paper and corrugated cardboard for roofs, with painted cones for the lighthouse. Small stones were put around the base to look like the rocky coastline." The result, she says, was "charming."

Kris Zuidema says that Janet Conner, art teacher at Edna Libby School, always adds a great deal to the bookperson visits. She prepared students for Kevin Hawkes's illustrator visit by "teaching them the vocabulary of principles of design such as line, texture, form, rhythm, composition, foreground, middle ground, background, and color." To connect with *The Princess and the Beggar* by Anne Sibley O'Brien, students made Korean festival masks from paper, and to connect with *Talking Walls*, which Anne illustrated, Janet had students make a craft from every culture represented in the book. For instance, to go with the Great Wall of China, they used paper plates to create "dragon plates." "The Great Zimbabwe" inspired cloth prints.

 The Katie Davis Project

Author/illustrator Katie Davis includes slides in her presentations to older students or adults. "I bring tons of visuals like overhead projected images, huge posters, original art and early sketches, and an enormous pile of 40 book dummies created through the editing process while I worked on *I Hate to Go to Bed!*" she says. "Everyone I present to learns story construction, sequencing, and how an idea transforms from a thought to a published book. I even tell them how scary it is to talk and draw in front of a group because I make lots of mistakes! They also learn how to do simple drawings of emotions. I tell them about mistakes I've made while writing and illustrating my books, and they discover the research that went into making *Who Hops?* scientifically accurate."

Whenever Katie visits a school or library, she tailors her presentation to the age group, reading (at least) her most recent book and following the reading with a highly interactive illustrating and storytelling session. She says, "Volunteers join me up front where I ask each to make a different facial expression expressing an emotion. They touch their faces to try to figure out what the expression looks like. Then I draw those expressions on the animals from *Who Hops?*, and we create a new narrative story with them." Katie is also designing a project where she will ask the school to have students bring in a large photograph either from home or from a magazine. She will bring tracing paper and show them how to draw a cartoon face with the real face as a guide. Kelly Agar, a kindergarten teacher at George Washington School in White Plains, New York, where Katie did an illustrator visit, says, "In Katie's presentation, she talks about facial expressions and how she draws them. This has really had an impact on my students' drawing. They pay much more attention to the face and its features when they're drawing.

"Before Katie came to our school, the kids were introduced to her through her Web site (http://www.katiedavis.com). By the time Katie arrived, the kids were very excited and familiar with her style. The classes had such a great time, we didn't want it to end there. My colleagues Sandra Rodriguez and Michael Downey and I brainstormed some activities and decided that we would each choose a verb per class. For example, I chose *sing* and *run*. (I have a morning and an afternoon class, so that's why I had two verbs.)

"My classes discussed and researched things that sing and things that run. Using inventive spelling, the students wrote about [them]. They worked at their individual levels. Some children were only able to write initial consonants. Others were able to write two or three sentences.

"Then our art teacher, Dana Devito, worked with the children on paintings. We tried to keep with a style similar to Katie's—bright colors and simple subject matter. After the paintings were done, we went to work on the frames. (Any great work of art needs a fitting frame.) We decided on colors and techniques which would complement the paintings. The children chose from a selection of colors and instruments. Then they were free to decorate the frames as they chose. The final products were amazing!

"We hung the pieces of work from all six kindergarten classes in the hallway (their writing was hung below their paintings), and invited family and friends to our gallery opening. Refreshments were served and all the artwork was enjoyed. After everyone was full of cookies and juice, we went back to where this began and read *Who Hops?*, which is now a class favorite.

"In addition, during Katie's visit, she drew pictures and told a story as she went. I hung those drawings in my classroom, and the children used them as a springboard to creating new stories involving the same characters. As I reviewed our activities, I thought it would have been fun to have incorporated Physical Education by having the students physically do each movement. This would have been an opportunity to include another curriculum area."

After the project was over, Kelly sent some samples from the Kindergarten Gallery to Katie and wrote, "You were such an integral part of this whole project that the boys and girls wanted to share some of their work with you. Everybody wanted to send pictures of their work, but that just wasn't possible, so I chose three to give you an idea of what we did. The gallery opening was a huge success! I have to tell you, you are forever ingrained in these kids' hearts! They loved you and still talk about you."

Susan Ayers, a third-grade teacher at Longfellow Elementary School, describes a rather unusual preparation for the visit of Jacqueline Briggs Martin, after her class unanimously chose *Higgins Bend Song and Dance* as their favorite of Jacqueline's books. "We loved the large fish, Oscar, who could not be caught, and the fisherman who was determined to catch him. To build enthusiasm for Jacqueline's visit and to enhance our discussion of interesting 'endings' of stories, we made fish-print/Oscar-print T-shirts." A parent who worked at a fish processing plant donated five flounder. Susan and parent volunteers then helped the students paint the fish, using special fabric paints. The T-shirts were laid on the fish and "carefully patted." The fish were then washed, and new students took their turns painting and patting. "The end result," says Susan, "was a class of 25 happy, fishy-smelling, enthusiastic children, ready to greet, learn from, and converse with Jacqueline Briggs Martin." Jacqueline adds that "students who may never before have actually worked with fish made something they could wear and keep to remind them of the visit.

Another teacher combined art and writing as she had her students make pockets such as the one Sarah Bryant wore in *Grandmother Bryant's Pocket*, an activity that Jacqueline says is a good example of something that "is closely tied to a book but which also expands—they get to make the pocket, in a way similar to the way the character in the book would have made it, and then they have to think about what would be important to put into the pocket, what defines them and is important to them." (The exact instructions for making the pocket are on Jacqueline's Web site at http://www.geocities. com/Athens/Forum/1090.)

Jane has worked with schools that were interested in focusing on the illustration process of picture books. Several times, she has provided the written version of a soon-to-be-published story, which the librarian or teacher has then read aloud, letting students create their own illustrations. "I did this with a Grand Forks school the fall before *Miro in the Kingdom of the Sun* was published," she says, "and we told the students—in all honesty—that no one, including me, knew what the illustrations in the book would look like, so their vision was as valid as any. In the spring, after the book was published, I returned to the school and used overhead transparencies to show various scenes—how a student imagined it and how David Frampton imagined the same scene. I still use some of those pictures to show how different people can imagine the same scene so differently."

An Inca Theme

Often one book can be the focus of a multisubject approach to learning. Many schools already study Inca culture somewhere in the curriculum, and Jane has sometimes been asked to focus on the Incas with certain grade levels, because of her retelling of an Inca folktale, *Miro in the Kingdom of the Sun*. "Social studies and geography connections with that picture book are obvious," Jane says, "because the book is full of details of Inca daily life, woven into the story. And the Incas were the first people to cultivate potatoes—a good hook that can be used with even the youngest classes. But connections have been made to many other subject areas as well."

Art: Teachers have encouraged older students to take symbols from Inca culture and use them to create prints (even pencil on Styrofoam, overlaid with paint, will work), somewhat like the wood blocks used by illustrator David Frampton in the book. Art teacher Bob Auclair at Longfellow School in Portland, Maine, had his students create dramatic two- and three-dimensional punched-copper pieces, replicating the patterns and motifs in Inca art.

Science: Teachers have used the volcanoes mentioned in the story to spark volcano research. "There's a connection between the volcanoes in the area and all that Inca gold," Jane says. "Students can go into Volcano World on the Web and even ask a volcanologist if they get stumped figuring it out" (http://volcano.und.nodak.edu).

Math: The Incas used counting knots somewhat like an abacus to keep track of the things in their storage rooms. Students have also measured out the 22- by 17-foot space that the Incas filled with gold and silver to try to preserve the life of their emperor.

Reading: Compare *Miro in the Kingdom of the Sun* with "The Search for the Magic Lake" by Genevieve Barlow in *Latin American Tales*.

RERERENCES

Anderson, Lisa. *Proud to Be Me, Peewee Platypus*. Pleasant Ridge, MI: Ridge Enterprises, 1990.

Barlow, Genevieve. *Latin American Tales: From the Pampas to the Pyramids of Mexico*. With illustrations by William M. Hutchinson. Chicago: Rand McNally, 1966.

Bartoletti, Susan Campbell. *Growing Up in Coal Country*. Boston: Houghton Mifflin, 1996.

Bernier-Grand, Carmen T. *In the Shade of the Nispero Tree*. New York: Orchard, 1999.

——. *Juan Bobo: Four Folktales from Puerto Rico*. With illustrations by Ernesto Ramos Nieves. New York: HarperTrophy, 1994.

——. *Poet and Politician of Puerto Rico: Don Luis Muñoz Marin*. New York: Orchard, 1995.

Billingsley, Franny. *The Folk Keeper*. New York: Atheneum, 1999.

——. "Searching for a Plot." *Book Links* 6 (July 1997): 13–17.

——. *Well Wished*. New York: Atheneum, 1997.

Burnett, Frances Hodgson. *A Little Princess; Being the Whole Story of Sara Crewe Now Told for the First Time*. With illustrations by Ethel Fanklin Betts. New York: Scribner, 1938. Re-issue, 1974.

Davis, Katie. *I Hate to Go to Bed!* San Diego: Harcourt, 1999.

——. *Who Hops?* San Diego: Harcourt, 1998.

Falwell, Cathryn. *The Letter Jesters*. Boston: Houghton Mifflin, 1994.

——. *Shape Space*. New York: Clarion, 1992.

Gibbons, Gail. *Sunken Treasure*. New York: Crowell, 1988.

Greene, Rhonda Gowler. *When a Line Bends . . . a Shape Begins*. With illustrations by James Kaczman. New York: Houghton, 1997.

Hobbs, Will. *Far North*. New York: Morrow, 1996.

Hopkinson, Deborah. *Birdie's Lighthouse*. With illustrations by Kimberly Bulcken Root. New York: Atheneum, 1997.

——. *Sweet Clara and the Freedom Quilt*. With illustrations by James Ransome. New York: Knopf, 1993.

Jacobson, Jennifer Richard. *A Net of Stars*. With illustrations by Greg Shed. New York: Dial, 1998.

Knight, Margy Burns. *Talking Walls*. With Illustrations by Anne Sibley O'Brien. Gardiner, ME: Tilbury House, 1992.

——. *Welcoming Babies*. With Illustrations by Anne Sibley O'Brien. Gardiner, ME: Tilbury House, 1994.

Kurtz, Jane. *Miro in the Kingdom of the Sun*. With illustrations by David Frampton. Boston: Houghton Mifflin, 1996.

——. *River Friendly, River Wild*. With illustrations by Neil Brennan. New York: Simon & Schuster, Forthcoming.

——. *The Storyteller's Beads*. San Diego: Harcourt, 1998.

Kurtz, Jane and Christopher. *Only a Pigeon*. With illustrations by E. B. Lewis. New York: Simon & Schuster, 1997.

Lewis, Valerie, and Walter Mayes. *Valerie and Walter's Best Books for Children: A Lively, Opinionated Guide*. New York: Avon, 1998.

Martin, Jacqueline Briggs. *Bizzy Bones and the Lost Quilt*. With illustrations by Stella Qrmai. New York: Lothrop, Lee & Shepard, 1988.

——. *Bizzy Bones and Moosemouse*. With illustrations by Stella Qrmai. New York: Lothrop, Lee & Shepard, 1986.

——. *Bizzy Bones and Uncle Ezra*. With illustrations by Stella Qrmai. New York: Lothrop, Lee & Shepard, 1984.

——. *The Finest Horse in Town*. With illustrations by Susan Gaber. New York: HarperCollins, 1992.

——. *Good Times on Grandfather Mountain*. With illustrations by Susan Gaber. New York: HarperCollins, 1992.

——. *Grandmother Bryant's Pocket*. With illustrations by Petra Mathers. Boston: Houghton Mifflin, 1996.

——. *Higgins Bend Song and Dance*. With illustrations by Brad Sneed. Boston: Houghton Mifflin, 1997.

——. *Snowflake Bentley*. With illustrations by Mary Azarian. Boston: Houghton Mifflin, 1998.

Mead, Alice. *Junebug*. New York: Farrar, 1995.

O'Brien, Anne Sibley. *The Princess and the Beggar: A Korean Folktale*. New York: Scholastic, 1993.

Pfitsch, Patricia. *Keeper of the Light*. New York: Simon & Schuster, 1997.

Regan, Dian Curtis. *The Kissing Contest*. New York: Scholastic, 1990.

——. *Monster of the Month Club*. With illustrations by Laura Cornell. New York: Henry Holt, 1994.

——. *Mystery of the Disappearing Dogs*. Ghost Twins Series. New York: Scholastic, 1995.

——. *Princess Nevermore*. New York: Scholastic, 1995.

Rosenberg, Liz. *Monster Mama*. With illustrations by Stephen Gammell. New York: Philomel, 1993.

Suen, Anastasia. *Man on the Moon*. New York: Viking, 1997.

Wardlaw, Lee. *Me + Math = Headache*. With illustrations by Deborah Stouffer. Santa Barbara, CA: Red Hen Press, 1986.

Whittington, Mary. "Ahvel." In *Vampires*, edited by Jane Yolen and Martin Greenberg. New York: HarperTrophy, 1991.

——. "Leaves." In *Bruce Coville's Book of Ghosts II: More Tales to Haunt You*, compiled and edited by Bruce Coville. New York: Scholastic, 1997.

——. "Somewhere a Puppy Cries." In *The Haunted House*, edited by Jane Yolen and Martin Greenberg. New York: HarperTrophy, 1995.

Wood, Audrey. *Heckedy Peg*. With illustrations by Don Wood. San Diego: Harcourt, 1987.

Chapter Six

Other Opportunities to Meet Bookpeople

Perhaps, for whatever reason, an author visit to your school just isn't possible. Don't give up! Creative book lovers across the country have long been working on bringing children and books together, and many possibilities—other than the bookperson visit to the school—exist to tap into or to inspire you to try something similar.

THE PUBLIC LIBRARY

A first logical step is to talk with your public library. Elizabeth Vollrath, youth services librarian at Portage County Public Library in Stevens Point, Wisconsin, describes the possibilities this way: "We have wonderful school–public library cooperation in our county. I started and still coordinate a group of librarians representing libraries of all kinds in our county—public, schools (public and parochial), university, and private business. We meet every other month or so to share information and ideas. Two of our most successful joint projects were 'Portage County Reads' and 'Count on Reading in Portage County,' where all of us involved our patrons in reading through activities geared to the setting. For example, schools held Read-Ins, decorated classroom doors with favorite books, and did Reading Is Fundamental distributions. The public library branches had a book fair, storytelling, and a trivia day for young adults. They also had patrons vote for their favorite books and organized family read-ins. An insurance library had a book swap.

"The university library prepared displays. I had a resolution signed by the county board, and we had lots of newpaper coverage. PTOs donated prizes. A local bank provided money for each school and public library to provide a book for a drawing. I brought in a storyteller to visit each school to kick off one of the programs. For another, I had songster Tom Pease do the final program for several hundred people. (I was fortunate to get local donations for these events.)

"Other things we have done jointly have included bringing in authors. We share costs, have the author visit certain schools during the day, and then have a program and book signing at the main library at night. We divide up duties such as arranging hotels, picking up the speakers at airports, and eating with them. It has been very rewarding."

Not every public library can be of help, but many can. In Williston, North Dakota, thanks to a grant from the North Dakota Library Association, Jane says rural and town schools were able to send busloads of students to the public library to hear her speak. She recently spoke in the elementary school in the small town of Fosston, Minnesota, because of a speaker's program organized by hardworking volunteers in the public library. In Oklahoma, according to author Dian Curtis Regan, the Center for the Book tries to coordinate Oklahoma authors and libraries in various parts of the state. "They ask authors to let them know when they are doing various functions in different cities and whether they can travel around the area and do appearances in libraries."

Bookpeople and Public Librarians Behind the Scenes

Even without public presentations, connections between public libraries and bookpeople can be useful. When Jane was making a trip out to Portland, Oregon, to visit her family and speak at Oregon Reading Association, she mentioned the trip to a librarian friend and was asked if she would be willing to do a presentation for the Portland Public Libraries' youth librarians. "I was happy to donate my time to help get the word out about my books," Jane says, "but I wasn't sure what librarians need from an author. As I stood in the room facing a table full of librarians, I told them that. I also told them that I could venture a few guesses: Librarians sometimes organize programs for kids; they sometimes offer booktalks to kids or teachers; and finally, simply as book lovers, they might be curious—as most reader seem to be—about the stories behind the books. 'All of the above,' they said."

So Jane gave a presentation that lasted for about an hour and a half and covered all of those areas. She used overhead transparencies to show the programs she gives in schools and also to illustrate how teachers have used the materials she makes available. She brought items from her box of realia for the librarians to see, smell, touch, taste, and hear. For each of her books, she offered a short-hand "hook" of how teachers are using them—linking *Pulling the Lion's Tail* with *Sarah Plain and Tall*, for instance, or using *The Storyteller's Beads* as "the first good read-aloud novel for the Africa unit," or using *Trouble* in a mapping unit or *Fire on the Mountain* as part of a values curriculum or *Only a Pigeon* in units on cities or pets. Finally, Jane briefly described how each of her books was conceived and born.

THE YOUNG AUTHORS CONFERENCE

What a Successful Young Authors Conference Looks Like

One time-honored option is the young authors conference, some version of which is held in many communities. The University of Alabama at Birmingham's (UAB) young authors conference (YAC) is an example of one that has successfully run for many years. The YAC steering committee of 20 to 25 people includes area teachers, administrators, and university personnel. The university's School of Education supports the conference as do area reading councils.

Each year, information packets are sent to each principal in the 10 surrounding county and city school systems. Depending on enrollment, each school is given a number of students who can attend. Schools are responsible for selecting the specific students and for sending a certain number of chaperones. "Each year," says Clark Underbakke, a member of the YAC committee, "we also get some phone requests from people who have heard about the conference either through the proverbial grapevine or seen it mentioned in the newspaper. Of course those people are more than welcome to join us. The more the merrier! We usually have around 4,000 children and adults who attend—4,000, not 400. It is a *whopper* of a day!"

Each child pays a nominal fee (around $4) to attend. This way, Clark says, the conference pays for itself. He stresses that it is "*not* a moneymaker . . . any proceeds go directly back into the conference in some way."

Once students arrive on the UAB campus, they are assigned, by grade level, to a specific building. An author or illustrator has also been assigned to that building. Clark explains that the children rotate through a series of activities. They listen to talks by the bookperson and have the opportunity to purchase books and have them autographed—"a *favorite* activity! The authors and illustrators take a great deal of time with each student . . . pose for pictures, draw pictures in the books, look at the students' writing. Each author/illustrator usually speaks three times, depending upon how many children are in the building, and usually signs books twice." Children also have a snack and a time to attend a session with one of various types of entertainers—storytellers, clowns, musicians, and magicians. Another highlight, Clark says, is when students share the work they brought with them. "At this time, they are given their certificate of attendance, signed by W. Ann Reynolds, a president of UAB, herself! These are highly coveted and hang on bedroom walls for years. . . . Hooray!"

Young Authors Conferences Handle Glitches, Too

Of course, not every young authors conference runs completely smoothly. To illustrate that young authors conferences can have horror stories, too, an author says, "I haven't had any really bad school visits, but the time I was part of the Lone Star Awards had its downside. The Lone Star program was a writing contest for every school in a district. The winners for each grade came to Austin to get their certificates, shake hands with a real author, and take part in a grade-appropriate workshop conducted by the most grade-appropriate author. It started at eleven o'clock and ran until two o'clock with no provision for lunch. Knowing my body chemistry as I do, I ate first *and* carried a snack, so there were no embarrassing incidents. The handshaking and all that went well enough, the only potential problem being the little girl who sneezed violently into her right hand before her turn to cross the stage and shake. I don't remember who the relevant author was, but when the girl, realizing what she had just done, hesitated, the author reached out and shook her hand firmly.

"The tough part was the workshop. We were in an auditorium. There were no side rooms. Each age group was given a space in the bleachers—well separated from each other, but not so far away that we couldn't hear each other. Plus, like all auditoriums, it echoed! And the space we had to work in was either the gym floor (if you were on level one) or the narrow space between the first bleacher and the railing (if you were on level two, as I was). There were no microphones. There was no provision for slides, bulletin boards, or anything large enough to be seen more than a foot away. And the lighting all came from the center of the auditorium, so I was backlit and my audience was in shadow.

"Fortunately, the kids, being all contest winners, were highly motivated, so we were able to soldier on and have productive sessions anyway, but I must ponder wistfully how much *more* productive we could have been with these wonderful kids if we'd had decent meeting space."

Scheduling an event as big as a young authors conference inevitably involves logistical complexities and sometimes problems. Each member of the YAC committee in Alabama is assigned to be in charge of a specific area such as buildings, entertainment, refreshments, certificates, signing, or lunch. The committee takes care not to schedule the event during a time when families may be unusually busy—holiday weekends, for instance. Clark notes that although the conference had two years where the weather did not cooperate, they have "never had a flop author or illustrator." Even in the bad weather years, "Nobody was hurt . . . and everyone still had a good time."

Jane knows about weather glitches. Her participation in a Minnesota young authors conference started off with weather warnings of an ice storm. Indeed, her car slid off the icy highway and she had to arrive at the planning meeting via state patrol. In this particular place, the local reading council, which organizes the young authors conference, invites area schools to submit a form specifying how they could use the visiting author in their classrooms. The winning school is awarded an author visit for the day before the conference. The next day—in the spirit of "the show must go on"—Jane was picked up and driven to the nearby school, while the local Amoco station towed her (undamaged) car to town. At the Saturday conference, Jane introduced her then brand-new book, *Miro in the Kingdom of the Sun*, to three different groups of students in the gymnasium, while area teachers and education students from the university worked with other students, in small groups, on their writing. "I'll always remember that conference," Jane says, "and not only because of that terrifying moment when I slid off the road. No, the big thrill was signing the very first copies of *Miro in the Kingdom of the Sun* and hearing the kids' gasps (they could see those bold illustrations to the very back of the auditorium) as I showed them David Frampton's giant crab and flying snake."

Where the Bookperson Is Primarily Inspiration

Author Helen Ketteman has participated in several different types of young authors conferences. At Middle Tennessee State University, for instance, she gave a speech to "a huge audience of kids and parents." She read from one of her books and then gave a slide presentation, much like one of her school visits, touching on "how books are created, how I go about writing a story, working with the editor, how important rewriting is, and how illustrators contribute their own creativity to the book." After the presentation, she answered questions from children. "It did feel a bit odd," Helen admits, "not having a little more contact with the kids, but this is the way the conference was organized, and it ran very smoothly. The kids were wonderful and very attentive during my talk, even though it came at the end of the day."

 Author Spotlight: Helen Ketteman

Helen says, "I grew up in Harlem, Georgia, at a time when there were no sports teams for girls, and when there wasn't much for kids on television (yes, it was invented). What did I do for fun? I read books. Reading stretched my imagination and helped me become a writer today.

"When I first started writing, I lived in Seattle, Washington. I thought the first story I ever wrote was wonderful and would sell right away. Guess what? It didn't. I had a lot to learn about writing for children. I wrote books for three and a half years before I sold my first one. If something is really important to you, you have to stick with it.

Children's lives have changed a lot since I was a child. They have many good (and some not so good) programs to watch on television. They have movies made especially for them, video games, computers, and the Internet to keep them entertained. But reading is still important, because it opens imaginations and gets people thinking, 'What if?' "

Helen's latest books are *Grandma's Cat, Bubba the Cowboy Prince, Heat Wave,* and *I Remember Papa.*

Where the Bookperson Is a Writing Resource

Jane and Helen have also been resource authors at the type of young authors conference where the author works directly with a group of students, emphasizing some writing technique. Jane says, "In those cases, I still talk about some elements from my regular school presentation—how much my stories come out of my real life, for instance. But I also tend to read more from my work, pointing to specific examples of how I tried to achieve a certain effect or how dramatically a revision changed, say, the first paragraph of *The Storyteller's Beads,* which has not even one word left of its initial opening. I also have them try writing and reading their work to each other."

Helen describes one where she worked with small groups of about 40 first graders, with several teachers in the room as helpers. "I started with a story and talked about some of the things a story needs. Then we talked about creating good characters and created a character together." Helen notes that, because this conference was held in the fall, she chose to do this exercise verbally, since she was not sure the first graders would yet be adept at writing. "At the end of the session, the kids had about five minutes to begin creating their own character. They wrote character profiles, and the teachers and I walked around the room, talking to each kid, seeing what they were doing, and helping them spell words." At the end of the session, the children were taken somewhere else for a storytelling session, while Helen had a new group and repeated her workshop.

In the afternoon, she worked a second time with each group. This time, she started with a tall tale. After talking a bit about tall tales and exaggeration, she offered a character and "together, orally, we brainstormed a tall tale. I spent time trying to get the kids to open up their imaginations to all sorts of possibilities they wouldn't normally think of, since tall tales are more fantastic than normal stories."

 ## Starting Out

Yvonne Hanley, a Grand Forks library media specialist, describes what it was like to help launch a young authors conference that had not been held since the 1980s. Organized by local librarians and funded partly through the librarians' association and partly through the local educational foundation, the Grand Forks event was open to first through third graders who had written a book, either at home or school. The conference was free, but children needed to bring a parent and needed to apply through their school librarian. While some schools hold a competition to determine who can attend, this one was "first come, first served," for up to 320 youngsters.

Yvonne warns that unexpected community events can throw off preregistration numbers. In the case of Grand Forks, nice weather plus a one-year-later "we survived the flood" celebration cut into attendance; one-quarter to one-third of the children preregistered didn't show up. While half of the children met with illustrator Gary Harbo, the others were divided into small groups where a facilitator had them read aloud the story they had written. "Some facilitators were better than others at drawing the children out," Yvonne says. "We realized that in future years, we needed guidelines so that each group would run as effectively as possible." Some children were too shy to read stories aloud, she notes, and some facilitators let parents read in those cases, while others simply went on to the next child. A local school administrator also did a magic show for the children. Yvonne says he later commented it was a wonderful experience, one of his best ever—"probably for the same reason these young authors conferences tend to be successful: they appeal to a select number of kids who are excited about such things."

Funding for future events, however, is going to be a challenge. The organizing committee plans to ask area schools to raise money for the project through their parent-teacher organizations and also to seek corporate sponsorship.

Working with Older Students

At an annual young authors conference in Thief River Falls, Minnesota, fifth through eighth graders from area schools, some quite rural, ride the bus to Northland Community Technical College, where the conference is held over two school days. Northwest Service Cooperative, a not-for-profit regional unit that serves several school districts, arranges for 10 to 11 authors and storytellers to work, in small groups, with about 500 students from 30 districts. Each presenter leads three breakout sessions, 50 minutes each, on a writing topic related to the year's theme. (For example, the theme was Creative and Courageous in 1998.) The students receive T-shirts autographed by all the participating authors and storytellers, and also have a chance to buy books written by the presenters. Mary Morken, student academic coordinator for Northwest Service Cooperative, decided to try a young authors conference after she heard about a similar program run by one of the metro service cooperatives. The purpose, she says, "is to celebrate writing and to inspire and encourage students to become even more effective writers."

Author Mary Casanova, who has been a resource person at the Thief River Falls conference as well as at several other young authors conferences for older students, says that, more than with her school visits, the focus is on writing and that "the students are like sponges, eager to soak up useful tips and inspiration." For one thing, she points out, "Students usually attend voluntarily and are already able writers." With this in mind, she says, "I draw on my own work as we interact, but the focus is on helping them gain skills and confidence in their own writing ability. I find myself recharged from a young authors conference, especially at the end of my sessions when the students share from their own writing." Often, she says, students from the conferences will keep in touch with her through her Web site.

 Practical Issues to Think About

How to fund a conference is one big issue, of course. Avoiding scheduling conflicts is another tricky one. The bigger the conference, the more challenging the details of organizing the day itself. The Illinois statewide young authors conference, for instance, held at Illinois State University in Normal, has more than 1,000 participants. Author Patricia Rae Wolff, who has been a speaker at the conference, commented in her local Society of Children's Book Writers and Illustrators newsletter that "the logistics of moving 1,300 children around a large campus with each group having a different schedule of places and events is . . . well, mind-boggling."

Choosing participants is also something for organizers to think about. In Illinois, teachers keep the conference in mind throughout the whole school year as they work with their students on writing. From all the writing samples submitted, each school district chooses at least one, and that student is invited to attend the conference. "Even at this young level," says Patricia, "the writers are up against formidable odds. They must adhere to very specific submission guidelines. Very few, comparatively, will succeed (and attend the conference). They are already learning to be writers."

Some conference organizers are uneasy about setting up conference participation as a competition and find other ways to handle the selection of which students will attend. Others point out that gifted writers should have a chance to compete and excel in the ways gifted athletes do. If you are considering starting a young authors conference, don't forget to discuss this issue.

Benefits of a Young Authors Conference

Mary Morken calls the conference she organizes "a stimulating experience. It's grown every year and has always been an exciting event, bringing authors to our region, which is quite isolated. Students don't have the chance to meet authors otherwise." Clark Underbakke echoes Mary's comments. "The long-lasting impact of the conference is what makes me know the conference works: When a student running for student council cites the conference in his or her experiences or list of honors . . . when a student starts fifth grade and can still remember going to young authors in first grade—including who the author was, what the student wrote, what the student shared, and all." Jo-Ann Portalupi, who taught children's literature at UAB and also worked on the steering committee, agrees that "for many of our local children, this opportunity to share their writing with peers and to be inspired by a published author is a highlight in their lives." She cites a "sad but telling" example. An obituary from the local paper told "a sad story of a school-age child who died way too young. On the short list of her accomplishments was mentioned that she had been a participant in the young authors conference."

Patricia Rae Wolff could "see and feel the enthusiasm and excitement" as students moved around the Illinois State University campus carrying the special book bags they were given. "From an author's perspective," she says, "what makes these author presentations different from a regular author presentation in schools is the very talented children who are chosen to attend this conference. Their enthusiasm for reading and writing just bubbles out with their questions. They want to know what it's like to be a writer because many of them already profess wanting to be writers when they grow up. They want to learn from us how they can become better writers. They want to know things about being a writer that teachers and parents can't tell them." After attending sessions with writers who publish books for their age levels, Patricia says, students gather in an auditorium to ask a panel of writers "some surprisingly astute questions. Then each child is individually called to the stage by name to receive a certificate and a copy of a book signed by the author whose presentation he or she attended. What a joy for any writer, old or young, to attend this conference!"

PIGGYBACKING SCHOOL VISITS WITH CONFERENCES

Sometimes, having a young authors conference in your community can be a good way to swing a school visit. "Generally," Clark says, "the young authors steering committee gets 'first dibs' at hosting an author or illustrator at their school. This is by no means a private clique . . . we just hear about who is coming before the general public. Any school interested in hosting a guest could contact Maryann Manning at UAB, and she would do what she could. Our authors and illustrators have also done book signings at local bookstores and spoken at local libraries."

Other conferences may help, too. Each year, Jane helps organize a children's literature conference at the University of North Dakota, where at least one author is brought to the state—many of them for the very first time. "Some authors, including Avi," she says, "tell us they made time for our conference specifically because they have never been in North Dakota before." Not all authors have time to extend their stay long enough to include school visits, but some do. Peter Cumming brought Arctic clothing and artifacts into Grand Forks classrooms the year he spoke at the conference. Recently, Walter the Giant Storyteller spent a whole week stirring both children and adults into huge enthusiasm about books. Sometimes a piggyback visit like this is the only practical way to get authors into some schools. "Sometimes," Jane says, "schools even ask us specifically if we can bring such-and-such an author, because they would love to team up with us in a school visit. Often we can't. Sometimes we can."

The North Dakota Library Association (NDLA) is another example of a conference that brings authors to various spots around the state. Each year, they try to have the winners of the Flickertail (children's choice) Award attend. School children from the city where the NDLA conerence is being held usually have a chance to hear the authors at the same time.

A Good Reason to Connect with Your Local SCBWI Chapter

Tricia Gardella, a regional advisor for Society of Children's Book Writers and Illustrators (SCBWI) and herself a children's author, organizes a conference every year where she brings three to five authors and illustrators to her part of California to speak at a daylong SCBWI conference for would-be children's authors. The bookpeople bunk at her ranch for several days ahead of time, eating such delicious tidbits as her family's famous homemade ravioli. (Using her contacts from many years of feeding authors during these conference weeks—and her memories of great times around the table—Tricia recently edited *Writers in the Kitchen: Children's Book Authors Share Memories of Their Favorite Recipes*.)

Each morning, everyone hops into Tricia's van and she drives along twisting mountain roads from school to school—often three or four schools per day, even making visits to one-room schoolhouses. When the group reaches a school, the authors and illustrators fan out, each speaking in one classroom (selected by the school). An hour later, everyone converges back on the van. On to the next school! Tricia funds the program with a $2,000 donation from her local newspaper, a $150 contribution from each school, and SCBWI funds that pick up some of the authors' travel expenses.

She also constantly experiments with new ways to reach children and get them excited about books. In 1998, for instance, she provided area schools with a number of tickets to a book signing party at a local pizza parlor. Classroom teachers picked their own ways to select a few students who would enjoy connecting one-on-one with the book people. At the pizza parlor, parents had the chance to buy books; children were served free pizza; and everyone was invited to participate in a bubble gum chewing contest with Lee Wardlaw, who had recently published *Bubblemania: The Chewy History of Bubble Gum*.

 ### Author Spotlight: Tricia Gardella

Tricia Gardella says, "I live on a cattle ranch in the gold country of central California, have two grown daughters, a grown son, six grandsons, and one granddaughter (all in preschool—what inspiration!). I've been a reading addict since I discovered that lining up those shapes made words and have loved playing with words ever since. I began writing in October 1985. Why I waited so long is the question. My books include *Just Like My Dad*, *Casey's New Hat*, and *Writers in the Kitchen: Children's Book Authors Share Memories of Their Favorite Recipes*, recipes and memories of children's authors and illustrators on favorite foods from childhood. And *Blackberry Booties*, a new picture book, is due to see print in 2000.

I've sold stories to *Highlights*, *Ladybug*, *The Friend*, and other children's magazines. I've had a ceramics studio; designed, manufactured, and distributed (nationwide) a musical critter I called a Drimble; and am a fiber artist—spinner, weaver, knitter, and crocheter. My designs continue to appear in such publications as *Pac-O-Fun*, *Crafts 'n' Things*, *Leisure Arts*, and others.

I am the north-central California regional advisor for the Society of Children's Book Writers and Illustrators. I've been writing a weekly review column ("Picture This") for seven years and have taught community classes on writing for children. In my spare time I love to work in my yard, travel, and meet my writer friends at conferences.

Audrey Conant, a school library media specialist and the information skills chair of the Maine Association of School Libraries, describes an author's festival held in Eureka, California, directed by the children's librarian of the Humboldt County Library. Sixty authors are invited. Twenty who are willing to waive their fee—only transportation, meals, and lodging are provided—attend each year. "They are housed at the city's fine traditional hotel, the Eureka Inn," Audrey says. "The authors are chosen via a committee and are preferably recommended by eyewitness accounts. A number of them are repeat visitors. Some authors value contact with students as a way of keeping in touch with an age level and acquiring permanent 'clients.' It's also a status thing."

Some authors, notes Tricia Gardella (who is herself one of the repeat visiting authors), "have been attending since the festival was first established." Most of the authors come from California because few others can handle the transportation costs.

Wednesday evening includes a reception and a chance to meet with local press. On Thursday, volunteer drivers take each author to various nearby schools. The authors then regroup that evening to attend a potluck supper. Friday includes more school visits and an evening banquet, where each author says a few words to the audience, and a raffle is held for 20 autographed books. On Saturday afternoon, the organizers sponsor a four-hour book sale and signing.

Funding for the conference comes from the book sale and raffle. "This is an example," Audrey says, "of a service that bridges home, school, and public—that involves cooperation and effort between educators, school librarians, and public librarians." The payoff? Each year, a certain number of classrooms and schools "benefit from real contact with real authors."

From an author's point of view, says Tricia, the conference is "exhausting, because schools are so spread out and you don't travel with other authors. But it's worth it. The redwoods make a gorgeous setting. Eureka is a city of charming old Victorian houses that date back to the booming lumber days of the early twentieth century." It's also great, she adds, because it gives her the chance to become friends with new authors and to reconnect with close author friends who make a point of attending.

PIGGYBACKING WITH BOOKSTORE APPEARANCES

Another option that may be a possibility, particularly if you are a classroom teacher who lives near an independently owned bookstore, is to check with a nearby bookstore and see whether they sponsor events where you might be able to bring your class to meet an author. One California author, Kathleen Duey, notes, "I almost never just sign books anymore. I insist that the stores get school classes in—a field trip/free author for them, an audience for me."

Kathleen has a send-home sheet with information about her and her books that she faxes ahead of time to teachers. When a class comes to the bookstore, they will see Kathleen's books and hear her "talking about literacy or telling stories from diaries and journals I've read, or describing people I have met or talked to on the phone who were colorfully helpful with my research, or talking about the months and years that can be packed into the tiny word 'revision.' "

A Bookstore Presentation

"History," says Kathleen, "is the story of everyone's extended family." Whether in a bookstore presentation or a school visit, she works to "help kids see their own place in history as inescapable, unique, and critically important. It's my belief that the future is shaped by all of us—that every life matters. So I talk about history, how everyone's family is a long line of every-day heroes who survived, who did not give up . . . or none of us would be here, now."

Her great grandfather, she says, "is a perfect illustration of an ordinary man who survived extraordinary danger." She shows students a picture of him and his family and tells them, "The three-year-old in that Indian woman's lap is my grandfather." He was a farmer, but he had "one brave, heroic night and did not give up or give in." As a Union soldier coming home from the Civil War, he was in a transport ship, the *Sultana*, that blew up. Though no one has heard about the *Sultana* because it sank about five days after Lincoln was shot, that night, more people died than died on the *Titanic*.

Kathleen's great grandfather, she says, had to fight to live, "and was fighting for my life and my sons' as well, though of course he could not have known that—trying to keep his head above the dark floodwaters of the Mississippi in the middle of a stormy night. I tell kids that when their own lives call upon them for courage and persistence, to remember that they never know who and what in the future depends on them."

Kathleen also talks about "the 3,000-year-old conversation—literacy. I try to give kids some sense of their heritage in the written word. I talk about letters that kept families, lovers, enemies engaged over decades of separation. I talk about ideas and how they spread in print." In short, she says, she talks about "how the world is changed by those who write" and about how bookstores and libraries are "treasure houses for all this wonderful inheritance—the places where it is stored—where we bring the new books and let people decide if they are worth keeping around for five years or five months or five centuries."

As Kathleen points out, the bookstore option can be a very appealing one, both for an author wanting to spread the word about her speaking capabilities and for a school that doesn't know if a certain author would be worth the time and money. "I think a lot of schools," she says, "have been burned by lousy author visits where they put out big money for someone who writes wonderful books but can't speak worth beans."

The catch—if this is a catch—is that clearly what makes such an event worthwhile for the bookstore and the author is book sales. Depending on how the bookstore arranges things, a teacher may have to distribute book lists and collect money, much as with those ubiquitous book-club sheets we all know and some of us love. The payoff, however, in addition to a free author visit, is that children are encouraged to think of books as valuable things worth owning, collecting, and reading and of bookstores as friendly and fun places to spend time. (For more on book sales and autographs, see chapter 10.)

Include as many people in the field trip as possible, Kathleen advises. "Include parent volunteers and maybe bring the media specialist/librarian along if he or she wasn't coming—maybe even the principal or any other administrative people possible. Pick a good speaker, so that the idea that author visits might be worthwhile begins to grow at school." Be sure to manage the book sheets well, probably sending them home a couple of times. If book sales are good, Kathleen points out, the bookstore, too, will want to do it again.

Author Spotlight: Kathleen Duey

Researching and writing her many historical novels has made Kathleen Duey acutely aware of the human conversation we think of as literacy. She is always delighted at the deep connection kids feel with authors. Books form a bridge that arches above differences in age, color, religion, gender, background, economic status, and whatever else might lie between writer and reader.

Literacy, Kathleen says, is the real star at any author's school visit. Using anecdotes from the hundreds of diaries and journals she has read, Kathleen strives to help kids feel as if they are connected to the whole human family—and all of its written knowledge—by birthright. If they can read, they can listen. If they will learn to write well, they can speak, and we are all waiting to hear what they have to say.

Kathleen is the author of two ongoing series of historical novels, *American Diaries*, with 12 titles available now, and *Survival*, with 10 titles in print. She also has several nonfiction and other fiction titles in print plus many new projects in the works.

AND ONE LAST POSSIBILITY

Perhaps nothing we've suggested so far feels feasible for your school. Is it time to give up? Sigh and say that all the bookpeople goodies will just have to go to other schools, other places? Crawl off in despair? Not at all. In part III, we will introduce you to some of the newest and most innovative ways of connecting with bookpeople through the use of methods that draw on the most basic technology (pen and paper) to the most advanced.

REFERENCES

Duey, Kathleen. *Sarah Anne Hartford, Massachusetts, 1651*; *Emma Eileen Grove, Mississippi River, 1865*; *Anisett Lundberg, California Gold Fields, 1851*; *Mary Alice Peale, Philadelphia, 1779*; *Willow Chase, Kansas Territory, 1857*; *Ellen Elizabeth Hawkins, Texas, 1887*; *Alexia Ellery Finsdale, San Francisco, 1905*; *Evie Peach, St. Louis 1857*; *Celou Sudden Shout, Wind River, 1826*; *Summer MacCleary, Virginia Colony, 1749*; *Agnes May Gleason, Walsenburg, Colorado, 1932*; *Amelina Carrett, Thibodaux, Louisiana, 1860*. American Diaries Series. New York: Aladdin, 1996–1999.

——. *Titanic*; *Earthquake, San Francisco, 1906*; *Blizzard, Estes Park, Colorado, 1887*; *Fire, Chicago 1876*; *Flood, Mayersville, Mississippi, 1927*; *Death Valley, California, 1849*; *Cave-in, Pennsylvania, 1859*; *Trainwreck, Kansas, 1892*; *Hurricane, New England, 1840*. Survival Series. New York: Aladdin, 1998–1999.

Gardella, Tricia. *Blackberry Booties*. With illustrations by Glo Coalson. New York: Orchard. Forthcoming.

——. *Casey's New Hat*. With illustrations by Margot Apple. Boston: Houghton Mifflin, 1997.

——. *Just Like My Dad*. With illustrations by Margot Apple. New York: HarperCollins, 1993.

——. *Writers in the Kitchen: Children's Book Authors Share Memories of Their Favorite Recipes*. Honesdale, PA: Boyds Mills, 1998.

Ketteman, Helen. *Bubba the Cowboy Prince (A Fractured Texas Tale)*. With illustrations by James Warhola. New York: Scholastic, 1997.

——. *Grandma's Cat*. With illustrations by Marsha Lynn Winborn. Boston: Houghton Mifflin, 1996.

——. *Heat Wave*. With illustrations by Scott Goto. New York: Walker, 1998.

——. *I Remember Papa*. With illustrations by Greg Shed. New York: Dial, 1998.

Kurtz, Jane. *Miro in the Kingdom of the Sun*. With illustrations by David Frampton. Boston: Houghton Mifflin, 1996.

MacLachlan, Patricia. *Sarah Plain and Tall*. New York: HarperCollins, 1985.

Wardlaw, Lee. *Bubblemania: The Chewy History of Bubble Gum*. With illustrations by Sandra Forrest. New York: Aladdin, 1997.

Part II

Alternative Connections with Bookpeople

We no longer live in a world circumscribed by boundaries of time zones and geographical location, though all adults remember that world quite well. Many of our children, however—the children we teach and link with authors, illustrators, and storytellers—have no memory of such a world. They know only the world that includes virtual opportunities and connections of every sort. If you haven't yet explored that world, or you have only gotten the first two toes on each foot wet, we invite you to learn more about this virtual world, rich in communication and information unavailable a generation ago.

In fact, it seems that many of us haven't explored the possibilities very thoroughly. When asked about the response to several online projects she has taken part in, author Jackie French Koller said, "I think this will all change as more and more schools come online, and more and more teachers become educated to the possibilities, but it's pretty slow out there right now." Author Wendie C. Old reiterates this opinion. "I expect to do more [virtual connecting] as time goes on and as teachers begin to become more computer savvy." Many adults, it seems, have been slow to dip into virtual waters, or perhaps many school and library funding sources have simply been slow to provide the dollars needed for equipment and connections.

The good news is that despite hesitation by some, and low funding for many, there are a tremendous number of exciting opportunities to connect with bookpeople in the virtual world. We invite you to explore the connections beyond your classroom or library walls!

Chapter Seven

Mail Connections

Enter ▷ PERSONAL MAIL

Fan Mail

The oldest and most reliable way for readers to connect with the creator of a book or story they love is by mailing a letter. How many times, over the years, Toni has helped one of her young library patrons seeking the address of an author! Teachers love to assign a letter-to-the-author/illustrator. Kids love to write to authors and illustrators, too. And authors and illustrators love to get letters from their readers, especially the ones that come from the reader's heart.

As articles and speeches have pointed out, it's crucial to be respectful of the limits many book-people—especially famous ones—need to draw around their time for creating new projects. Warn children that they may not get an answer to their letters, and recognize that publishers don't always forward letters promptly. If it's anywhere near the end of the school year, have children include their home addresses on the letters. Author Dian Curtis Regan says, "It's disheartening to receive those letters and know that either school is already out or will be out by the time the author's answer is received. I hate thinking about how bad the kids feel who don't get a response, when other kids are receiving letters from authors. And it's all a matter of timing."

Fan Mail

"I'm not even halfway through your book & I already love it! I have read 52 books since August and yours is the best—so far. And I'm not just saying that to make you feel better."

—Snail mail addressed to author Dian Curtis Regan,
author of *Monster of the Month Club*

"Do you make more money or less money than normal people?"

—Snail mail addressed to author Dian Curtis Regan,
author of *The Friendship of Milly and Tug*

"I think it's inspiring that you followed your dream and became a writer. You have inspired me to follow my dream of becoming a doctor, so someday if you're ever in Virginia and you feel sick, feel free to drop in."

—Snail mail addressed to author Jackie French Koller,
author of The Dragonling series

Author Spotlight: Jackie French Koller

Jackie French Koller was born in a Native American long-house in the woods of New England. As she grew, she lived, among other places, in a great castle in England, in an orphanage, in a covered wagon heading west, in outer space, and in the jungles of Africa, where she was exuberantly courted by Tarzan.

These are all lies, of course, but they are also all true, because, as a child, Jackie French Koller lived as vividly inside her own imagination as she did inside the four walls of her home. As she grew, Jackie tried her hand at an assortment of careers and college majors, but it wasn't until she married and had children that she discovered her life's passion—books. The road to publication would prove long and arduous, but finally in 1989, 16 years after she had written her first story, *Impy for Always* was published. Since then, more than two dozen books have followed, with many more in the works.

Now Jackie French Koller lives, among other places, in a longhouse in the woods of New England, in a tenement flat in depression–era New York, in a spooky old house that she shares with a monster, with a dragon in a distant, alien world, and, oh yes, with her family on a mountain in western Massachusetts.

You can visit Jackie at her Web page at http://geocities.com/ ~jackiekoller/.

Fan Mail

"Your books will live forever. I hope you live to 99 or 100 but who cares."

—Snail mail addressed to author Jane Yolen, author of Caldecott-winner *Owl Moon*

"I was going to write to Mark Twain or Enid Blyton but they are dead, so I am writing to you."

—Snail mail addressed to author Jane Yolen, co-author of *Armageddon Summer*

Author Spotlight: Jane Yolen

"I have always been an overachiever, but I must admit that I still cannot believe I actually have over 200 books in print. The reason is—I love writing. I even love rewriting.

"I have been writing since I was very young. In first grade I wrote the class musical, and I was the author of the script, the lyrics, and the music! It was a play about vegetables and I also played the lead carrot. We ended up in a salad together.

"Over the years I have been extremely lucky in that my books and stories have won innumerable awards. Some of the most famous are the Caldecott for *Owl Moon*; the Caldecott Honor for *The Emperor and the Kite*; the Nebula for "Sister Emily's Lightship"; the Jewish Book Award for *The Devil's Arithmetic*;

the Christopher Medal for *The Seeing Stick*; the World Fantasy Award for *Favorite Folktales from Around the World*; and four body-of-work awards, as well as two honorary degrees.

"But awards sit on shelves and need dusting. The best rewards come in writing books that change lives.

"Nowadays I am on a new adventure—writing books with my three grown kids. I cowrite books and stories and poems with my daughter Heidi E. Y. Stemple; I do music books with my musician son Adam Stemple; I write poetry and text to go with the astonishingly beautiful photos by my son Jason Stemple.

"When my three grandchildren grow up—I may write with them as well."

Fan Mail

"I haven't read any of your books but I know I'd like them."

—Snail mail addressed to author Jacqueline Briggs Martin,
author of *Snowflake Bentley*

"My teacher is making me write you this letter. Thank you for coming to our school and talking about *A Vampire Named Fred*.
Your only fan, David."

—Snail mail addressed to author Bill Crider

"Thank you for sharing your book about wolves. Are you writing one about cats? If so I have information."

—Snail mail addressed to author Kay Winters,
author of *Wolf Watch*

 Author Spotlight: Kay Winters

It's never too late to follow your dream! In 1992, Kay Winters quit her job as a classroom teacher and college instructor and began a new career writing children's books. *Did You See What I Saw? Poems About School* came out in 1996, followed by *The Teeny Tiny Ghost*, *Wolf Watch*, *Where Are the Bears?*, and *How Will the Easter Bunny Know?* Kay writes picture books and early chapter books, both fiction and nonfiction. She loves learning about the various topics in her books. "Being a writer lets me do what I love best! First I have adventures, then I read about the place, or the subject, or the people in the book, and finally I have a chance to play with the words. I try to make each one count." When she is not reading, writing, speaking at conferences, or doing school visits, Kay is traveling with her husband Earl. They have been on a walking tour of the Cotswolds, explored the pyramids in Tikal, and ridden elephants in Thailand. Kay and Earl live in an old stone farmhouse in Quakertown, Bucks County, Pennsylvania. They have wild turkeys and twin fawns who visit daily during the summer. Kay advises other teachers with a yen to write to "Go for it and *persist!*"

Fan Mail

"If I were you before turning in *Absurd, Said the Bird* I would have looked around for a book that was similar. I personally don't read books because I have exactly 150 books in my room, and none of them are read yet."

—Snail mail addressed to author Tricia Gardella,
author of *Just Like My Dad*

Fan E-Mail

What's new about letters to book and story creators? E-mail letters to the author, illustrator, or storyteller are the new twist in communications with bookpeople. As the presence of E-mail capability on school, library, and home computers grows, so does the opportunity to engage in virtual communications with the creators of books and stories.

Many authors have enthusiastically greeted the opportunity to connect so easily with their readers and fans. Author Haemi Balgassi welcomes E-mail from her readers. "I enjoy hearing from readers via E-mail. I'm still new enough at this to think, 'Wow! This person actually read something I wrote!' I get a rush every time I hear from readers—especially the children. And, in cases where students request interviews for school assignments, I think E-mail is a huge convenience over both the telephone and snail mail. If distance is a factor, it's likely to be less expensive than phone calls—and less awkward for both parties; a young interviewer might be nervous on the phone, and the author might feel more pressured to respond quickly instead of thinking the questions through. Plus, snail mail can't compete with E-mail's speed. Most students are working against a deadline and need quick replies." Like Haemi, author Deborah Hopkinson has her E-mail address posted on her amazon.com (one of the major online bookstores, http://www.amazon.com) interview page as well as on her own personal Web page. "I love E-mail from fans. . . . [It is] so cool. That someone takes the time to let you know their response to your work is terrific."

Author Roland Smith, also an enthusiast, actively encourages E-mail communications from his readers. "At each school [I visit] I encourage the children to E-mail their questions to me. I give the E-mail address to children for several reasons: 1) Children who are sincerely interested in writing are often shy kids (not always, of course) who are reluctant to ask their questions in front of three hundred classmates. E-mail gives them a chance to do it privately. 2) Good questions oftentimes occur after I've left and the kids have had time to think about the visit. 3) It gives the teachers a chance to do follow-up to a visit. It costs a lot of money for a school to have an author come in. Using E-mail, the visit can continue indefinitely, i.e., they read one of my books in class, discuss it, send the questions, and discuss it some more. 4) Selfishly . . . it is a lot easier and less expensive for me to answer fan E-mail than it is for me to deal with and answer fan snail mail. There are no envelopes, stamps, stationery, or printers, and I can reply instantly from anywhere in the world with my laptop. So far this has not been a big burden; it's been a real joy to hear from them."

Many other authors and illustrators also enjoy E-mail communications from their readers but express some reservations about the time it might take should the volume grow. Jackie French Koller enjoys electronic fan mail and has not yet found the demand of corresponding electronically too great to handle. "I do allow kids to E-mail me from my Web site, and I don't find the volume too much to handle—yet. When and if I do, I'll take the link off. A few of them have started up a back-and-forth dialogue, but it doesn't last very long and they're off to other things." Jaqueline Briggs Martin, too, has had limited E-mail communications from her readers. "I've received some E-mail from people who've read [my Web page], but not over a dozen messages probably. I'm not sure how

I feel about E-mail from students. I think I'd be willing to say yes to it, though I do see a danger in getting overwhelmed. But I think contact is so important I'd be willing to put up with the danger—and just know I'd have to deal with it if it occurred." For her part, Jane says, "The main thing is that I often get follow-up letters or other letters from students that I have to answer via snail mail and, though I'm sorry to admit this, the truth is that they go into my *huge* to-do stack and don't always get answered right away. E-mail is not only so easy, it's also pressing in a way . . . that post stares up at me from my E-mail box . . . and so my answers are much more timely than they would have been via snail mail. I often feel guilty about how I deal with fan letters, so I am gloriously glad to have an easier way to connect with kids."

Even some authors who now find their volume of E-mail manageable mention apprehensions about increased volume in the future. Illustrator Chris Soentpiet is already at that place. "I have had wonderful opportunities to connect with teachers and young readers. The downfall of E-mail services is my inability to respond to each E-mail, especially with younger audiences who may be seeking an E-mail pen pal. . . . If I do not respond to their second or third request, the young . . . readers get disappointed." For her part, author Dian Curtis Regan has made a decision to exclude her personal E-mail address for this very reason. "I'm possessive of my E-mail address, and presently receive far too much daily E-mail. Therefore, I'd rather readers write to me via snail mail," she says. However, for a year after *Monsters in Cyberspace* was published, Dian did "share" a screen name with the book's main character, earthgirl7, and chatted with readers who E-mailed the character, letting them know, of course, that earthgirl7 was a fictional character.

Other authors, such as Deborah Morris, consider E-mail, no matter the volume, just another requirement of the job. "I've been deluged with great E-mail!" she says. When asked about the danger of being overloaded with the task of answering it all, she says, "Oh well! That's an author's job and, in my mind, responsibility. I answer all snail-mail letters as well. And frankly, the E-mail letters are much easier to respond to!" Like Roland Smith, she cites speed, low cost, and instant delivery as advantages of E-mail over snail mail. In addition, Deborah says that she likes the fact that it is more casual, more like a conversation with her readers. Although she admits that it eats into her time, she has set it as a priority. "I just think it's important, so I put it on the 'must-do' list. I do answer most of my fan mail and young writers' questions in the wee hours, though."

Author Spotlight: Deborah Morris

One of the nation's leading writers of real-life dramas, Deborah Morris has written more than 100 magazine articles and 12 books, including the young-adult book series Real Kids, Real Adventures. Her work has been translated into as many as 10 languages and featured in *Reader's Digest*, *Family Circle*, *Good Housekeeping*, and other publications. She also cowrote the young adult Christian bestseller *What Would Jesus Do?* and coproduced two reality-based television movies: *Dancing in the Dark* (Lifetime, 1995), and *Angel Flight Down* (ABC, 1996). In addition, she is creator/coproducer of the *Real Kids, Real Adventures* television series based on her books, airing in the United States on the Discovery Channel and in Canada on Global Television. Deborah lives in Garland, Texas.

To learn more about Deborah Morris, visit her Web site at http://www.realkids.com.

Teacher Monica Edinger, The Dalton School, New York City, who has had some wonderful on-line experiences with authors and scholars of children's literature, notes that she does worry about the implications of this ready communication. "I guess I feel strongly that we teachers should be very careful not to impose on authors. If they want the exchange—great. . . . I mention this because I don't want to encourage teachers and librarians to respond to this by indiscriminately requiring children to write authors and scholars. I think these sorts of experiences are wonderful, but cannot be planned; rather, they just appear, should be done once, and then the children should be left with the memory of a special personal connection with an author or scholar." We agree with Monica and share her concerns. Before we introduce the wonderful opportunities available to you and the children you teach or serve, we'd like to add our advice: In using E-mail to communicate, please be respectful of the time and privacy of authors, illustrators, and storytellers, and share this attitude of respect with the children you teach.

Fan Mail

Even in E-mail, the personality and charm of the writer come trumpeting through. Referring to an earlier E-mail correspondence with an author, a student writes:

"Yes I remember the day when I lost the address to my favorite author's Web page and wrote her this wonderful letter about how much I loved her books, and her page and how could she please send me the URL.

"You know what she does? She sends me the URL. Not that that's bad, I mean, it's good that she sent it to me. But here I had written an extremely personal letter to my idolized (well idolized is going a bit far but I like to embellish) author, and she simply sends me a plain URL. I mean, I know she's busy but she could at least say, 'thanks for the letter' or 'I love hearing from my fans.' "

The student passes on a bit of advice, should the author ever find herself in a similar circumstance:

"So this is what you must do; you must say: Thanks for the incredibly cool letter. You can find my books at _____.

"OK? that's not too hard is it?"

—E-mail addressed to author Deborah Morris

"Hello again: . . . I am the one who wrote to you about wanting to be a 'super star playright' about a week ago. Sitting with me is my friend . . . who is my partner in writing. Ahhhhhhhhhhhhhhhhh, first we would like to say thank you a thousand times for actually reading my E-mail . . . WOW—you are coolness trapped in human form. THANK YOU.

—E-mail addressed to author Deborah Morris,
author of the Real Kids Read Adventures series

"I first picked up your book, *Are You Alone on Purpose*, at the local bookstore. After reading it I impatiently waited for your next book, but to no avail. Your first was incredible, but what now?"

—E-mail addressed to young adult author Nancy Werlin*

*Nancy assured her fan that help was on the way. Her second novel, *The Killer's Cousin*, was published only three months after she received this letter and went on to win the 1999 Edgar Award.

Author Spotlight: Nancy Werlin

"For me, there's a tremendous excitement in writing about teenagers. In some ways this is ironic, since I remember every minute of being a teenager with a feeling of huge relief that it's over. During those years, beneath a (mostly) quiet front, I seethed with helpless rage: not only at the typical adult targets, but also at the lock-step, self-policed behavior of most of my peers. I knew that at core I was meant to be an adult—not even 18 or 21, but at least 35.

"What strikes me now, however, is the sheer dramatic power of all that teenage emotion and passion. I'm not romantic about it; my own discomfort and misery at that age is too vivid a memory for that. But it's irresistible material for a writer to work with: anything, literally, is possible for a teenager. And, since this is a time in which so many of us—such as myself—work out our core identities, you can write book after book in which characters are floundering at the beginning, but, by the end, have a solid grasp of who they are and what they want. That process is unique for each individual, and never grows stale.

"There is nothing more satisfying than guiding a teenage character safely, despite both internal and external hazards, along that personal journey."

Nancy Werlin's third novel, *Locked Inside*, will be published in spring 2000.

CLASSROOM E-MAIL

Preparation for a Real-Space Visit

Beyond personal E-mail from students, many teachers and librarians have made use of E-mail as a way for their students to connect with authors in advance of a real-space visit, as a follow-up to a visit, or even in lieu of a visit. School counselor Karl Holzmuller and several classroom teachers at Clear Lake Elementary School, Sedro-Wooley S. D., Washington, prepared five classes of elementary students for a visit with author Deborah Hopkinson (whom Karl had met on CHILD_LIT, a children's literature discussion listserv) in a variety of ways. "This preparation extended over several weeks and included reading her books with the class in a kind of large-group literature-circle format. We studied the historical setting of the books, looked at maps to orient ourselves as to where Clara and Birdie lived, and spent considerable time with 'graphic organizers' doing character maps of the two girls. We also did some Venn diagrams comparing and contrasting Clara and Birdie. . . . I found the whole process of preparation to be rewarding and felt it would be essential for both the children and Deborah.

"The students developed questions they wanted to ask Deborah based on our studies. Each class worked together on their list of questions, which were then E-mailed to Deborah. The children felt like they knew her by the time the visit occurred. I feel the use of E-mail was a very important part of all of this. There is a kind of immediacy through E-mail that is not possible through regular mail. I think it aids continuity in a teaching/studying process in that momentum of interest and engagement in the project can be more easily maintained. . . . The students responded very positively throughout this whole project. They checked the classroom E-mail every morning and were thrilled when there was a message back. I believe their whole experience was sharpened by the personal contact. I have enjoyed using the Internet and E-mail to help establish these contacts. My advice [to teachers and librarians] would be to not hesitate to try it. I feel if an author offers [his or her] E-mail address then [he or she is] welcoming that kind of contact."

E-Mail in Lieu of a Visit

Some authors and illustrators have had the opportunity to communicate electronically with entire classes of students who are studying their work, even when they are not able to visit in person. Contacts between the librarians/teachers and these book creators happen in a variety of ways, from personal acquaintance, to acquaintance through online connections such as listservs and writers' boards, to contact through addresses posted on Web pages. Jane advises teachers and librarians who have an idea for an E-mail project to ask, in the initial contact, what that author can handle in terms of a time commitment. In many cases, time and willingness on the part of the author/illustrator and the teacher are all it takes to get a worthwhile project started.

 A Classroom/Author E-Mail Connection

In spring 1999, Jane was putting the finishing touches on her first early middle-grade novel, *I'm Sorry, Almira Ann*, and was eager to see how young readers would respond to it. Laura Pellerin, second-grade teacher at Longfellow School in Portland, Maine, happened to be studying the westward movement. Voila! Toni made the connection. Jane sent the class a copy of the draft she was working on, along with copies of the artwork to be inserted in the chapters, and Laura got busy reading the book aloud to her class, discussing both content and clarity. Students then wrote letters to Jane, offering feedback and asking questions (see **Letters from Laura Pellerin's Class to Jane Kurtz**, below). Students had an opportunity to feel that they were part of the process. Jane had an opportunity to hear early reader feedback, and everyone learned more about the westward movement!

Letters from Laura Pellerin's Class to Jane Kurtz

"Dear Jane,

How did you think of the goat scene? Why don't you put at least two pictures per chapter? Please make a sequel. Here are some ideas for pictures: Soda Springs, Sarah's Trade, the goat scene, and a picture of the smashing storm. We liked chapters 9 and 10 a lot because they were very humorous. Did Almira Ann and Sarah ever encounter any buffalo?"

—Wagon Wheels

"Dear Jane,

We liked when Grandma was nicer to Sarah. What was the temperature at the Soda Springs body of water? We liked when Sarah gave Almira Ann the lemonade and the new Queen Victoria. We liked when Sarah and Almira Ann made friends. We liked when Sarah's Mama helped Sarah with the new Queen Victoria for Almira Ann. You should have more describing words on the part where Sarah gave Almira Ann the lemonade.

—The Four Covered Wagons

Jane responded by telling the Wagon Wheels that each person has a different job to do in making books, and, alas, deciding how many pictures to include is not part of her job. She also sent them this description taken from an 1846 letter: "The Sody Spring is aquite acuriosity there is a great many of them Just boiling rite up out of the groung take alitle sugar and desolve it in alittle water and then dip up acup full and drink it before it looses it gass it is fristrate I drank ahal of galon of it you will see several Spring Sprouting up out ove the river it is quite asite to see."

When undertaking such a project, there are many considerations. Not only must the time demands of the author/illustrator be kept in mind, but those of the teacher or librarian must be considered too, as the varying experiences of author/librarian Wendie C. Old and author David Lubar reveal. When a reading teacher from a school north of Philadelphia posted a query to the AOL (America Online) Children's Writers' Board looking for local authors interested in participating in a yearlong project involving monthly E-mail with students in her school, both Wendie and David responded. Books of the participating authors would be made available to classes paired with an author, and the authors would be paid for their commitment and time.

David Lubar's experience with this project was very satisfying. "I loved the program. The person in charge, Laura Johnson, started out by sending me a letter from each kid, along with a photo. This made me feel that I was in touch with real people and not just names on a screen. The loose structure allowed me to give them whatever seemed best suited for the moment. For example, when they complained that the ending of one of my stories was too abrupt, I suggested that they show me how the story should end. When I got their endings, many of which used some sort of surprise, I realized I had a great opportunity to discuss foreshadowing. I explained how a surprise shouldn't come out of the blue and gave them some examples how they could weave clues into their endings. In little ways like this, I think I was able to show them some of the craft that lies behind writing a story. I also used them as a critique group, sending them chapters of the first draft of a novel. Their feedback was great. I think it was also important for them to see that books don't spring fully formed from empty space, but come by way of a long process. . . . All of this evolved as we experimented with the best way to use the technology. I'd imagine that each person who tried something like this would develop a different approach."

Wendie's experience, however, was somewhat disappointing, as communications fell by the wayside in a busy classroom. She comments, "All-in-all, I enjoy E-mail conversations with kids and teachers. But teachers have other things they have to do and this is additional work for them to organize as a yearlong project. I can see how this got put onto the back burner." Don't underestimate the amount of time such a project might take!

Author Spotlight: Wendie C. Old

Wendie C. Old, children's librarian with the Harford County Public Library in Maryland, also writes children's books. She believes that "People who read, succeed."

Her nine books include seven biographies and two picture books. (Because she worked with three friends to write it, the picture book, *Busy Toes*, came out under the pen name of C. W. Bowie.) She writes her biographies trying to make "dead guys come to life," attempting to capture the personality of the person.

She lives in an eighteenth-century stone farmhouse north of Baltimore City, Maryland. At home, Wendie is surrounded by two huge hairy dogs, two shedding cats, and a thousand-pound horse.

E-Mail Critiques

Author Bruce Balan also had the experience of connecting with a class who critiqued his work. A mutual friend of Bruce's and librarian Debbie Abilock, from Nueva School, in Hillsborough, California, put them in touch for the project. Bruce sent Abilock a first draft of each of the first two books in his Cyber.Kdz series, *In Search of Scum* and *A Picture's Worth*, which she photocopied for her students. The students E-mailed their comments to the author. Bruce says that some of the student comments were helpful, but most important was the fun and the connection with the kids. Bruce would do it again, depending on his schedule and deadlines, and offers advice to those who might consider such a project. "Let kids know they may not get responses immediately. Tell the kids to limit comments to constructive criticism—not chat. Give the author an 'out' if it isn't working for him [or] her. But make sure he [or] she is committed before starting. Remind everyone that this is fun, and don't let them forget that."

Author Spotlight: Bruce Balan

If Bruce Balan isn't writing at his computer, he can probably be found at sea on his sailboat. Bruce's love of the ocean inspired his most recent book *Buoy, Home at Sea* (published in 10 languages), while his experience in the high-tech field led to the development of his Cyber.kdz series. The author of 12 books for young people, including *Pie in the Sky* and *The Cherry Migration*, Bruce has visited hundreds of schools and is sure that it's "the best part about being an author." He is the technology advisor to the Society of Children's Book Writers and Illustrators and sits on the board of directors of SCBWI and The Read In! Foundation. His Web site, Bruce Balan's Office (http://cyber.kdz.com/balan), was the first site created by a North American author. Bruce lives in the San Francisco Bay area with his wife, Dana, and their dog and cat, Brandie and Bacardi. His favorite saying is "Never tie your shoes when standing in lava." If he could be any animal in the world he'd choose a porpoise. His favorite food is the smelt and lard sandwich (though he refuses to eat them). His favorite words are "snork, lobster, and duck."

American author Dian Curtis Regan, who is living for three years in Puerto La Cruz, Venezuela, has been involved in an exciting project with a special school and its students. A book she is working on is set at the Colorado School for the Deaf and Blind, in Colorado Springs, Colorado. "I grew up one block from the school, so it holds a big part of my childhood memories," Dian says. In researching the book, she visited the school on a trip to the United States, took pictures of the campus, talked to several teachers, the librarian, and a principal, and got to sit in on a class with blind students. Back in Venezuela, she and the students made plans to keep in touch. "Since we all are online, we have made plans to communicate while I am writing the book. . . . I think this is a wonderful two-way street. I will be able to ask the students questions about what it's like living and going to school not being able to see. And they will be able to ask an author questions about how the information they provide works its way into the story. I'm looking forward to the experience. Also, I donated books to the school and they are transcribing them into Braille, which I think is very cool."

E-Mail for Continued Conversation

Finally, storyteller Robin Moore has experimented with the use of E-mail in his CyberResidency: Imagination Restoration Via the Internet. In a successful pilot program at Hartwood Elementary School in Pittsburgh, Pennsylvania, Robin first met the students during a live visit in the fall. He presented a full day of performances and workshops to all students in the school. The following spring, he returned for a full-day follow-up visit and an evening assembly for families. In between, he engaged in an ongoing dialogue with students through the Internet. They E-mailed him the writing they were working on, based on techniques Robin had taught them during his fall visit. Robin responded via E-mail with his comments. He also sent them successive drafts of the book he was working on. Students responded via E-mail with their comments.

This ongoing "conversation" with students allowed Robin to follow up with students in a manner not possible with a single school visit. What's more, he says, he was able to share the progress of his own work over the course of several months. "Students gained a real insight into the rigors of making a book. When the completed book appears on the bookshelves, students will have a very real sense of participation in the book project."

"In addition to learning about story writing and story creating," Robin says, "students gained a very practical, hands-on understanding of how to use the Internet—an innovation which has revolutionized the writing business and will have beneficial effects on every imaginable profession. Internet literacy will expand the horizons of every student, regardless of the field they choose."

Storyteller Spotlight: Robin Moore

Robin Moore's family has lived in the mountains of central Pennsylvania for nearly 200 years. Digging deep into his North American and Celtic roots, Robin has presented more than 5,000 storytelling programs and workshops at schools, museums, conferences, festivals, and on radio and television. He has written 14 books published internationally by HarperCollins, Random House, and Simon & Schuster. His titles include *The Bread Sister of Sinking Creek* and *Maggie Among the Seneca*. His book *Awakening the Hidden Storyteller* is now available as an audiocassette. Although he is best known for his historical fiction novels about life on the frontier, all of his work is focused on celebrating the power of the human imagination. He lives with his family in a stone farmhouse on a small patch of land in Montgomery County, Pennsylvania.

For more information, visit Robin's Web site at http://www.robin-moore.com.

Ongoing E-Mail

Not only has Jackie French Koller received E-mail from kids through her Web sites, she's received letters from teachers, too! With one of these teachers, she engaged in an organized E-mail project. "A second-grade teacher was doing the Dragonling books with her class, and she asked if they could E-mail me as they read and I agreed. She broke the students into groups of five, and the groups took turns coming up with questions about the readings. I would get one group's questions every couple of days. I would respond, and they would share their response with the other students. This worked well because the number of messages was manageable, yet I was still able to personalize them. Every child in the group got to put his or her name on the message, and I would respond to them by name." Although Jackie was not paid for this pioneer project, she says that she is likely to charge for her involvement in future projects, as it was quite time-consuming.

Jane has been equally pleased with the wonderful experiences she has had in connecting with classes of children using E-mail in lieu of a real-space visit, particularly an experience with teacher Monica Edinger's students. Monica says that she and her students "spent a year of interacting with texts and authors, writing letters, thinking hard about history, all sorts of things." Jane had been enchanted and intrigued by Monica's descriptions of the work she did with her students and books on CHILD_LIT, to which they both belonged. "I told her I was eager for kid feedback on *The Storyteller's Beads* and asked if she'd like to read it with her class and let me correspond with them." Monica agreed that this would be a wonderful culmination of her students' year of study. The class read the novel, just after its release, in three segments, and at the end of each wrote to Jane via E-mail with their responses. Jane, in turn, wrote a class letter each time, addressing each child's comments individually. Monica says, "It was an amazingly rich experience, not easily reproducible." However, she says, "similar experiences can occur, and do, in classrooms, if teachers are open and flexible." The project owes its success, Monica says, to two factors First, her students' full year of experiences with texts, authors, and letters, and second, her own personal connection with Jane through CHILD_LIT. "This was a lot of hard work for all—it wasn't a quick superficial 'letter to an author' sort of thing. The online element happened because Jane already knew me from my posts on CHILD_LIT and offered to do this, guessing it might be a good experience." Despite the hard work, the experience was a rewarding and affirming one for author, teacher, and students (see **Letters from Monica Edinger's Class to Jane Kurtz**, below).

Letters from Monica Edinger's Class to Jane Kurtz

"I loved the mysterious writing in your book *The Storyteller's Beads*. It's a great book so far! I like the strange words, so my class and I want to know how to pronounce the following: markato, gahbis, and tukul. Thank you."

"Our class is studying the pilgrims. Even though you are writing a sort of memoir and we are writing a time travel story book, they are similar because they involve composite characters and tell about a true time. I love your dramatic first chapter. I love how it makes you want to read on."

"I think that the book is really good. When you were talking about how thirsty and hot they were I felt thirsty and dusty since there is such good description. Is there a difference between the red terror and the white terror besides the name? Do you know what illness Rahel had? And did you have any experiences with hyenas, since you mention them so often?"

"Hello! I've learned a lot about Ethiopia by reading some of your book. It was not a subject I particularly would have chosen to read about, but now that my teacher has read a little bit of it, I would love to learn more about Africa."

"Did you have to do a lot of research to write this story? How long did it take writing the story up to an editing stage? Besides living in Ethiopia do you have anything in common with Sahay and Rahel?"

"I love your book. It is really touching. I think it helps people understand the awful things that happen to people around the world. You have the coolest vocabulary ever."

"Thank you for the letter. It was nice of you to reply. Emma got her letter read first so she got lucky and got the longest response."

"Dear Jane, It's Keith again. I would like to thank you for responding to my letter. Sometimes if you write to an author or a sports player it takes so long for them to write you back. Sometimes you never get a letter back."

Deborah Hopkinson, who holds a full-time day job in addition to her writing and has some time limitations on travel, has nevertheless had many opportunities to make connections with her readers by exchanging E-mail in lieu of visits with classes of students who are reading her books. Third-grade students from Alta Vista School, Los Gatos, California, under the direction of librarian Laura Manthey, read and discussed Deborah's picture book *Sweet Clara and the Freedom Quilt* with suggestions from the author. Students generated a list of questions for Deborah that Laura E-mailed to her. Deborah responded by E-mail as well. "The students really enjoyed this exchange and came up with some very good questions. Some would have liked to E-mail her on their own, but I think it was more efficient for all of us to send her a compilation in order to avoid duplication. They really liked getting such a quick response—much faster than we would have gotten if we'd sent letters to her editor. I'd love to do it with more authors/illustrators."

Questions from Laura Manthey's Students to Deborah Hopkinson

- "Do you have a husband, children, a daughter named Clara?"
- "Do you look like the people in the book?"
- "Do you have a friend named Jack or an aunt named Rachel?"
- "Is there a real Freedom Quilt?"
- "Do you have a secret place you like to go . . . like Sweet Clara did when she drew in the dirt?"
- "Have you written other books about freedom?"
- "Did you ever have to run away like Sweet Clara?"

It was very unlikely that Deborah would ever travel to Kwigillingok, Alaska, on the frozen tundra where students were studying quilts and quilting. However, teacher Lara Crome-Guthrie E-mailed Deborah after reading her posts on KIDLIT, another online children's literature discussion listserv. She asked the author whether her Yup'ik students, quite isolated from the outside world, might write to her after reading *Sweet Clara and the Freedom Quilt*. Deborah agreed. The correspondence had a wonderful impact on classroom learning. Lara wrote, "The kids talk about your book all the time. I show them pictures of different quilts, or quilts I make, and they say, 'Mrs. Guthrie, it looks like *Sweet Clara and the Freedom Quilt*!' " This communication is a remarkable example of the capacity of E-mail to remove the physical walls of the classroom, the boundaries of geography, and the barriers of culture that separate students and children's story- and bookmakers from each other.

FORMAL E-MAIL PROGRAMS

Some E-mail connections go beyond the individual or the single classroom project. These connections allow authors to interact with student writers in a finely tuned project or allow young writers to gain access to an author who will mentor them as they pursue their own writing.

Authors Mentoring Authors Online: A Writers Workshop

In an ambitious E-mail project designed to make connections between authors and students, Title I math and reading specialist Carla Hurchalla initiated Authors Mentoring Authors Online: A Writers Workshop. The goal of the two-week summer program, held at The Write Place computer lab at Delmar Elementary School, Delmar, Maryland, was for students to gain experience in creative writing through a mentorship with a well-known children's author. Carla hoped that students would learn to write children's books through an authentic opportunity to interact with published authors of children's books. The workshop met for nine consecutive weekdays, three hours per day. Each day began with a 30-minute mini lesson centered around the craft of writing. Carla used the work of each author, in turn, as a model for the lessons. After setting daily goals for themselves and enjoying some free-writing time, the students engaged in formalized writing time for an hour and a half. "Surprisingly," Carla says, "the children wrote and revised nonstop for the entire time! They loved what they were doing."

Mini Lesson: Jane Kurtz

Carla used Jane's book *Trouble* as a model for employing the five senses in writing. She says, "As I read the book, the students jotted down when and how they used their senses to get pictures of what was going on in the story."

 Mini Lesson: Rick Walton

Carla used *Once There Was a Bull . . . (Frog)* by Rick Walton as an example of how an author can create a piece based on wordplays. She says, "It is truly a wonderful model of having fun with words. The apprentice authors had great fun experimenting with words based on Rick's example."

 Mini Lesson: Susan Taylor Brown

Carla used Susan Taylor Brown's *Did Not, Did So* as a great example of using everyday occurrences and memories to create a great story. "Every student has had experiences with siblings similar to the ones presented in the story, so the apprentices could easily see the simplicity in turning their own experiences into stories." Carla adds, "This is also a good example to use when you get the complaint from students [who] don't know what to write about [because] nothing exciting ever happens to them."

Mini Lesson: Karleen Bradford

Carla used excerpts from *There Will Be Wolves* by Karleen Bradford as a model of how historically accurate facts can be interwoven in fiction to create a masterpiece. "The readers can learn about history as they enjoy a wonderfully good piece of fiction," she says. "This was the first time for many of the apprentices to have any experience with historical fiction."

Organization

Students began the program by reading E-mail messages sent by their mentor authors, the author's Web page (if available), and copies of the author's books. The students then established an E-mail relationship with their mentors. With their mentors, students explored possible ideas for their books, discussed ways in which the ideas could be developed, submitted drafts for critique, and received feedback on their ideas and progress. The final edited stories were published, with graphic illustrations using the students' media of choice, both in hard copy and on a Web page. As a culminating activity, parents were invited to celebrate the publication of student books. Carla enjoyed the project and has plans to continue it in future years. "The most satisfaction I gained was from the students who had an attitude change. They all enjoyed writing but many felt that when they wrote something, what they wrote was good enough and did not need revision. When the apprentices saw the time that the authors gave to them and the suggestions that they made, many were awestruck. The mentor authors also offered so much encouragement that the students wanted to revise and follow their suggestions. I really never expected the vast amount of support that the authors gave to their apprentices."

Author Connections

The participating authors enjoyed the project as well. When Carla contacted him, author Rick Walton was eager for a chance to explore electronic opportunities for connection. "Public appearances take a lot of time and energy, so I've been interested in how the Internet and E-mail can be used to make 'public' connections that are less time and energy consuming. I thought this would be a good opportunity to try out something new, to learn something, and maybe to teach something." Rick's experience with his student was rewarding for both of them. He offered his student specific comments on the story he was working on, while trying to put them into a larger context that would allow the student to learn principles that would transfer to his future writing. Rick's student proved to be very good at taking suggestions and seemed to appreciate them. Rick was pleased with the experience and can even imagine ways that it could be expanded for older students. "For young writers, I thought the program lasted about the right amount of time. I can see, however, the possibility of having similar programs with more advanced writers, where the interaction goes for weeks or months."

Author Spotlight: Rick Walton

Rick Walton became a children's writer because, after trying almost every other career in the book, he finally realized that writing for kids was one of the few things that he both enjoyed and was good at. Since that realization, he has had more than 30 books published, with about a dozen more scheduled for publication over the next couple of years. His works include picture books, riddle books, activity books, a collection of poetry, and educational software. His books have been featured on the IRA Children's Choice list, on *Reading Rainbow*, and on *CBS This Morning*.

Rick lives in Provo, Utah, with his wife, Ann, whom he calls "the brains of the household" and who also writes for kids, programs computers, masters Rick's Web site (http://users.itsnet. com/~rickwalton), and does all the home repair that Rick never learned how to do. It was Ann, who grew up in a computer family and who has eight siblings and a father in the computer industry, who dragged Rick kicking and screaming into the computer age. Now Rick doesn't understand how anyone can survive without word-processing programs, E-mail, and their own Web site.

Rick and Ann have four children, all of whom are learning to love reading, writing, and computers.

Author Susan Taylor Brown was equally enthusiastic about her experience with the Authors Mentoring Authors program. "I think the [E-mail] contact was very valuable. . . . I got a letter back from the facilitator of the program who told me that my student was quite surprised that I really wrote back and that I sounded like I really cared. The one-on-one contact with someone already doing a job the student admired, well, it was very important to that particular student." Susan says that she could see improvements in her student's writing each day, but she felt that her gains in self-esteem were even greater. "It was interesting to me to realize that I wrote to her as one writer to another, an experienced writer to a beginner. I didn't think of her as a fifth-grade student. When she asked me how to improve an opening of a story, I told her the same thing that I would tell a beginning adult writer. I think she responded well to being treated that way. . . . "

Author Spotlight: Susan Taylor Brown

"I have always loved to write, but if a gypsy had ever predicted that I would grow up to be a professional writer, I would have laughed. Writers were special, and I didn't feel special. I was a lonely kid who talked to herself about places that didn't exist and people that no one else could see. I also knew the main reason I couldn't be a writer wasn't that I couldn't tell stories, but because my handwriting was sloppy; no one would ever want my autograph! My mom used to make me practice my penmanship during summer vacation.

"I'm an only child, and while growing up in Concord, California, I lived in a neighborhood without any other kids. My imagination became my best friend. Well, except for bedtime when I imagined lots of scary things. That's when I started rewriting my favorite television shows, and of course, I made myself the star.

"I'm not afraid to go to sleep at night anymore, and I'm lucky enough to have my favorite job in the world, writing children's books. (I'm still working on the handwriting part.) I've sold seven children's books so far, including *The Very Patient Pony* and *A Pony Named Midnight*. Alas, there are no horses living with me in San Jose, California. To learn more about me, visit my Web site at http://www.flash.net/~susan23."

Author Karleen Bradford, another of the project's mentors, notes that the student she worked with was pleased and enthusiastic about the program. "I would be very happy to participate again," she says. "I think the chance for students to work with published authors who are encouraging and 'human' is invaluable." Susan Taylor Brown says she felt the same kind of thrill participating in this project that she feels in writing for children—that of making a difference in a child's life. "To let a child know his [or] her words have value, whether written or spoken; to believe in a child and thereby help a child believe in him [or] herself and his [or] her own unique abilities; to be privy to the growth of a child writer as he [or] she experiences the joy of playing with words . . . these are just some of the reasons I'd do it again."

Author Spotlight: Karleen Bradford

Karleen Bradford is an award-winning Canadian author of 15 books for children and young adults. She grew up in Argentina, returning to Canada to take a B.A. in English at the University of Toronto. There she met a young geography student who somehow morphed into a foreign service officer with the Canadian Government. As a result, she has spent the last 34 years traveling from country to country. Many of the places she and her husband lived in have become settings for her books. Her husband is now retired, however, and they have returned to their roots on the shores of Georgian Bay in Owen Sound, Ontario. There they share their lives with an inherited feisty old tabby cat and a boisterous young German shepherd. Three adult children and one grandchild live comfortably near. She has written several historical novels, the most recent being a trilogy about the

Crusades. Like Tolkien in his "Essay on Fairies," however, she "desired dragons with a profound desire," and her latest book is a fantasy called *Dragonfire*. There are two sequels to come. To learn more about Karleen Bradford, visit her Web page at http://www.makersgallery.com/bradford.

Once Upon a Computer

Canadian author Margriet Ruurs has also created an online mentoring program for young writers. Through Once Upon a Computer, Margriet mentors children one-on-one without the prohibitions of jetting off to schools around the continent. Once Upon a Computer, Margriet says, "was born out of the wish to be able to encourage individual children to write stories and/or poetry. After doing school visits, and talking to 600 kids in a gym, I always felt that I would have liked to be able to talk to kids on a personal basis, especially those kids who want to write and think they can't." So five years ago, Margriet launched Once Upon a Computer.

Using E-mail, Margriet offers an eight-week writing program to students in grades four and up on all aspects of creative writing, from generating ideas, to plotting fiction, writing poetry, and the editing process. She sends her students many lists of children's books to read as well, offering them a personal reader's advisory service. After the first few lessons, Margriet's students begin to work on their own story or poem. Like Carla's students, the kids E-mail their rough drafts to Margriet, who offers revision suggestions.

Teachers learn about Once Upon a Computer through the workshop information that Margriet sends to schools. But even more often, she finds that teachers tell each other about the program. Generally, students are enrolled on an individual basis, usually by a teacher or a school librarian, with the school funding the program, often from gifted or special education monies. Because Margriet can work with up to 20 students at a time, she often has from four to 12 students enrolled simultaneously from a single school. In addition, parents sometimes inquire and enroll their children, especially home-schooling parents.

Margriet sees many advantages to instructing via E-mail. It has allowed her to work with students in places where she couldn't visit them, such as Australia. "It also allows a kind of privacy that lets the student write in much more trusting ways than if they worked with me face-to-face," she says. "I have even worked with a student who turned out to be very physically disabled. I had no idea of this until her teacher wrote to tell me. I'm sure that I might have treated her in a different manner, had I seen her, but because of the computer, I treated her as a competent writer, which she was. Her teacher told me that she had never seen this child so committed, so eager to come to school and write! That was reward enough for me." Finally, she says, writing by E-mail is advantageous because it allows her to be at home, accessing her students' writing when it suits her. "At the same time, it allows the student to work during school or after school or even at home. It's very convenient. They can print off lessons and keep a binder of their writing, or they can just keep everything in a computer file."

Indeed, parents, teachers, and students have been enthusiastic about Once Upon a Computer. The program is gaining in popularity as an enrichment program in many schools, and Margriet is enthusiastic, too. "I have loved to be able to encourage kids to write. To show them the joy of writing, of playing with language and creating your very own stories or poems. I have seen kids gain confidence in their own writing skills and thrive! While they write, I encourage them to read more. I send them lists of books and tell them about my own favorite books. I have often put two kids in touch with each other if they shared similar interests. When children know that there is someone out there who cares and who likes their writing, they love it."

Teachers interested in learning more about Once Upon a Computer may contact Margriet Ruurs at ruurs@junction.net.

Author Spotlight: Margriet Ruurs

Margriet Ruurs has been writing children's and educational materials for a long time. "I love to use my imagination and dream up stories!" she says. Margriet likes to work in schools telling children about being a writer and sharing her love of playing with language. She has seven books published, including picture books *Emma's Eggs*, *Emma and the Coyote*, and *A Mountain Alphabet*, as well as a classroom resource book entitled *On the Write Track*, designed to introduce intermediate students to the writing process.

Having been born and raised in The Netherlands, Margriet is bilingual. She writes and translates into Dutch and English and especially likes to write poetry. She has a master's degree in education. Margriet and her family have lived in many places, including California, Oregon, Alberta, the Yukon, and British Columbia. They like hiking, camping, and traveling. Once they traveled for a whole year!

Margriet now lives in British Columbia's Okanagan Valley. She conducts readings, writing workshops, and teachers' in-service workshops in schools around North America and via E-mail. What she likes to do most is get children excited about reading good books and writing their own stories!

E-MAIL INTERVIEWS

Finally, using E-mail for a slightly different purpose, are those who are conducting interviews with their favorite bookpeople via E-mail. Haemi Balgassi has been interviewed by several students who contacted and interviewed her by E-mail in order to complete school book reports or author interview assignments. While Haemi has enjoyed the interviews for the most part, during one week she received three such requests from students in three different locales and had to forward her answers to the first student's questions to the next two, for lack of time. Bookpeople are generous with their online time for the most part, but we'd like to remind teachers and librarians of the necessity of respecting their time. You'll see from the set of interview questions addressed to Deborah Morris (see **Online Interview Questions**, below and the thoughtful responses to interview questions given by Haemi Balgassi and **Online Interview with Haemi Balgassi**, pp. 119–120), that an interview is a time-consuming project.

Online Interview Questions

Dear Deborah Morris :
Hello . . . I am doing a project for 9th grade English. We are supposed to do a report and a speech on a career we would like to pursue. I have chosen to be a writer. I love to write, and would like to get some background on how to continue leading myself to this goal. So I have a couple questions I would like to ask you, if you have the time in your busy schedule to help me out. Just answer the questions below and please send them back before mid January. Thanks a lot and I really appreciate it!

1. How did you get interested in your line of work?

2. How did you prepare for this career? (college, special courses, vocational school, etc.)

3. What special interests or skills do you need for your job?

4. What school subjects were most useful to you?

5. What are your job responsibilities?

6. What do you like most about your job?

7. What do you like least about your job?

8. Do you see yourself in this field 10 or 20 years from now? If yes, in what capacity? If no, why not?

9. What is a typical beginning salary for a person in your occupation?

10. What is a typical salary for a person with 5 to 10 years of experience in your occupation?

11. How many hours must you work in the average week?

12. Does your job allow enough time for leisure activities or to be with your family?

13. What are some different jobs you have had? Were they helpful in directing you to your present position or in helping you for your position? If so, how?

14. Would you recommend any part-time or summer jobs as preparation for your occupation?

15. Do you have any regrets about your preparation for your job, or are there any subjects in school that you wish you had taken to prepare you for your job?

16. Do you have any other advice for someone interested in entering your field?

17. What are some of the businesses or careers that a person in your occupation might be employed in?

18. How do you get the ideas for what you write?

19. How did you get your book(s) published? What steps did you have to take?

20. Were you rejected many times before your book(s) actually got accepted? How long did it take to actually get your book(s) published?

21. What books have you had published?

Thank you for helping me with my project!

—E-mail interview questions addressed to author Deborah Morris

Online Interview with Haemi Balgassi

Q: At about what age did you begin writing?

A: *I fell in love with creative writing in the fourth grade, after I won a creative writing contest, and since then I've found that I express myself most effectively through the written word. In speaking, I feel clumsy in comparison.*

Q: If I were ever to become an author, about how much money could I expect to make?

A: *It depends. Most writers I know supplement their writing income with another source (e.g., I also speak at schools about my books). As in many professions, there is a tiny segment that makes a huge income. . . . This is the exception, however. To answer your question more directly, your writing income would really depend on how well your books sell, or how many magazine stories/articles you sell per year. For my books, I received an advance amount against future royalties of 5 to 10 percent (depending on whether I have to split with an illustrator).*

Q: What is your favorite thing about writing?

A: *The euphoric satisfaction I feel when I've successfully finished a story!*

Q: About how long, from the time you begin, does it take you to complete a book?

A: *Depends on the book.* Peacebound Trains, *my illustrated chapter book, took longer than* Tae's Sonata, *my middle-grade novel, the text of which is 10 times the length of* Peacebound Trains. *For me, the actual writing of the book (including all revision stages) can take anywhere from a few months to a year or more.*

Q: Why did you choose to become an author?

A: *I can't imagine being happier doing anything else (professionally speaking).*

Q: What was your biggest step towards becoming an author?

A: *The birth of my older daughter, Adria, inspired me greatly. In discovering children's books with her, I was drawn to writing children's books myself.*

Q: Are there any bad points about the profession? If so, what are they?

A: *I've learned to be a more patient person because of this business. The waiting can be agonizing. Editors can take months (sometimes years) to let the writer know that they want to buy the work (sometimes they take that long to say no!). Once the book is published, it can be a struggle to get it into bookstores. With so much competition (I read somewhere that there are some 50,000 books published a year—not all children's books, of course), it can be a challenge to make YOUR book stand out. Even if a book is given a shot at a bookstore, its shelf life is often limited. Many booksellers feel it makes better business sense to give shelf space to established books that sell quickly (or new titles by best-selling authors who've already proven their track record). Many writers I know lament the fact that new books by new or lesser known authors just aren't given enough of a chance to gain an audience anymore.*

Q: As a child, were there any authors that influenced you? Please explain.

A: *Writers who impressed me the most include F. Scott Fitzgerald, William Faulkner, John Steinbeck, Dr. Seuss, and Judy Blume. I greatly admire Dr. Seuss's genius for creative brevity. As an adolescent, I enjoyed Judy Blume's books because her writing voice rings so true. She remains one of my favorites.*

Q: Do you have a certain standard, set by yourself or by your publisher, that you have to meet when writing a book?

A: *My personal philosophy is this: I don't compete with other writers and books. I compete with myself and my previous written works. With everything I write, I work to become better at my craft.*

Q: As a child, did you enjoy reading? What kind of books did you read?

A: *Oh, yes—books were my best friends! I enjoyed everything from Nancy Drew to Faulkner's great novels. A few titles that stand out are Fitzgerald's* The Great Gatsby, *Louisa May Alcott's* Little Women, *Robin McKinley's* Beauty, *and just about every Judy Blume title. The only books that didn't appeal to me were Westerns and science fiction.*

Q: I thank you very kindly for your time in completing this interview. I am sure that it will help me to better understand your profession.

A: *You're very welcome. All best with your report, Haemi.*

⌨ REFERENCES

Balan, Bruce. *Buoy, Home at Sea*. With illustrations by Raul Colon. New York: Delacorte, 1988.

——. *The Cherry Migration*. With illustrations by Dan Lane. San Diego: Green Tiger, 1988.

——. *In Search of Scum*; *A Picture's Worth*; *The Great NASA Flu*; *Blackout in the Amazon*; *In Pursuit of Picasso*; *When the Chips Are Down*. Cyber.kdz Series. New York: Camelot, 1997–1998.

——. *Pie in the Sky*. With illustrations by Clare Skilbeck. New York: Viking, 1993.

Balgassi, Haemi. *Peacebound Trains*. With illustrations by Chris Soentpiet. New York: Clarion, 1996.

——. *Tae's Sonata*. New York: Clarion, 1997.

Bowie, C. W. *Busy Toes*. With illustrations by Fred Willingham. Dallas: Whispering Coyote, 1998.

Bradford, Karleen. *Dragonfire*. Toronto: HarperCollins Canada Ltd., 1998.

——. *There Will Be Wolves*. New York: Lodestar, 1996.

Brown, Susan Taylor. *Did Not, Did So*. With illustrations by Liz McIntosh. Bothell, WA: The Wright Group, 1996.

——. *A Pony Named Midnight*. With illustrations by Linda Sniffen. Boise, ID: Writer's Press, 1998.

——. *The Very Patient Pony*. With illustrations by Linda Sniffen. Boise, ID: Writer's Press, 1998.

Crider, Bill. *A Vampire Named Fred*. Lufkin, TX: Ellen C. Temple Publishing, 1990.

Gardella, Tricia. *Just Like My Dad*. With illustrations by Margot Apple. New York: HarperCollins, 1993.

Hopkinson, Deborah. *Sweet Clara and the Freedom Quilt*. With illustrations by James Ransome. New York: Knopf, 1993.

Koller, Jackie French. *The Dragonling*; *A Dragon in the Family*; *Dragon Quest*; *Dragons of Krad*; *Dragon Trouble*; *Dragons and Kings*. The Dragonling Series. New York: Minstrel, 1995–1997.

——. *Impy for Always*. With illustrations by Carol Newsom. Boston: Little Brown, 1989.

Kurtz, Jane. *I'm Sorry, Almira Ann*. New York: Holt, 1999.

——. *The Storyteller's Beads*. New York: Harcourt, 1998.

——. *Trouble*. With illustrations by Durga Bernhard. New York: Harcourt, 1997.

Martin, Jacqueline Briggs. *Snowflake Bentley*. With illustrations by Mary Azarian. Boston: Houghton Mifflin, 1998.

Moore, Robin. *Awakening the Hidden Storyteller*, audiocassette. Boston: Shambhala, 1991.

——. *The Bread Sister of Sinking Creek*. New York: HarperCollins, 1992.

——. *Maggie Among The Seneca*. New York: HarperCollins, 1990.

Morris, Deborah. *Shark Attack*; *Over the Edge*; *Tornado!*; *Runaway Bus!*; *Lightning Strike*; *Firestorm!*; *Adrift in the Atlantic*; *Runaway Hot Air Balloon!*; *Explosion!*; *Glacier Rescue*. Real Kids, Real Adventures Series. New York: Berkley, 1997–1998.

Morris, Deborah, and Garrett Ward Sheldon. *What Would Jesus Do?* Nashville: Broadman & Holman, 1997.

Regan, Dian Curtis. *The Friendship of Milly and Tug*. With illustrations by Jennifer Danza. New York: Holt, 1999.

——. *Monster of the Month Club*. With illustrations by Laura Cornell. New York: Holt, 1994.

——. *Monsters in Cyberspace*. With illustrations by Melissa Sweet. New York: Holt, 1997.

Ruurs, Margriet. *Emma and the Coyote*. With illustrations by Barbara Spurll. Toronto, Ontario: Stoddart, 1999.

——. *Emma's Eggs*. With illustrations by Barbara Spurll. Toronto, Ontario: Stoddart, 1996.

——. *A Mountain Alphabet*. With illustrations by Andrew Kiss. Toronto, Ontario: Tundra, 1996.

——. *On the Write Track*. Vancouver, British Columbia: Pacific Educational Press, 1993.

Walton, Rick. *Once There Was a Bull . . . (Frog)*. With illustrations by Greg Hally. Salt Lake City, UT: Gibbs Smith, 1995.

Werlin, Nancy. *Are You Alone on Purpose?* Boston: Houghton Mifflin, 1994.

——. *The Killer's Cousin*. New York: Delacorte, 1998.

——. *Locked Inside*. New York: Delacorte. Forthcoming.

Winters, Kay. *Did You See What I Saw? Poems About School*. New York: Viking, 1996.

——. *How Will the Easter Bunny Know?* With illustrations by Martha Weston. New York: Bantam Doubleday Dell, 1999.

——. *The Teeny Tiny Ghost*. With illustrations by Lynn Munsinger. New York: HarperCollins, 1997.

——. *Where Are the Bears?* With illustrations by Brian Lies. New York: Bantam Doubleday Dell, 1998.

——. *Wolf Watch*. With illustrations by Laura Regan. New York: Simon & Schuster, 1997.

Yolen, Jane. *The Devil's Arithmetic*. New York: Viking, 1988.

——. *The Emperor and the Kite*. With illustrations by Ed Young. New York: Philomel, 1988.

——. *Owl Moon*. With illustrations by John Schoenherr. New York: Philomel, 1987.

——. *The Seeing Stick*. With illustrations by Remy Charlip and Demetra Maraslis. New York: Crowell, 1977.

Yolen, Jane, ed. *Favorite Folktales from Around the World*. New York: Pantheon, 1986.

——. "Sister Emily's Lightship." In *Starlight*, edited by Patrick Neilsen Hayden. New York: Tor, 1996.

Yolen, Jane, and Bruce Coville. *Armageddon Summer*. New York: Harcourt, 1998.

Chapter Eight

Real-Time Connections

Nothing beats a live visit from a bookperson! Author Deborah Morris says, "The advantage to personal visits is that I get to read the kids' body language, and they get to touch me, hug me, and feel personally connected." Similarly, author Roland Smith reflects on the benefits of live encounters. "Seeing an author in person lets the kids know that authors are normal people, just like their parents, just like the kids are. At least this is what I try to convey when I'm there. 'If I can do this, you can do this.' Teleconferences, E-mail, snail mail all have their place, but I don't think they leave as much of an impact as live-in-person." Still, there are times and places where real-space visits just aren't possible.

VIRTUAL VISITS

When it is not possible to host a live visit with an author or illustrator, though, it may still be possible to have a real-time electronic visit. More and more authors are open to "virtual visits" using "chat rooms." A chat room is simply an Internet site set up to allow several Internet users to log on from separate sites and "chat" simultaneously. Chatting has become a popular vehicle for communication over the Internet. Chatters sit at their own computers to type their messages and what they type appears on the other chatters' screens. It is even possible, using real-time video cameras, for the visitor and his or her audience to see each other.

Advantages for All

There are advantages in virtual visits, not only for librarians, teaching, and children who would like to meet and discuss the books of an author or illustrator, but for the bookperson too. Roland Smith says, "School visits are very time consuming and take you away from your first passion, which is writing, to say nothing of the travel involved, which takes you away from home. I was on the road for nearly five months last year (1997) doing school visits and conferences." Virtual visits, while they still draw the author/illustrator away from his or her writing or art, do not require leaving home. Yet they do allow for connection with readers in a personal and significant way, and with more of the excitement of a live visit than E-mail can provide.

Deborah Morris, who does many self-styled Virtual Author Visits, finds them advantageous for both schools and herself because they are less expensive (authors and illustrators do charge for such visits, which normally last from 45 minutes to an hour, but the fee is only the cost for a single session, normally, and of course there are no travel costs), the kids love the technology involved, and no travel is required. "The biggest advantage to Virtual Visits is that I don't have to travel. I travel a *lot* and it gets wearing. With Virtual Visits, depending on whether the schools are really up-to-date and/or daring, they might or might not use the real-time video cam. With a video cam, I have to actually be dressed. If we're just using graphics, I can do a visit in my PJs and bunny slippers. The Internet is a wonderful thing."

Haemi Balgassi is especially enthusiastic about virtual visiting. "It is luxurious to sit at my own desk, still wearing my robe, sipping my morning juice. I enjoy doing live school visits as well; it's enormously satisfying to interact with young readers in person. But, the chat-room visit had several benefits. Every student was prepared with a question, even those who might have been too shy to speak up in a live visit. And, there's no room for a disruptive student in a chat-room visit, at least, none that I could see!" For Haemi, there have been other advantages too. "At the time of one chat room visit, I was unable to travel because of a complicated pregnancy. A live visit wouldn't have been feasible. Virtual visits allow authors to conveniently and inexpensively 'travel' to faraway schools."

Making Contact with the Bookperson

As with real-space visits, authors and illustrators are contacted to schedule visits in a variety of ways. Bookpeople may be contacted through snail mail, E-mail, or even through their publishers. Often, though, for virtual visits, the first contact is electronic. Deborah Morris advertises her Virtual Author Visits on her Web site (see **Virtual Author Visits**, below). However, she still receives many bookings through word-of-mouth, which is where most of her live school bookings come from as well.

 Virtual Author Visits

Schools with tight budgets don't have to miss out on the rewarding experience of bringing an author in to "talk" with the students. If a school is connected to the Internet, Deborah can chat with students and answer their questions electronically for as little as $100! Her Virtual Author Visit uses a variety of technologies, including real-time chat areas, live video broadcasts, and RealAudio. 30–45 min.

Reprinted from "Author Presentations K–12" in Real Kids, Real Adventures by Deborah Morris. http://www.realkids.com/programs.htm. Permission granted by the author.

Virtual Variety: Types of Visits

There can be as much variety in virtual visits as there is in live visits. Jackie French Koller has had wonderful experiences with her real-time chats with individual classes. "Teachers set up the chats in advance, get the books, and prepare the kids. They take turns typing in their questions, and the whole class gets to see the answers via overhead projector." In a different sort of visit, she was the "guest author" at a school technology fair—a fun experience, she says. "A monitor was set up, and my books and photo were on display beside it, and as students and parents came through the fair they would stop and 'chat.' " This type of chat would work equally well for a public library book discussion group.

In yet another twist on virtual author visits, Haemi Balgassi participated in a Young Author's Day conference at Woods Road School, an elementary school in Belle Mead, New Jersey, via a virtual visit. The Woods Road Young Author's Day event coordinator contacted Haemi after visiting her homepage and invited her to be the Internet author for the school's 1997 Young Author's Day. They also hosted another author for the day in a live visit. Haemi visited with fifth graders, their parents, and their teachers via an Internet chat room. The teacher typed their questions at a computer station while the students viewed their questions and the author's responses, as well as her homepage, on a large overhead projection screen. This allowed students to see photographs of Haemi and her family as they chatted with her. They had read Haemi's picture book *Peacebound Trains* and were prepared to ask questions about Haemi's books and her writing life in the 50-minute visit. The school also offered Haemi's books for sale. Purchased books were then forwarded to the author for autographing and return postage was reimbursed.

This virtual Young Author's Day visit was an exhilarating experience for Haemi. "Doing the visit in 'real time' made it exciting, I believe, for the students as well as myself. I was staring at a chat-room screen . . . and I knew that at that same moment, hundreds of miles away, there were real kids staring at the same chat-room screen—kids who had read my book, who were now eager to share their comments and questions. I looked forward to seeing what they'd ask next. The minutes flew by!" Haemi proclaims the visit a complete success. "I enjoyed it immensely! It was very rewarding to be able to 'speak' to the students in live time, and I was pleased and impressed with their comments and questions. It was obvious that they put a lot of thought into this visit."

Caveats

However, because technology carries with it the potential for glitches, there are also possible disadvantages to virtual visits. "Minutes before the visit was scheduled to begin, I had difficulty signing on to my Internet server. I was starting to feel frantic, thinking of the students who were waiting for me to enter the chat room . . . what if I couldn't get online? Thankfully, I made it into the chat room a minute or two before the designated hour. It made me think, though; both parties are really at the mercy of their software, and one has to hope that there won't be a power outage at either end."

To help prevent some potential problems, Haemi offers some advice. "It's a good idea to arrange for a trial meeting (with the teacher who will conduct the visit) in the designated chat room a day or two before the actual visit, especially if the author isn't used to Internet chat rooms. This way, the author can familiarize herself with where (which Internet Relay Chat Channel and room) she has to go. Also, be sure both parties make available to each other appropriate phone numbers for the time of the visit so they'll be informed if either party has run into problems (e.g., loss of power). If I hadn't been able to log on for my Woods Road visit, I would have been stuck with no immediate way to let the school know."

Young Author's Day Virtual Visit

"Thank you Haemi! The fifth graders, as well as all of the parents, teachers, and visitors in the room for your chat want to let you know what a wonderful time they had! It is a really neat experience, kind of weird when it's over . . . kind of like you want it to go on and on. I thought the questions and answers were terrific."

—Thank you note to children's author Haemi Balgassi after her Virtual Visit at the Woods Road School Young Author's Day

REAL-TIME CHATS AT MANAGED SITES

Real-time chats are not always organized and orchestrated by the authors and teachers/librarians involved. Some real-time chats, bigger than a single author and a single class, or even a single school, or library, meeting in a designated chat room, take place at managed sites.

The Random House Children's Author Chat Series

A successful example of chats at a managed site is The Random House Children's Author Chat Series, conceived by Steve O'Keefe, director of Internet publicity services at The Tenagra Corporation, Houston, Texas, hosted at The EduCenter at Talk City (http://www.talkcity.com/educenter).

At the time of the program's inception, Steve was something of a visionary; there was nothing comparable online. The first series of five author chats on two venues was launched in the spring of 1998, at the Talk City EduCenter, geared toward teachers and librarians, and simultaneously at AOL's Parent Soup, geared toward parents and children. Guest authors in the first series were Barbara Park, Mary Pope Osborne, Sally Warner, Jack Prelutsky, and Stan and Jan Berenstain.

Steve, who was enthusiastic about the success of this first endeavor, says, "When companies are market driven, they think about how to sell books with gamey stuff, glitzy Web sites, etc., and neglect things with educational value. . . . Chat tours for authors are something that should be done by publishers and demanded by teachers and librarians rather than PR fluff." He sees The Random House Author Chat Series as a smarter way to spend book promotion dollars. Because production costs are very low, chats cost far less than an author tour, yet allow the author to visit with people all over the country. Furthermore, Steve was quite taken aback by just how much the authors enjoyed the experience! He sees these chats as a wave of the future. "More publishers will do this," he predicts. "When a book comes out, they will plan a chat tour covering multiple sites and services."

Steve contends that a site-managed chat is often a better option for both authors and teachers/librarians. However, he says, some publishers tried hosting author chats at their own sites and gave it up because "no one showed up and the author couldn't connect. They didn't realize the complexity." As manager of the Random House project, Steve removed all obstacles and simplified the process. First, he located venues with chat-room moderators who would audit all chats. Because the Random House chats would be moderated, a requirement for listing in the Yahooligans Chat Calendar, the Author Series was listed there, attracting a larger audience as a result. In addition, the Random House chats were streamlined for authors. Ghost typists were provided, eliminating the need for the author to log into a chat room or even to be online. Questions were transmitted to the author by phone, eliminating the need for the author to install appropriate software on his or her machine. It also eliminated the worry about computer crashes or problems in logging on. Each of the chats, as a result, was a smooth and lively interchange between author and readership.

Steve added a daytime author chat to the series in fall 1998, allowing school library media specialists, teachers, and students to become participants. Steve, who understands the limitations of technology budgets in many schools, stayed away from state-of-the-art technology in designing the Author Chat Series. "It is important to use the lowest common denominator," he says, "to scale down to the lowest possible entry point, keeping it as plain as possible but still useful." Because of the desire to connect with the school audience, video and audio chatting are still in the future. However, during March 2000, Random will again run a live chat sponsored by Target Stores' Take Charge of Education initiative.

A Girl's World Online Clubhouse

Author Judith Harlan, whose *Girl Talk: Staying Strong, Feeling Good, Sticking Together* is a testament to her concern that preteen girls remain empowered as they enter adolescence, has connected with her readers through A Girl's World Online Clubhouse Web site (http://www.agirlsworld.com). Not only does Judith serve as an advisor on that site, empowerment suggestions from her book appear on Girl Talk Adventures daily, and she hosts chats on the site as well.

At A Girl's World Online Clubhouse, editor and publisher Karen Willson maintains careful control over who may attend the chats, intended for girls age 7 to 17. It is necessary to be a Gold Key Member in order to enter the chat site. After that, all attendees and the host are on an equal footing. Karen encourages participation by adults involved with girls. "Any teacher or librarian can get a Gold Key membership for her class for free by writing me an E-mail at editor@agirlsworld.com In the subject area write: Partners in Education."

Judith says, "Talking with these girls (most of whom are 10 to 12 years old) is a challenge. They don't just sit and listen. If you don't answer them, they put it in capital letters and return, return, return!" Judith enjoys the fact that they get excited about the discussion and that they ask questions. "Some," she says, "are quite touching. It's really a cozy connection. They feel like they know me. They call me Judith." In fact, Judith says, it can be a challenge to stay in charge in a chat room. "You don't have the clout of being the biggest person in the room. You have to keep them interested in the topic."

Judith suggests that the chats at A Girl's World Online Clubhouse might be a wonderful project for a public young adult or children's librarian. If the librarian were to keep track of upcoming chats using the Chat Calendar at the site, and become a Gold Key Member, the chats could be promoted in advance and attended by young library patrons. For some authors who don't take part in live visits, Judith notes, the only way young readers will find contact with them is through such sites.

The whole idea of virtual visits and Web site chats is a wonderful way to connect, Judith says, but "to do the visits along with writing can make it more than a full-time job." Besides, she says, virtual visits and chats do have their limitations. "They are not as personal as going and talking with [the kids] in person. . . . It can be warm but in person is much more powerful." For Judith, the mission is to let people know "that there are lots of things that girls can do themselves to be whole and empowered." Virtual author chats help her to do that, allowing her to share "the strength, the ideas of the girls." When she does, she feels that she has "made an impact on a girl's life."

Author Spotlight: Judith Harlan

When I first sat down at a computer back in 1983, I was still in love with my Selectric typewriter. Boy, was I fickle! I immediately switched my adoration to this newfangled computer contraption. Here was a machine that deleted words, moved whole lines of type, and made it so that never again would I have to re-type a manuscript! When I first got onto the Web, I fell in love again. Here was a whole world of information, data, accessible experts. For a children's nonfiction writer, this was a world of wonder. Through it, I've met people who share my goals of empowering girls and expanding horizons for boys. My children's books show up in several places on the Web, many of them through no direct effort on my part but simply as a result of the seeds I've planted around the world of the Web. I hope that my work will continue to include both print and Web media; both, I believe, are invaluable tools for reaching into the lives of children and sharing ideas with them on a personal, powerful level. For more information about me and my books, visit my Web page at http://www.west.net/~jharlan."

THE READ IN!

Even broader in scope than real-time chats at managed sites is The Read In!, an annual daylong international reading project for children in kindergarten through twelfth grade sponsored by The Read In Foundation, Inc. The program integrates the language arts curriculum with technology to create a full day of collaborative experience and learning throughout the world via the Internet.

The Read In! began in 1994 as the culminating activity for a yearlong electronic connection between the class of teacher Jan Brown, Dutcher Elementary, Turlock, California, and the class of teacher Dolores Willoughby, Grand Avenue Elementary, Chickasha, Oklahoma. Dutcher computer technician Jane Coffey orchestrated that first Read In! between the two classes. The next year she contacted R. L. Stine, who has become a fan of the program and who wrote a nice note of welcome to potential participants that helped the project expand to 5,400 participants. Coffey solicited a volunteer staff and, using library books to guide her, incorporated as a foundation. In 1997, The Read In! involved more than 140,000 participants at more than 1,300 schools. In 1998, the program grew to 303,023 participants in 15 countries: Argentina, Australia, Bolivia, Canada, Colombia, England, Germany, Guatemala, Israel, Japan, Malaysia, Pakistan, South Africa, Turkey, and the United States, plus the Virgin Islands. Jane Coffey, now computer technician at Dennis Earl Elementary, Turlock, California, and current The Read In! and Read In Foundation, Inc., president and program director, hopes it will continue to grow. "Our goal is to reach and include as many kids as possible and to get them to *read*!"

According to The Read In! Foundations guidlines, some of which are listed on their Web site (http://www.readin.org/start.htm), "The Day Of The Read In! is the culmination of several weeks of online participation by teachers and students, during which they share descriptions of their schools and interesting geographical facts, and often establish dialogues between schools that continue throughout the school year." All of this interaction leads up to the event which organizers refer to as the "Day Of."

Objectives for The Read In!

We hope that students are . . .

- Encouraged to read.

- Helped to foster the love of and need for literature through online participation, activities in the classroom, and scheduled "live chats."

- Guided and encouraged to use telecommunications to share suggested reading lists.

- Encouraged to collaborate with their peers on a project.

- Given the opportunity to communicate "live" online, if site resources are available.

- Encouraged and instructed in use of the Internet specifically, and telecommunications in general, in a meaningful curriculum-based project.

Student Outcomes and Goals for The Read In!

At the conclusion of this project, students will have . . .

- Learned to use telecommunications to communicate with peers in live "chats," to experience and participate in a curriculum-based online project, and to use the Internet to research and supplement the curriculum areas under discussion.

- Learned from their peers through cooperative, hands on experiences and real time activities both on- and offline.

- Practiced brainstorming skills in a large group setting when developing suggested reading lists, compiling "Total Minutes Read" lists, evaluating the day in post-event E-mail exchanges, and posting to bulletin boards.

- Experienced and valued others' opinions and expressed their own.

- Learned the need for and the love of reading from their peers, their teachers, and on-and offline celebrities and special guests.

- Helped compile a database of literature, to be distributed to each participating class following The Read In!

- Discussed various forms of literature in both off- and online discussions.

- Enjoyed themselves, relaxed, and had fun reading and observing others enjoying the pleasures of reading!

Activities for The Read In!

Students . . .

• Learn to access and search the Internet for literary sources.

• Participate in live chats on the Day Of The Read In!

• Participate in E-mail exchanges with others.

• Contribute to and compile a database of suggested reading and books read to share with all participants.

Individually, students are encouraged to . . .

• Post information.

• Use Internet searching techniques to locate literary sources online.

• Learn to correspond with peers through E-mail.

• Develop a sense of global awareness and community as part of a worldwide audience.

• Learn that telecommunications enhances the Language Arts curriculum in a unique, personal way.

On the day of The Read In! students, authors, and moderators take part in a global chat via the Internet. Participating schools use their Internet connection and chat software to gather together for a day of celebration of literacy. For those schools without Internet access, it is possible to participate from an alternate community facility, such as a public library, bookstore, or municipal building with Internet access.

The Author Perspective

Karleen Bradford, a participating Read In! author, describes the day. "I was connected through a local school [Keppel-Sarawak Public School, Owen Sound, Sarawak County, Ontario, Canada] that was participating and did workshops and readings during the day as well as going online. It was an incredible event. I arrived to find the halls and library floor filled up with kids on blankets, in sleeping bags, and with pillows and stuffed animals, all reading like crazy. The school had set up a kind of thermometer which kept track of how many reading hours were being racked up during the day. I can't remember the total, but it was impressive. The kids were having a great time, but what really impressed me was the silence—they were really reading! The school had also set up a TV in the library tuned into The Read In!, so kids could watch other kids and authors communicating. They were especially thrilled when I was on. . . . There were guest writers and visitors in their classrooms for the whole day. Big radio and TV coverage for such a small town as Owen Sound, too. Authors participating were from all over North America, Hawaii, England. Lots of very well-known names. There were over 300,000 kids from all over the world. It was really exciting. Until our server bumped me off!"

The English teacher at the school had requested that Karleen do readings and visits with classes during the day as well, so she stayed on for the remainder of the day. "The whole day at the school was fun, and I was impressed by the enthusiasm of the kids and the teachers. It is a small country school and everybody in it took part in the whole project wholeheartedly."

Aside from the local server disconnecting Karleen during her chat, The Read In! at the Keppel-Sarawak Public School proceeded just as organizers would have hoped, with kids sprawled everywhere, reading together, and celebrating reading. Additionally, the day is scheduled to allow classes to meet in designated chat areas to chat with kids at other schools across the globe about the day's events, the books they are reading, and books they'd like to recommend. Furthermore, students are able to speak with an ever-changing list of authors.

Jackie French Koller, another participating Read In! author, is equally enthusiastic about the annual affair. "The Read In! is an amazing event. I've been involved for two years and it gets bigger and more exciting each year. Hundreds of thousands of students participate all over the world . . . there are dozens of authors lined up online all day, changing every half hour. Teachers get the schedule ahead of time so they can get the books and prepare the kids, then they tune in when the authors of their choice are on live."

The Librarian Perspective

In many schools The Read In! is orchestrated by the school librarian. For school library media specialist Margaret Vital at Madison Junior High School in Madison, Maine, The Read In! was just what she needed as the new librarian in her school. "This will be my third year with The Read In! My first year was exciting, and scary. It was my first year as the librarian at Madison Junior High, and I was looking for something that would excite and involve the staff and students with reading. Well, I hit the jackpot! The staff became interested and excited about the project and I was able to involve all grades, five through eight. This included the technology staff, support staff, volunteers, teachers, and students. We had 25 computers online and had virtually no problems throughout the day."

Margaret describes the many preparations and yearlong activities her students have engaged in as Read In! participants. "The Read In! brings a celebration of reading and integrating curriculum throughout our school. . . . [An] eighth grade geography class drew a world map and tracked the sites as they registered for the big day. Math classes charted and totaled books and hours read by students. Students and classrooms kept track of the hours they had read during the year, becoming familiar with the authors who were online for the ["Day Of"] as they waited for the big day. A book report contest was held, and [an] eighth grader's . . . report was submitted to The Read In! where he won a $50 savings bond from Microsoft. Students made posters, book covers, kites, shirts, license plates with symbols, and slogans representing their favorite authors, books, or book characters. Prizes, gift certificates to our school book fair, were awarded at each grade level.

"This year [1998] The Read In! event took place during spring vacation, but we still ran a week of reading activities. The day of the event students and staff dressed as their favorite book characters. Reading teachers offered a grade, equivalent to one test grade, for coming to class in costume as a character from a book, fiction or nonfiction, they had read during the year. . . . We are fortunate to have 25 computers online in the computer room, and reading teachers bring in their classes at scheduled 30-minute intervals. However, it is possible to participate with only one computer. It is what you want the day to be, doing as much or as little as fits your schedule and school. The main objective is the celebration of reading throughout the world, linking students and authors together . . . The Read In! has blossomed the last three years and is more exciting than ever to be a part of." In fact, Margaret is so enthusiastic that she has become The Read In! volunteer coordinator for New England.

The Administrator Perspective

The Read In! participant, board member, and treasurer Bruce Balan is a Read In! enthusiast as well. "The Read In! is a perfect example of the [Internet] at its best. It is the creation of a new project that could *not* exist without 'the Wire.' And it is a project that is win-win-win all around: for authors, teachers, and students. The best part is the sense of excitement and community that surrounds the event. . . . I also love this event because it shows how technology enhances literacy and the written word. Many people are afraid that the [Internet] will destroy books. No way. Now a reader can get connected with books and authors in a way never before possible . . . I love it."

President and program director Jane Coffey looks ahead to the future of the program. "What do we expect? Hard to imagine! I am constantly being asked if I 'expected' the project to be this large . . . and yes, I did . . . I love telecommunications and love working with both the kids and the authors, so the fact that they could use this to communicate was a 'natural' and a simple idea for entire site participation . . . and it is *fun* and exciting!

"The future is limited only by the technology . . . I imagine children around the world enjoying chatting for several days, not just one . . . and at periodic intervals during the school year (in fact, we are in the process of attempting to make that a reality as I type) . . . if one goes by past figures, and we double *each* year, we should expect over a half-million this year!"

References

Balgassi, Haemi. *Peacebound Trains*. With illustrations by Chris Soentpiet. New York: Clarion, 1996.

Harlan, Judith. *Girl Talk: Staying Strong, Feeling Good, Sticking Together*. New York: Walker, 1997.

Chapter Nine

Alternate Connections

SOURCES OF CONTACTS ON THE WEB

Lists on the Web

Many author contacts arise from personal acquaintance or word of mouth. But not every teacher or librarian knows, or even knows of, the many children's authors and illustrators who are available for real-space visits or who have an electronic presence and a willingness to connect with readers in that realm. Luckily, there are many sites on the Internet that will provide you with an opportunity to explore connections with new and well-known authors, illustrators, and storytellers. At the sites listed below, you will be able to browse a list of authors, illustrators, and/or storytellers and, in some cases, read a bit about the bookperson's site. The links on these pages are all hot links, so you can click and go from there!

Click and Go

Authors and Illustrators on the Web

http://www.acs.ucalgary.ca/~dkbrown/authors.html

This is one of the many pages of The Children's Literature Web Guide: Internet Resources Related to Books for Children and Young Adults, managed by David K. Brown, director, Doucette Library of Teaching Resources, University of Calgary, Calgary, Alberta, Canada. Each listing includes a one-sentence description of the site. In cases of classic authors where more than one Web page exists, there are multiple links.

Authors and Illustrators Who Visit Schools

http://www.teleport.com/~authilus/

This page is a location source for professional authors and illustrators who present school programs. An overview of the presenter's work and awards, as well as available programs, fee structure, and contact information, is provided so that schools can contact the bookpeople directly.

The Canadian Teacher-Librarians' Resource Pages: Canadian Authors and Illustrators of Books for Children and Young Adults on the World Wide Web

http://www.nlc-bnc.ca/services/ekidauth.htm

The site, maintained by the National Library of Canada, provides an alphabetical list of personal and organizational Web pages of Canadian children's authors and illustrators. Many authors and illustrators have links to both primary and secondary sites.

133

Canadian Society of Children's Authors, Illustrators and Performers (CANSCAIP); Membership List

http://www.interlog.com/~canscaip/members.html

Maintained by the Canadian Society of Children's Authors, Illustrators and Performers, this page lists all members (active professionals in their fields), provides a one-sentence description of the work of many members, and makes a notation regarding recent work. It also provides regularly updated E-mail and Web page links to those CANSCAIP members who are online.

CBC Online; Author & Illustrator Links

http://www.cbcbooks.org/navigation/teaindex.htm

Sponsored by the Children's Book Council, this page is a part of the CBC guide for teachers and librarians and offers links to the personal Web sites of authors who have at least one published book with CBC member publishers.

Children's Book Authors Who Visit Schools

http://www.snowcrest.net/kidpower/authors2.html

Sponsored by Kid Power, a counseling center specializing in play therapy, this page lists links to the Web sites of children's book authors who visit schools. Also included is an FAQ (Frequently Asked Questions) about school visits.

Fairrosa Cyber Library of Children's Literature; Author/Illustrator Information and Links

http://www.dalton.org/libraries/fairrosa/cl.authors.html

Maintained by librarian Roxanne Hsu Feldman, this extensive list with short descriptors includes author sites beyond personal Web pages, including the brief pages posted by publishers, Web interviews, and listings for several authors whose Web presence is limited to the catalog information for the de Grummond Collection at the McCain Library and Archives, University of Southern Mississippi.

The National Storytelling Directory

http://www.storynet.org/newdir/

At this highly useful, searchable directory page of the National Storytelling Association site, it is possible to search the database by teller's name, address, E-mail, location, and travel region, as well as by the information on a teller's personal Web site. Listings include E-mail addresses and hot links to personal Web pages where available.

Society of Children's Book Writers and Illustrators (SCBWI); Members Page

http://scbwi.org/member.htm

Maintained by the Society of Children's Book Writers and Illustrators, this page links to the personal Web sites of some of SCBWI's full members. Although it is not a comprehensive list of all full (published) members, it is a growing list that includes a one-sentence description of each Web page.

The Storytelling Ring

http://www.tiac.net/users/papajoe/ring.htm

A ring of sites featuring storytelling resources, organizations, events, and tellers themselves. The Member's Index (follow the List Site link) allows you to link to the individual Web sites of tellers.

Vandergrift's Children's Literature Page; Learning about the Author and Illustrator Pages

http://www.scils.rutgers.edu/special/kay/author.html

A highly comprehensive list of more than 500 links to children's and young adult author/illustrator sites, as well as adult authors commonly read by young adults, appears on this regularly updated site maintained by Professor Kay E. Vandergrift, Rutgers University, New Brunswick, New Jersey. Entries include author/illustrator personal Web pages, pages posted by publishers, sites Vandergrift maintains herself, and sites maintained by other site owners.

Yahoo Children's Author Index

http://www.yahoo.com/Arts/Humanities/Literature/Genres/Children_s/Authors/

Yahoo Young Adult Author Index

http://www.yahoo.com/Arts/Humanities/Literature/Genres/Young_Adult/Authors/

Yahoo Illustrators' Index

http://www.yahoo.com/Arts/Humanities/Literature/Genres/Children_s/Illustrators/

The Yahoo search engine lists of children's and young adult authors' and illustrators' personal and institutional Web pages include listings for several authors/illustrators not on other lists.

Publisher Sites

In addition to these online lists, many publishers also maintain a list of their authors/illustrators who are available for appearances. For real-space visits, this is often a preferred way to contact an author you don't know. However, contacting the publisher generally precludes direct contact with the author. The publisher representative will supply you with a list of the company's authors and illustrators from which to choose, and then you will work through the representative to negotiate dates, times, and fees for the visit. For virtual connections with authors and illustrators, the Web itself is your best resource.

AUTHOR/ILLUSTRATOR PERSONAL WEB PAGES

Most of the links in the previous lists will take you to authors' and illustrators' personal Web pages. Authors design their pages with many goals in mind. Some of them simply hope to familiarize the reading public with themselves and their work. These pages will typically include a photograph, a brief biography, and cover art from published books with annotations and sometimes clips from reviews. Even these pages, of course, are helpful to you and your students if you are studying the work of a particular author, or if students are conducting individual author/illustrator studies. If the page includes an E-mail link, you will be able to contact the author electronically and explore possibilities for real-space or virtual connections. In fact, more and more authors and illustrators are including live and electronic "visiting" information right on their Web pages, allowing you to explore options and fees before contacting the author. These basic pages, then, can be useful resources.

However, the richest resources are Web pages that have been written with teachers, librarians, and kids in mind. The authors and illustrators on these pages are eager to provide information not only about themselves and their books but about how their books tie into the curriculum. Such pages may have extensive bibliographies of other useful titles and links to sites that tie in with the content of the author's books. They might even include simple or complex lesson or unit plans, free for the printing! These pages put the author or illustrator's work into a broader context and allow the teacher or librarian to plan instructional units to include the author's work. Combine this opportunity with the possibility of E-mail connections or virtual author visits, and instruction is both deeper and more meaningful.

A Cautionary Note from Anna Grossnickle Hines Regarding "Book Activities"

Note to parents and teachers: Follow-up discussion and activities can be a good way to expand a child's reflection and understanding, but please don't turn them into a chore. THE MOST IMPORTANT THING IS READING SHOULD BE FUN. A friend of mine was trying to help her son choose something to take to school to do when he finished his assigned work. She suggested he take the book he was reading at the time. "No!" he said. "If my teacher finds out I'm reading that she'll make me do a report!"

Reprinted from "Things to Do!" in *Anna Grossnickle Hines Writer and Illustrator of Books for Kids* by Anna Grossnickle Hines (http://www.aghines.com). Permission granted by the author.

Jane Kurtz

http://www.norshore.net/~JaneKurtz

Jane's site goes far beyond the usual biographical information and synopsis and review of her books. Because Jane grew up in Ethiopia, and the country is both inspiration for and subject of many of her books, her site includes a page, with photographs, on her 1997 trip to Ethiopia. In addition, for each of her books, Jane has written a curriculum guide. Each begins with connections to other books, a wonderful resource for both teachers and librarians, especially those who are preparing for a real-space or virtual visit with her, but helpful for any group focusing on her books.

For example, Jane has retold several traditional folktales, *Fire on the Mountain* (Ethiopia), *Pulling the Lion's Tail* (Ethiopia), *Trouble* (Eritrea), and *Miro in the Kingdom of the Sun* (Peru). On her Web pages for these books, she offers many suggestions for other sources of retellings of the same stories. Teachers and librarians are encouraged to share other versions of the stories with students in order to give the stories a broader context. When Jane visited Toni's school, activities that arose out of the many comparisons included writing yet another version of the stories and Double Bubble comparison charts.

Jane also emphasizes the many aspects of cultural and physical geography that underlie or come into play in her books. She offers many suggestions for studying the continent of Africa, the countries of Ethiopia and Eritrea, and the Inca empire. She also provides bibliographic information for many other books and links to Web sites that will enhance these geographical studies, from map activities to the Volcano World Web site, to questions about the role of gold in Inca culture. Jane updates her page regularly to reflect her own new publications as well as new tie-in books others have published and projects classes of kids have undertaken when studying her books or during a visit.

Jackie French Koller

http://www.geocities.com/~jackiekoller

Children's and young adult author Jackie French Koller actually maintains three sites. This address takes you to her general site, with its many pages, including a biographical page and pages on each of the genres she writes, picture books, chapter books, and novels. Her main site also includes links to her two other sites, Zantor's Home Page, named after Zantor the Dragon from Jackie's Dragonling series and designed just for children, and Jackie French Koller's Teacher Resource Center, designed for teachers.

Jackie's Teacher Resource Center is a comprehensive site dedicated to instructional activities to accompany each of Jackie's books, from her picture books through her young adult novels. All of the activity pages are designed to print out and duplicate for students. They are plain black text on white backgrounds, some with large white areas for students to fill in. Suggested activities range from discussion questions and writing activities to historical research projects and a comprehensive curriculum guide for *The Dragonling*. In addition, Jackie has started a page entitled Teacher's Idea Exchange. Here, she invites teachers to share the exciting things they are doing with her books in the classroom. "The design—particularly of the Teacher Resource Center—is to help teachers integrate my books into their curriculums and my hope [is] that it [will] become interactive—a place where teachers [can] communicate not only with me, but with each other to share ideas and build on the basics I provide. I would like to see teachers make more use of the interactive features of the Web sites. I welcome reader reviews from students, and I have an idea exchange for teachers, but so far there has been little response in either of these areas. I also have a trivia section on my Dragonling Web site and I welcome kids to send me their own trivia questions for posting. I've gotten a few of these, but again, nothing like I'd hoped," Jackie says.

Deborah Hopkinson

http://people.whitman.edu/~hopkinda

Children's author Deborah Hopkinson has created a curriculum-rich site that provides an excellent base from which to teach her books. For each of her published picture books, Deborah's focus is on using the book in the classroom Her wonderful historical fiction lends itself to exciting curriculum studies, and Deborah ensures that teachers and librarians will know just the sorts of connections they can make between her books and the content standards they are teaching to.

Deborah writes, "One of the most exciting things about writing *Sweet Clara and the Freedom Quilt* has been to discover that she now has a life of her own in the capable and creative hands of teachers across the country! There have been actual *Sweet Clara* quilt replicas sewn, as well as "story quilts" developed by students. Some teachers have used the quilt to teach about math, measuring, and mapmaking. Others have used the entire school as an underground railroad and spent a day taking their classes on a mock escape. They've learned beautiful and haunting songs, like 'Follow the Drinking Gourd,' and even cooked their own food."

Deborah offers a list of Web sites in a series of categories that connect with her books. For instance, for *Sweet Clara and the Freedom Quilt*, she has lists of Web sites under each of the following categories:

- Slavery and the underground railroad

- Quilts and quilters

- Geography and economics

- Strong female characters

- Patterns and math

- Other: Character Education, Multicultural, History, Music

Each Web site listed in a category includes the title, the Web address, and a one- or two-sentence description of the contents of the page. Many are lesson plans developed by other teachers that use *Sweet Clara* to teach a curriculum concept. Others are bibliographies or sites that provide teachers or librarians with information that can be used in planning their own activity, lesson, or unit.

Deborah has made the same kinds of links available on her *Birdie's Lighthouse* page. She includes a list of Web sites under each of the following categories:

- Lighthouses and lighthouse links
- Journal and letter writing
- Historical fiction in the classroom
- Weather, hurricanes, and storms

In addition, Deborah adds her own bibliographies and suggested activities under some of these categories. Also included in the Weather category is the address for an E-mail discussion list focused on teaching weather and environmental issues in K–12 classrooms. Deborah addresses the topic of using the Internet to locate sites that connect with a unit of study, lighthouses in this case, in her teacher in-service workshops and in her article, "Shining Light on History" in the November 1997 issue of *Book Links*.

Anna Grossnickle Hines

http://www.aghines.com

Children's author and illustrator Anna Grossnickle Hines has created a multifaceted site that will be especially useful to primary-grade teachers. The site includes a special page, Things to Do! designed to offer many activities to accompany her picture books. She includes both Things to Think and Talk About sections, with many discussion questions for each book, and Things to Do sections, which include mapping activities, genealogy activities, nature and science activities, story starters and writing suggestions, and art activities. Because Anna is the illustrator of her own books, she also posts Coloring Pages, line drawings of art taken from her books that can be printed and duplicated.

As are so many authors and illustrators, Anna is eager to hear what teachers are doing to extend children's learning in relation to her books. On her page, she actively solicits information about projects that teachers and librarians have done with kids and posts them on her Web site. "In May [1998] I went to a school in Blairsville, Pennsylvania. For several weeks ahead of time, along with reading my books to the kids, the librarian and reading specialist used my Web page with the children and teachers. Many of them had done some of the activities I suggested and the kids were *super* enthusiastic. It was kind of like they knew me already. A second grade class was dressed in T-shirts they had painted with 'My Wild Garden' [based on Anna's book *Miss Emma's Wild Garden*], and the kindergarten presented me with a book that they had made. I thought these were wonderful activities and asked if I could add them to my Web page." Anna has a link from the Things to Do page to these projects, and photographs of them as well—a teacher-friendly effort.

Cynthia Leitich Smith

http://homepage.interaccess.com/~cynthias/index.htm

Children's author Cynthia Leitich Smith, a newcomer on the children's book scene, created an extraordinary Web site even before the publication of her first book, a picture book titled *Jingle Dancer* to be published by HarperCollins in 2000. Although her publication date was still in the future, she saw no reason to wait to encourage reading and learning via her Web site. Because Cynthia is a mixed-blood member of the Muscogee (Creek) Nation and her husband is Japanese-German American, Cynthia is dedicated to providing readers, teachers, and librarians in particular, a resource guide for Native American, Japanese and Japanese American, and multiracial themed literature.

Cynthia's site includes pages dedicated to Books Featuring Mixed-Race Characters, Kids' and YA Books about Contemporary Native People, Kids' and YA Books about Historical Native Americans, Native American Literature Reading List, and Books with Japanese and Japanese American Characters. She takes a friendly approach to offering insights, bibliographies, and numerous related resources about children's and young adult books, reading, and support organizations and activities. Each page includes annotated bibliographies of what Cynthia considers to be the best books available for children and young adults in each category. Her exceptional annotations include notation of tribal affiliation of the authors and illustrators, synopses of the books, discussions of related themes, and citation of awards.

Particularly extraordinary are the links that Cynthia provides, within each annotation, to interviews, homepages, and biographies of authors and illustrators, as well as to bibliographies on the subjects or themes of the books and to appropriate tribal or cultural sites. She has taken care to ensure that all tribal sites are legitimate, noting that there is much erroneous information on the Web related to Native peoples, in particular. "It's important that teachers not pull down a culturally inconsistent or made-up traditional story, for example, and so unnecessary when there is information available from knowledgeable sources on the Web. What I've done is sift for them." For both the Japanese and Japanese-American page and the Native American pages, Cynthia includes related reading for adults, again with links to book and education sites.

On Cynthia's site, a teacher or librarian can begin with one of the featured topics or individual books and use that entry as a starting point for locating solid related sources. It can serve as the only launching pad, whether you are planning a whole unit or your next day's lesson plan. Whenever possible, the source of the linked site is listed, along with a summary of what of interest that site may hold. For example, some museums offer teacher guides online or online information about obtaining them. Cynthia's site will give you that information. Although some of the books highlighted are tied to certain communities, it's not an exclusively multicultural site. The spirit is broad and inclusive with a primary focus on encouraging reading and learning. Cynthia says, "If you need to know your best on- and off-line sources related to these categories, including related online background information, this is the place to look." She is absolutely right!

Author Spotlight: Cynthia Leitich Smith

"I was born on New Year's Eve 1967 in the middle of one of the worst snowstorms in Kansas City history, less than a year after my Grampa Scott passed on. My mom missed four parties that night. Four. I know all this because I've been told and told. Just like I know about another winter night, way back when Grampa Scott and his brothers and his sisters tried to run off from Indian boarding school. Just like I know about Great Grampa Hilterbran's philosophy on the fish in Oklahoma. Maybe it came from all that storytelling, but even though I grew up (or as close as I plan to get to it) and went off to journalism school and law school, the first thing I set down to do with my whole heart and a serious mind was to write for children. I'm proud to consider myself still a beginner and look forward to the release of my first children's picture book from HarperCollins Junior Books in spring 2000. It's about a contemporary Muscogee- (Creek) Ojibway girl getting her regalia together to jingle dance at a powwow. That reminds me, I love a powwow. It's a great place to hear a story."

MANAGED INTERNET SITES FOR AUTHOR INTERACTION

Scholastic Network

Scholastic Network (http://www.scholasticnetwork.com), a comprehensive commercial educational site that offers free subscriptions to schools as well as to individuals, offers opportunities for teachers, librarians, and students to connect with Scholastic authors and illustrators in two projects, Authors Online and Writing with Writers.

Authors Online

Authors Online is designed on the premise that the best way to get kids in grades kindergarten through 10 excited about reading is to offer them opportunities to interview the authors and illustrators of their favorite books in one of two ways. Most discussions take place on a bulletin board with a single visitor in residence for several weeks. A few authors/illustrators visit in a live chat room for a one-hour chat moderated by a Scholastic editor. All bulletin board and live author chat transcripts are archived after the author/illustrator visit is complete and may be accessed through the Scholastic Network site.

Authors Online can be a full class experience or can be the activity of a small group or an individual. Because the Authors Online Calendar is posted at the beginning of the academic year, teachers and librarians can plan reading around upcoming author/illustrator residencies and appearances. A photograph and background information, including an author/illustrator biography, FAQ, and bibliography, is posted a week in advance of the residency, allowing students to come to their interactions as well prepared as we hope they are prior to a live visit. From this base of knowledge, students are able to create meaningful questions to post on the bulletin board or to ask the author during a live chat. Author Dian Curtis Regan, an author-in-residence in the Scholastic Authors Online program, chose the bulletin board approach. Scholastic put up a display "introducing" Dian to her audience and then invited classes or individual students to post questions to her. She was free to check in at her convenience and answer questions individually or group them together before answering. Dian enjoyed her residency. "As a former schoolteacher, I wish this had been available when I was in the classroom. I definitely would have planned units around the upcoming featured authors. What a great lesson plan—read a book, then go directly to the author to ask questions!"

Writing with Writers

Writing with Writers is the second program Scholastic Network has designed for meaningful interaction between children and authors. Using a bulletin board format, this project allows students in grades three through eight to learn to write in specific genres and to submit their work to be read by children's authors. These authors provide warm-up activities, writing tips, and a sample of their own writing in the genre. In addition, they provide general comments, suggestions, and ideas about student writing as well as responding to some student writing. They do not, however, respond individually to each student's writing submission.

In spring 1998, author and folklorist Jane Yolen offered a workshop in myth writing. During the workshop, designed to be completed in daily lessons of two weeks' duration, or once a week over the full eight-week course of the project, Jane taught participants to write a myth. Learning proceeded from an autobiographical sketch Jane posted for her students, a myth she wrote to be used as a model, a series of writing tips and warm-up activities, and a myth writing assignment or challenge. Students were then able to publish their revised myths online at the Writing with Writers site.

Houghton Mifflin Education Place

In a similar, though less extensive, publisher site, Houghton Mifflin Education Place (http://www.eduplace.com) provides free, nonsubscription resources for teachers of kindergarten through grade eight, librarians, students, and parents. At its Author Spotlight site, which resides at The Reading/Language Arts Center (http://www.eduplace.com/rdg/index.html), you'll find book summaries, book reviews written by kids, author/illustrator articles and biographies, classroom connections, Internet links, and interviews. In addition to publisher book summaries, student book reviews (Kidviews) are solicited and selectively posted at the site, offering kids an opportunity to hone their reviewing skills for publication. Many cross-curricular teaching ideas are offered, and each Author Spotlight also includes a page of Internet links in all curriculum areas related to the author/ illustrator's work. These links are intended to extend the themes and curriculum connections of his or her stories, much as the links do on the personal author/illustrator Web sites above. Finally, during an author/illustrator residency, visitors may post interview questions from the site to the guest. The questions are then compiled, an interview is conducted with the visitor, and the transcript is posted on the site. Although this does not allow for direct interaction with the author, teachers, librarians, and students will find their author studies enhanced by a visit to the site.

Additional Web Sites

In addition to these publisher sites, author/illustrator interviews are popular at other sites as well. Online bookstores often post author interviews, many with hot links to the author/illustrator's Web site, and some with E-mail links. Amazon.com (http://www.amazon.com) has many posted author interviews; however, they are not interactive. Smaller online bookstores have carried the interview idea a step further, offering teachers, librarians, and students the opportunity to ask guests their own questions. Author Kathleen Duey tells of doing online interviews through children's specialty booksellers on the Web. One such store is Just for Kids (http://www.just-for-kids.com) where a month long "Electronic Dialog" with Kathleen took place using a bulletin board approach. Replies to questions were posted on the dialog page, and participants were notified when their questions were answered. Kathleen reports that it is "very simple and if you are used to talking through a keyboard, not inhibiting at all." Just for Kids hopes to offer more author dialogues in the future.

Opportunities to connect with authors and illustrators are growing on the Web. Although such projects as the AOL Author In Residence program and the Internet Public Library Ask the Author site are no longer active, they were early attempts to explore the possibilities that the Internet afforded for connections. As more schools gain Internet access and more teachers and librarians become aware of the opportunities available, successful projects will grow and spawn still others.

INTERACTIVE TELEVISION BROADCASTS

Beyond live visits, E-mail connections, and virtual visits are the somewhat uncharted waters of interactive satellite television (called ITV) for student connection with bookpeople. Some schools are making their own forays into the wilds of ITV interconnectedness. In addition, the Education Department of the Kennedy Center in Washington, D.C., and a commercial company, Planet Think: The Interactive Learning Network (formerly EMG), have also offered ITV visits to classrooms across the country and around the continent. These endeavors have met with success.

Owen Valley Middle School

Myrna Fields, media specialist, devised an exciting virtual visit program for Owen Valley Middle School in Spencer, Indiana, with two other area schools using a fiber optic link. The three schools entered an agreement to share Ben Mikaelsen as their yearlong artist-in-residence. To launch the program, Ben, from Montana State University, held a four-way distance session with eighth graders. At Owen Valley, one group of students was in the distance education room and several other classrooms of kids watched through closed-circuit television.

Myrna explains, "Ben started out with general comments about research because Owen Valley Middle School eighth graders were about to begin research projects of their own. Then he showed slides of some of the places, people, and things that he has researched and showed covers of his books. He allowed the students about 20 minutes for questions and he directed which school's turn it was to ask questions." After this virtual kickoff, the students went on to keep in weekly E-mail contact with Ben as he ventured off on a four-month road trip from his home in Bozeman, Montana, to the southern tip of South America. While Ben was on the road, the students read Ben's books. After Ben's return, each school engaged in a series of book discussions with him.

Speaking after the first interactive session, Myrna reported, "It was fantastic! All of the connections worked and the kids and Ben had a great session. . . . We were really pleased with the way this conference came out. . . . He is a very inspirational speaker and the kids loved him." And they might never have met him, if it weren't for the virtual link of interactive television!

Kennedy Center Performing Arts Series

In a joint enterprise with the Prince William Television Network, Manassas, Virginia, the John F. Kennedy Center for the Performing Arts Education Department (http://artsedge.kennedy-center.org/pwtv) began its program of live and interactive performances and discussions with Kennedy Center artists in a single event in 1993. The program continues seven years later. Programs feature artists and companies who perform at the Kennedy Center and explore the performing arts in the areas of music, dance, theater, and poetry. The events, originating at a high school with a program in broadcasting, are delivered over local cable television stations or via moveable C-Band satellite dish.

The distance learning program is advertised to schools across the country, says senior program director Ginger Rogers. "The live and interactive broadcast format of this televised series allows students to phone in, fax, and E-mail questions to the artists involved in the programs." During the two weeks following each live broadcast, teachers and students can connect to Internet Web sites specifically designed to coordinate with the series. A Study Guide containing dates and times of programs, information and activities for students, and Web site addresses is sent to each teacher who registers for the series. The programs themselves are one-hour live broadcasts to students in grades seven through twelve during which both the live and satellite audiences can question the visiting artist.

Poet and author Naomi Shahib Nye, who, in 1998, was the first guest poet in the series, recalls, "I was concerned about how it would work with live audience *and* satellite audience, but it seemed very natural, very fluent, in part thanks to the expert guiding hand and voice of Jim Haba, poet and poetry conductor, who kept things flowing smoothly, sat beside me, interacted with me, a sort of conversation-at-large."

Naomi comments that she and Jim wished after the "visit" that they had kept the live audience around for an additional half hour, "so that they could continue the dialogue without the extra 'hush' feeling, being on best behavior, for the larger audience . . . but they were terrific, the questions came from both live and satellite audiences, and it was amazing to me, these high-tech days, how everything was such a neat weave—talking about intimate things, poetry, close experience, to the wide horizon as well as those 1,000 audience eyes."

Planet Think

Another highly successful endeavor, Planet Think is a satellite network for interactive learning connecting more than 2 million students and teachers in 4,200 schools across the country. Planet Think produces eight channels of programming, six student channels by grade level and two adult channels for teachers and parents. *Cover to Cover* and *Author's Desk*, two programs produced by executive producer Cindy Beeson, offer the opportunity for students to connect live with authors, illustrators, and others in the publishing world, from a variety of publishing houses. Hundreds of authors and illustrators have been featured over the past five years. The shows, in fact, are two of the most popular programs that Planet Think offers.

Each "visit," Cindy says, is similar to a live-appearance visit with a shortened format. Cindy brings an author or illustrator into the Scottsdale, Arizona, Planet Think studios or to remote studio sites. Much like a radio talk show, schools that have requested to be wired for interactivity are able to ask questions of the guest and are kept online throughout the program. In the case of very popular authors, the opportunity to ask questions is rotated among the participating schools. Other schools will also be watching the program live, without asking questions. Because of the variance in time zones from Maine to Hawaii, each 30-minute program is broadcast two to four times during one day. In addition, all programs are recorded and can be downloaded or aired again upon request.

The Planet Think satellite programs are often enhanced with field-production video shot at the home or studio of the author or illustrator or with still photography shot from the bookperson's books as well as photos or slides they might contribute. For instance, when Cindy produced a show on author/illustrator Gerald McDermott, she included clips of a PBS special on him. When author/illustrator team Joanna Cole and Bruce Deegan were guests, Cindy filmed a clip behind the scenes in their homes. When author Kathleen Duey appeared, Cindy used a photograph of Kathleen's great grandfather, a Union soldier in the Civil War who was a passenger aboard the steamboat *Sultana* when it exploded in 1865, the inspiration for her book *Emma Eileen Grove: Mississippi, 1865.* When Cindy produced a program on cut-paper illustrator Robert Sabuda, she went to even greater lengths, shooting a video package in Quito, Ecuador, where Robert's book, *ABC Disney Pop-Up* was being assembled at the Carvajal manufacturing facility in South America. This video piece demonstrated the hand-assembly process of pop-up books, an industry that has existed in South America for the past 36 years.

One to two months prior to the broadcast of an author or illustrator visit, Planet Think creates print documents, or flyers, for distribution via broadcast fax and their FaxBack document retrieval system to subscribing schools all over the country. Teachers and librarians can order biographical, bibliographic, curriculum, and Web site information to help them prepare for the upcoming "visit." Materials include information prepared and/or supplied by the guest or designed by a Planet Think resource specialist in conjunction with the guest. Cindy also encourages students to ask her questions via the Internet or fax before the visit. She forwards questions to the author/illustrator after the visit as well.

As with real-space visits, it is always important for students to have read the visitor's work. Links to publishers' and distributors' sites assist schools in obtaining the books. Some authors, such as Will Hobbs, who has twice been a participant, stipulate that teachers read his books with their students, preferably aloud, in order to participate in the interactive visit. While Cindy can't guarantee that students will have done the requested reading, Educational Support Services does notify potential participants of the author's request as well as possible limitations by grade level. Beyond that, she hopes that the live interaction will serve as an impetus for the audience to go out and read the books.

Planet Think is a subscription-based, commercial-free educational service. All necessary hardware is provided as part of the subscription to the service. Because Planet Think sends an encoded signal, schools must have a satellite receiver capable of receiving the CODEC signal and televisions. Both are provided. Planet Think provides services to schools in many different financial circumstances. Some of them are Title I schools using government money designated for technology. In normal circumstances, technology funds could not be used to pay for bookperson appearances, but because of the nature of the service, technology funds are appropriately directed to Planet Think, creating an unusual opportunity for schools to tap into author and illustrator visits they might not have had the time or resources to participate in otherwise.

Young adult author Chris Crutcher was an early participant in the Planet Think project. His experience was a good one, he remembers. Because it is best to be accustomed to the format of live-television interview, Chris says, prior experiences in being on camera are helpful. For the audience, though, the barriers were few. "It doesn't take the kids long to warm up. It isn't quite as good as being there live, just because there is some piece of intimacy that you miss with the audience. You can only hear a few at a time, and you don't get to just hang around and talk afterward, but you reach a lot more kids, and once I was comfortable, which was fairly quickly, it was great."

Much like Chris, poet and author Naomi Shahib Nye enjoyed her experience with Planet Think. "Any way we may speak to one another in this world matters very much to a writer," she says. Though Naomi mentions the distance created by broadcasting from a studio, rather than being face-to-face with her audience, it was not prohibitive for her. "There's an odd remove (being in that little studio somewhere) coupled with an intimacy (the students' voices coming in loud and clear) that I find appealing, and touching. It doesn't bother me at all. I guess poets often feel they're talking into the wind or the air anyway, so the whole 'notion' of it does not feel abstract or strange. I like it!"

The only disadvantage that Naomi imagines is that she doesn't have the visual cues of an audience before her. "I don't get to see their beautiful faces as I speak, their gestures, grimaces, interest. . . . I *adored* making a whole classrooms of new friends in Hawaii through the EMG broadcast and was thrilled to meet those teachers later, who were as warm to me as if we had known each other for years. They said, 'Well, you visited us! We feel close to you!' What a gift!"

Author Spotlight: Naomi Shahib Nye

"I live a block from the sleepy little river in downtown San Antonio, Texas, with my photographer husband, Michael Nye, and our 12-year-old son, Madison. My dad was born in Jerusalem, Palestine, and my mom grew up in St. Louis—the two other places I have lived. Libraries have always been my richest oasis. Now our son likes to check out 50 books at once! My most recent books are *Fuel*, a book of poems, *The Space Between Our Footsteps: Poems & Paintings from the Middle East*, *Habibi*, a novel, and *Lullaby Raft*, a picture book. I try to write every day beginning at the sweet hour of four in the morning."

Author Kathleen Duey was also enthusiastic about her experience as a *Cover to Cover* guest author. She says, "in some ways it's easier than live visits; in other ways it's harder." The kids' questions, Kathleen says, were better than the questions she hears from a live audience. She attributes this to the teachers spending more time in advance helping kids write questions, knowing that they will be broadcast across the continent. One child, for instance, asked how Kathleen handles dialect in her regional books. "No one had ever asked me that question before!" As does Naomi, Kathleen mentions a drawback in not having visual cues from the audience. Nevertheless, like Chris, she sees significant advantages in reaching a very wide audience. In addition, sales spiked in the month of her visit. Kathleen attributes this sharp increase in sales to the show. When asked if she would participate in such a program again, Kathleen replied, "In a heartbeat."

Kathleen has several pieces of advice to offer to teachers and librarians who might be participating in an ITV author visit. "All of the preparation that is necessary for a live visit becomes more critical for a virtual visit of any kind. The author will need your help even more because there is no interaction." As with every visit, she says, the outcome will be dependent on the work done in advance. "There is no free lunch in the preparation." It is more critically important, she thinks, for kids to have an idea of who the author is. Kathleen suggests that creating an intimate atmosphere in the classroom will be even more important than with a live visit. She suggests having a theater-like atmosphere by using lights as segues. Choose question askers beforehand, with a few wild cards thrown in for fun, she says, and try a dry run of the questions. Practice getting back and forth to the microphone. Clear off student desks and have additional volunteers in the room to assist students. Finally, she suggests doing all of the celebratory things one does for a live author visit. "Decorate! Make posters! Blow up book covers! Don't neglect all of the things that you do for a live visit."

⌨ REFERENCES

Duey, Kathleen. *Emma Eileen Grove: Mississippi, 1865*. American Diaries Series. New York: Aladdin, 1996.

Hines, Anna Grossnickle. *Miss Emma's Wild Garden*. New York: Greenwillow, 1997.

Hopkinson, Deborah. *Birdie's Lighthouse*. With illustrations by Kimberly Bulcken Root. New York: Atheneum, 1997.

——. "Shining Light on History." *Book Links* 7 (November 1997): 35–40.

——. *Sweet Clara and the Freedom Quilt*. With illustrations by James Ransome. New York: Knopf, 1993.

Koller, Jackie French. *The Dragonling*; *A Dragon in the Family*; *Dragon Quest*; *Dragons of Krad*; *Dragon Trouble*; *Dragons and Kings*. The Dragonling Series. New York: Minstrel, 1995–1997.

Kurtz, Jane. *Fire on the Mountain*. With illustrations by E. B. Lewis. New York: Simon & Schuster, 1994.

——. *Miro in the Kingdom of the Sun*. With illustrations by David Frampton. Boston: Houghton Mifflin, 1996.

——. *Pulling the Lion's Tail*. With illustrations by Floyd Cooper. New York: Simon & Schuster, 1995.

——. *Trouble*. With illustrations by Durga Bernhard. New York: Harcourt, 1997.

Nye, Naomi Shahib. *Fuel*. Rochester, NY: BOA Editions Ltd., 1998.

——. *Habibi*. New York: Simon & Schuster, 1997.

——. *Lullaby Raft*. With illustrations by Vivienne Flesher. New York: Simon & Schuster, 1997.

——. *The Space Between Our Footsteps: Poems & Paintings from the Middle East*. New York: Simon & Schuster, 1998.

Sabuda, Robert. *ABC Disney Pop-Up*. New York: Disney Press, 1998.

Smith, Cynthia Leitich. *Jingle Dancer*. With illustrations by Cornelius Van Wright and Ying-Hwa Hu. New York: HarperCollins. Forthcoming.

Chapter Ten

A Potpourri of Resources and Props

We hope that by now you are thoroughly excited about the prospects of connecting well with authors, illustrators, and storytellers. This final chapter contains a potpourri of approaches and actual materials that can be used to help kids make a deep and lasting connection with books. Many bookpeople have props. Some of the props travel with the bookperson and can enhance a visit. Other props can be used to help readers connect with books, even if the bookperson is nowhere in sight. This last chapter deals with a variety of things that teachers and librarians have used—with or without the presence of the bookperson—to help make those all-important connections.

USE THE BOOKPERSON'S BOOKS WELL

Benefits of an Autographing Session

The most obvious and most valuable connection of all, when it comes to bookperson visits, is the book connection. We hope by now it's completely clear that if the bookperson has written a book or books, those should be treated as a valuable resource. Be creative! Some schools buy copies of an author's books to give away as prizes during the week of the visit or during the entire school year. In addition, many schools sponsor an autograph time. Don't forget that signings can even be part of cybervisits.

This type of book sale can be an important source of funding for future visits. Schools can generally get around a 40 percent discount by ordering the books from the publisher or a book distributor. Even passing on some of the discount to students (which many schools do), a school can raise several hundred dollars to go into the pot for next time. Libraries have also raised money this way. Author Lee Wardlaw spoke at a Friends of the Library dinner, for example, and donated 20 percent of the profit from book sales to the library. Some libraries make money from selling tickets to dinners with bookpeople and others from handling their own book sales at dinners or other events.

Book sales are also important to most bookpeople because connecting children with books is a major reason why they put up with the inconvenience of traveling away from home, taking time from their families and their writing. In fact, some bookpeople won't consider a school visit that doesn't have an autographing time attached because it lessens the impact of the visit.

Author Kathi Appelt speaks for many authors when she says, "I know, for myself, that an autographed book means a great deal to me. It's my way of knowing that a real live person wrote that book and the autograph makes me feel that it was written 'for me.' It makes the book important. And that's what I want for all kids—to know that books are important. To give them a place in their lives for books. One thing that concerns me is when I visit 'lower economic' schools and the librarian has made the decision not to sell my books. I understand the reasoning: The kids are so poor that offering a book for purchase would embarrass them; only the more well-to-do kids would be able to purchase a book, thus making the less well-to-do feel bad; if they purchase one of my books, they might miss a meal. These are very real concerns and I do understand them. But I'm not sure that it's the school's place to make that choice for that child.

"Many of these same schools hold an annual book fair. I wonder if the school would decide not to have a book fair based on the same reasons? It makes no sense to me. At least a couple of my books are in paperback and not that expensive, especially when a discount is usually built in. Sometimes, I'm afraid if I say anything, it will make me sound 'whiny,' as if all I care about is how many books I sell.

"But I've visited the poorest of poor schools in the lower Rio Grande Valley of Texas where 99 percent of the kids were on reduced breakfast and free lunch programs. Trust me, it doesn't get lower economically. I was there as part of a federal grant program that the schools had received. They sold lots of my books, and I could tell that the kids loved having them. I still love going to schools regardless of whether my books are sold or not, but I think this is something that we should all consider. Is it our place to decide whether a child should have an opportunity to own a signed book? My goal, when I visit schools is to let them know that *anyone* can become a writer if they work at it hard enough. Shouldn't *anyone* also be allowed to own a book?"

Author Spotlight: Kathi Appelt

Kathi Appelt grew up on the banks of the Chocolate Bayou in Houston, Texas. She began her writing career at the age of two when her mother handed her a fistful of crayons and told her she could draw on the inside walls of the garage. No longer an "up against the wall" writer, she now does most of her work on a desktop computer (although crayons and walls in the same room do stir up old yearnings). Her books for children include *Bat Jamboree*, illustrated by Melissa Sweet, which was named a Best Book for Children by *Child Magazine* in 1997, and *Just People and Other Poems for Young Readers*, photographed by Ken Appelt, which was named a Best Book for Young Adults by the American Library Association and a Book for the Teen Age by the New York Public Library. She and her husband Ken have two teenage sons, Jacob and Cooper, who both play the upright bass. They all live in College Station, Texas, with two goldfish, a gerbil, and two Manx cats.

How to Set up an Autographing Session

The autograph time can be held during school hours or can be structured as an evening time, drawing in parents. Author Lee Wardlaw describes a great visit that ended with two hours of book sales and autographing. "The school provided boxed dinner meals (hot dogs, chips, fruit, etc.) that the parents and kids could buy while they were enjoying the festivities." Jane points out that a school can even use combinations of times. When she spoke at Lyseth School in Portland, Maine, for instance, library media specialist Jo Coyne sponsored an eight to nine-thirty A.M. signing plus an evening signing. "In the morning," she says, "some parents zipped in on their way to work. Some parents sent money with their children, so that the children could go ahead and get the book and have it signed. In the evening, I told stories to families and then got a chance to talk with parents and kids as I signed their books. It was a wonderfully warm way to end a great author visit—seeing all those books of mine go out the door tucked under new readers' arms."

Toni tries to attach the author signings to some "event." Sometimes, it's possible for the author to *become* the event, as in the storytelling evening above. But generally, she says, "It's wise to schedule author signings in conjunction with some other schoolwide event—the book fair (which we have had great success with), an open house, or a curriculum night. This kind of event requires lots of advance planning, of course, but the rewards are worth the extra trouble."

Toni offers a few other hints that have helped her organize successful evening signings. "We set up the book sales in a very public place, the hallway all families must enter in order to get to the book fair. But whenever possible, we provide a rather secluded spot for the author to sign, a little room off of that hallway. It provides a chance for the author and her fans to speak one-on-one and lends a tone of specialness to the encounter. We use tablecloths and interesting fabric to create a celebratory atmosphere at the sales table and the signing table. And we always assign one person to be available to the visitor throughout the signing. This person keeps traffic moving, runs for snacks and drinks, opens books to the title page, and assists the visitor in any other way she needs assistance."

While having a family time for signing offers a little extra dimension to the bookperson visit, it's not the main ingredient for a successful signing. Many schools do not tackle parent involvement, but sell the books for several weeks before the bookperson visit and (crucial!) the day of the visit. Inevitably, excitement will peak on that day. Most authors are even willing to sign a few bookplates for those students who don't get organized until the day *after* the visit. The important thing is the chance for author and readers to connect over the books.

Author Mary Casanova says, "I value the time to sign books and speak with kids individually, asking something about them, shaking their hands, signing personalized messages. But this takes time. So I've come to think that the ideal schedule is three hours of presentation with plenty of time for book signing. Both speaking and signing are demanding, but it's the latter, I believe, that will make the biggest impact on a student. And, along those lines, whenever teachers can get books at a discount and pass along the discounted price to students, it means more kids can walk home with a signed book. To me, this is part of the magic and memory of a successful author visit."

Kathi says, "The signings I love most are when I get to meet with the kids. I know this isn't always possible, but it's much more fun for me to have the student hand me his or her book and have me sign it while they're there. That way I get a small visit and it makes me feel like my book is going to a real person. I enjoy the chitchat too, the one-on-one that is not always possible in a gathering of hundreds."

Finally, illustrating in vivid detail the magic and memory that can be part of a book signing, teacher Clark Underbakke offers the example of Deborah Norse Lattimore, "who painstakingly signed *hundreds* of books, some with Celtic messages, some with hieroglyphics, some with incredible dragons; whatever the book pertained to, she created an original of it on the title page of the book . . . even used several different colors of pen!" He also remembers a visit from Wil Clay, "who went through *boxes* of Sharpie markers as he drew portraits/caricatures of the children in their books. A true act of love."

PROPS FOR PRESENTATIONS

Many bookpeople bring things other than books along with them—sometimes many, many things. Author/illustrator Cathryn Falwell says, "I haul a tremendous amount of 'stuff' with me. I recruit kids to help truck it down school corridors, and it works out fine. Minivans are the godsend of children's book presenters!" For instance, she says, "*Dragon Tooth* has a child that creates a dragon from recycled materials. I have lots of junk I bring along to show kids how they can do that, too. I have little Velcro dots on all the stuff I bring, so I can zap it together quickly without waiting for tape and glue. Teachers have reported lots of projects that have sprung from these ideas." (Cathryn adds that a cynical neighbor comments on these "art-from-junk" projects: "This isn't recycling—it's delaying!")

Her book *Letter Jesters*, she adds, is "a kid's guide to letter forms—a kind of consciousness-raising about typefaces. So I have lots of hands-on things to show the kids about type styles, logos, letters, and other things. I can work in about 20 volunteers for this part. They seem to really enjoy the exercises!" In addition to the things she brings, she suggests "that kids look through magazines and newspapers and cut out different styles of letters. I also have photocopied sheets of a variety of styles and sizes of letterforms for them. Kids have created wonderful things with letters—using them as shapes, exploring their characteristics and uses. Since nearly all children have access to computers these days, and choose 'fonts' to create documents, it's great to give them a little knowledge about the styles they are choosing! I often segue into *Word Wizard*, which is about creating anagrams. If you have a chance to talk with the author a bit beforehand, ask what kinds of things he or she will be bringing along and what setup works best.

Bookpeople have used slides in their presentations for years. "I know I'm not a terrific public speaker," one author says, "but by giving the kids something to look at, I'm now comfortable even in big assemblies, and I get great comments about my school visits now." Slides can illustrate the process of making a book, an illustrator's techniques, the writer or illustrator's workplace or family, events that inspired a story, even how something looks in real life and then becomes a cartoon version of itself.

Other authors swear by color transparencies to achieve a similar effect. Those who prefer overhead transparencies point out that relatively few schools have slide projectors, but almost every school has overhead projectors. "Overheads are more forgiving when the light isn't great," one author points out. Another notes that using overheads gives her greater flexibility; she can make the program longer or shorter depending on the age of the students and the allotted time. Jane uses transparencies to show pictures of herself as a child in Ethiopia and illustrates the way her stories grew out of her real life. "I recently visited three schools in Wisconsin where no author before me had used color transparencies," she says. "The library media specialists made me feel like a technological genius. What a thrill! Alas, I had to admit that all you do is take a picture to a place like Kinkos Copies and pay a dollar or two, and they do the rest."

Whether slides or transparencies are used, it's important for the host school or library to prepare well ahead of time. Some rooms simply cannot be darkened enough even for transparencies. Bulbs blow out. Dark smudges on screens can be disconcerting. Strange angles distort pictures. Plan ahead!

Slides in the Public Library

Slide presentations can work well at a public library, too. Deborah Hopkinson shows slides of her picture books that illuminate the illustration and research process. For instance, she includes slides of Maria Mitchell's birthplace and of the slave cabins where James Ransome based his art for *Sweet Clara*. She also has a simple audience participation story on slides which works well with larger groups of children. Through questions and answers, she both tells stories through the slides and shows children things to look for to help improve "visual literacy," such as an artist's use of color and style.

She showed her slides in the Springfield, Oregon, public library in what she calls "the perfect example of cooperation and coordination among public library, school, and media." The author's visit was timed to coincide with National Library Week, and expenses were shared between and elementary school and a grant, funded from a proposal written by Judy Harold, children's services librarian at Springfield Public Library. Judy handled media, and the local newspaper came on Friday to interview students about what they had learned. A nice feature article appeared in Saturday morning's paper. That afternoon, about 50 people showed up for Deborah's 30-minute slide show and talk, followed by a craft project organized by the library. A local bookstore participated with a table so participants could buy books and get them autographed. "All in all," says Deborah, "a win-win situation."

AUTHOR CARDS

Ever seen a student who was in the acute throes of baseball card fever? If you have, you well understand the impetus behind Authorcards International, Inc., published by School Art Materials, P.O. Box 94082, Dept. A, Seattle, WA 98124 (800 752-4359). "These little cards are the best idea in years in my opinion," says author Joan Carris.

Author Spotlight: Joan Carris

Joan says, "I write for children because children's books are almost the last place in America to find fun and laughter in literature. Most writing today is either serious to the point of sorrow or else highly practical. Being practical is great, of course, and yet it is laughter that makes life worth living. Life will thrust quite enough misery down our throats, I figure, but literature should offer courage and hope and joy.

"In my own books for kids, thanks to delicious days of research, I've explored being a vet, a paleontologist, a kid in a British school, a neophyte artist, and a whole lot more—and all of it with humor. I hope I've taken my readers there with me because I believe that kids are inherently eager to learn while they giggle. When I talk to children or teachers in schools, I'm on a mission—making the link between reading and pleasure, knowing that language shapes our lives."

> Joan's still-in-print books include *Aunt Morbelia and the Screaming Skulls*, *Beware the Ravens*, and *Just a Little Ham*.

Author Jacqueline Briggs Martin has created her own author cards. On the front is a picture of her. On the back, she has a list of her books, some basic facts, and the following short biography: "Jacqueline Briggs Martin has always loved stories. She started writing books in 1975 because she and her young children enjoyed books so much. She gets ideas from her family, from books, magazines, and newspapers. And she says some ideas are just 'surprises.' Her advice to children is, 'Ask questions, try new things, do your best, but don't worry about making mistakes.' "

She says, "My student visits are usually focused—at least some of the time—on how writers often weave details from their own lives into their stories, and how important it is that we remember the details of our lives through journals, diaries, scrapbooks, or memory boxes. So this author card is a way for students to remember our visit and the things we have talked about."

CURRICULUM GUIDES

Many publishers provide curriculum guides to go along with some of their books. Harcourt Brace, for instance, developed one for *King Bidgood's in the Bathtub* by Audrey Wood that has activities in four different sections: "Preparing to Read," "While Reading," "After Reading," and "Across the Curriculum." In the last category, one activity suggests that teachers "mark off a large area on the floor with masking tape" to create a play bathtub and then let children dramatize the story. A final page lists other books that have Creative Curriculum Guides to go along with them. For obvious reasons, the publishers give out copies of their guides at conventions and are usually happy to make them available free of charge.

Some authors have also developed their own curriculum guides, sometimes with the help of teachers or librarians. Sherry Park, a library media specialist in the Edmond, Oklahoma, Public School System, for instance, put together an attractive and complete guide with four pages of activities about Dian Curtis Regan's *Princess Nevermore*. The first page gives a short plot summary, notes the book's honors, and quotes from its reviews. The middle pages suggest things to think about before, during, and after reading the book.

A Tip from "Before Reading" in the *Princess Nevermore* Guide

The author's office is home to 82 walruses. A walrus is buried in every one of her books. Tell students to watch for the walrus as they read.

Two pages of "Across the Curriculum" activities extend the reading experience. For example, a social studies activity notes that "Authors often choose to set a story in a real location. Why? Outer earth is a specific city where the author once lived. Recall landmarks mentioned in the story. (Clues: Caprock High, Canadian River, Wonderland Amusement Park.) Ask students to determine where the actual setting is. (Answer: Amarillo, Texas.)" The last three pages of the guide show a picture of Dian Curtis Regan, list her other books, and give a brief biography of both the author and the contributors.

Author Spotlight: Dian Curtis Regan

Dian Curtis Regan's first attempt at publication occurred at the age of eight. Three hundred dollars for an amusing anecdote, read the note in *Reader's Digest*. After asking her mom what an anecdote was, Dian mailed in her goldfish joke—the funniest anecdote she knew. It was handwritten in pencil on a page ripped from her Big Chief tablet. She did not enclose a SASE, because she did not know what it was or that she was supposed to enclose one.

Dian is still waiting to hear from *Reader's Digest*. While she waits, she writes books for young readers—mostly with the humor theme that caught her fancy at the age of eight. However, to date, she has never again written about goldfish.

A native of Colorado, Dian has also lived in Texas and Oklahoma. Presently, she writes from an apartment overlooking the Caribbean Sea in the city of Puerto La Cruz, Venezuela. In her spare time, she reads the anecdotes in *Reader's Digest*. Some of her newest books include *Monsters in Cyberspace*, *Monsters and My One True Love*, *Home for the Howl-i-days*, *Fangsgiving*, and *Dear Dr. Sillybear*.

Author Lee Wardlaw was thrilled when Sherry Park also put together "a *huge* curriculum guide stuffed full of ideas" to use with *Bubblemania*. Following are some of the many, many ideas that come from Lee and Sherry.

Have the students follow the recipe for making chewing gum found at the back of *Bubblemania: The Chewy History of Bubble Gum*. After the gum is made, each student (or small groups of students) may wish to try the following activities:

- Make up a fun name for the gum.

- Design a poster, or create a newspaper/magazine ad for the gum, complete with a catchy slogan.

- Write a gum commercial or jingle, then perform it for the class. If there is access to a video camera, film the commercials.

- Design bubble gum cards. Each card could feature the student, herself, or drawings of favorite heroes, authors, friends, teachers, pets, family members. Remember to include important statistics on the back of the card.

- Design the packaging for your gum.

Additional activities:

- Sponsor a Bubble Gum Cleanup Day. Kids who scrape up the most chewed wads could win Gum King or Queen certificates or prizes.

- Take a school survey. Ask fellow students such questions as this: What can you do with chewed bubble gum? How do you blow a big bubble? What is your favorite brand and why? Write up and publish the results in your school newspaper.

- Hold a classroom chewing gum test: determine which brands taste the best, which flavors last the longest, which gum is easiest to chew.

- Hold a bubble blowing contest. Make up your own rules, deciding how many pieces of gum may be chewed at the same time, how much time each contestant has to blow a bubble, how long the bubble must last, how the bubble will be measured, who will judge the contest.

Language Arts Activities:

- Write directions on how to blow a bodacious bubble. Test the directions on one another and revise as needed.

Social Studies:

- Create a time line of the development of chewing gum and bubble gum. Include the differing peoples and civilizations who have chewed, noting their locations and the material used to make the gum.

- Use the Internet to access a chat room in order to connect with a global classroom. Compare notes with key pals and exchange information about bubble gum. Or create a classroom bubble gum Web page, complete with fun facts about this sticky subject.

Math:

- Make a comparison chart of bubble gum projects, listing the weight, number of pieces, and cost. Determine the best buy.

- Let students make predictions for the amount chewed for the entire class each week. Keep a log of "chewing." Average. Compare with predictions. Devise other questions, such as these: length of chew, time of each chew, favorite flavors, how long flavors last. Predict, log, average, and discuss.

Science:

- John Bacon Curtis invented machines in the mid 1880s to produce his gum more efficiently. Inventions often happen in chains, as one discovery or invention may create a need for another. Choose an invention and trace its history. Make a timeline showing its development.

- Check the weight of bubble gum on the package. Weigh and compare. Chew it and weigh again. Use the scientific method to resolve any differences.

    Predict, research, investigate, test, and analyze the following problems:

    Does chewing gum contribute to tooth decay?

    How biodegradable is chewing gum?

    Can chocolate be a flavor for chewing gum?

Author Spotlight: Lee Wardlaw

"I started writing at age seven. My first book told the adventures of Teena Belle, who runs away from home to escape her 14 baby brothers and sisters. (My brother had just been born, so no doubt I was subconsciously expressing disapproval of my new job as Assistant Diaperer!) My mother typed the manuscript and bound it in a small folder: my first "published" book! With her support, and that of numerous teachers and librarians, I've been writing ever since: stories, poems, songs, plays, even radio commercials. Two of my most recent titles are a middle-grade novel, *101 Ways to Bug Your Parents*, and a picture book, *Bow-Wow Birthday*.

"After receiving my B.A. in education, I taught school for five years before choosing to write full-time. I've now written over 20 books for children, ranging from board books to young adult novels and have kept in tune with my readers by working as a reading tutor, library story lady, and Tooth Fairy (don't ask!). I also enjoy visiting schools, talking to kids about the creative process.

"Currently, I teach writing workshops at Santa Barbara City College; write a column for *Inklings*, an online newsletter for writers; and lecture frequently at conferences. I live in Santa Barbara, California, with my husband Craig, a winemaker; our son, Patterson; and two cats, Riesling and Beaujolais.

REALIA

Jane was in the middle of a writing residency when the idea came to her for her favorite prop, something she simply calls The Box. "I was talking to the students as I always do," she says, "about the importance of using the five senses in their writing. Suddenly, it struck me that I could be doing more to use the five senses in helping students connect with my own childhood experiences and with my books. For the remaining days of the residency, I gathered up things the students could see, smell, taste, touch, and hear from Ethiopia."

Some time later, Jane was talking with a library aide in California about ways to make books really come alive for kids. "I asked if she'd be interested in being a guinea pig for using The Box long-distance," Jane says. "I ended up mailing it to her, and she experimented with using it with her students."

Contents of The Box

Jane has created several versions of The Box, but there are some things she tries to be sure to include in each one:

- *Bere bere* spice so students can smell what the rich man would be smelling as he waits for his food in *Fire on the Mountain* and what Tekleh smells as he walks into the wedding scene in *Trouble*.

- A fly swish such as the one the last servant carries as he walks behind the rich man in *Fire on the Mountain*.

- A *shamma* so students can see and touch the cloak that Alemayu wraps around himself to survive up in the high mountains in *Fire on the Mountain*.

- A drum such as the one Almaz would play when she has managed to get some hair from the lion's tail (*Pulling the Lion's Tail*) and also such as Tekleh trades for in *Trouble*.

- Some eucalyptus leaves to smell so students can imagine themselves as Almaz, hiding behind the eucalyptus tree before she creeps up to the lion or as Onduahlem, walking to school in the crisp morning air of the city in *Only a Pigeon*.

- Pages that show the Amharic writing that Onduahlem studies in school.

- An amber bead, like the beads that Rahel touches to help her remember the important stories in *The Storyteller's Beads*.

Laura Manthey works in an area of California where most professional library media specialists have been cut from the schools for financial reasons. Luckily for her school, she has continued to bring a number of interesting resources into the library because of her background as a bookseller of children's books. After Jane sent The Box to her and they discussed the items via E-mail, Laura created a bulletin board with Jane's picture and two mountains—one with a fire on top—a map of Ethiopia, a book jacket, and other items. As the project began, she sent an E-mail to tell Jane some of the details about how it was going:

"Everything has gone so well. I have now read *Fire on the Mountain* to all first through fifth graders. That's 26 readings, by the way. Then I followed that up the next week with Ethiopia through the five senses: a huge hit as well." She started out showing her students maps of the world, then Africa, then Ethiopia to help them understand exactly where Ethiopia is. Then she played some of a tape Jane had made that explained a bit about the language and included Jane singing a song in Amharic, shared the sounds of a cowbell ("which very few kids recognized as such") and the sounds of a drum. After that, Laura passed around things to smell including coffee, eucalyptus, and spices. When students had all had a chance to touch obsidian, *shammas*, and baskets, Laura gave them an opportunity to taste pomegranate and an Ethiopian snack she had made (using Jane's recipe), *dabo colo*.

During the next week, Laura did different activities with different grades. For example, "the third graders drew pictures of one item for each of the five senses that is familiar or special to them here in San Jose. I just gave them a big piece of blank paper and markers, crayons, and colored pencils and told them to write or draw one thing for each of the senses. It was great for me to get to know a different aspect of their lives. They shared a lot, and it was interesting to see how they approached the project." Laura notes that she asked her students to think about how they would share their environment and lives with someone in Ethiopia and that "the results were quite amusing and a number of kids wished I could send their pictures to children in Ethiopia."

Fourth graders heard an explanation about how books are created. Laura read what Jane had explained about the illustrations "and how long it all takes" and then read the manuscript pages of *Pulling the Lion's Tail*, without showing any pictures. She gave each student a page to illustrate, asking them to use what they had learned through the reading of *Fire on the Mountain* and through the sharing of things in The Box.

Fifth graders did some research on Ethiopia. Laura pulled out reference materials and some books and magazines she thought would be helpful. She divided the groups into pairs and asked them to find the answers to various questions: What kind of animals are found in Ethiopia? What is the weather like in Ethiopia? What jobs do people do? What do people eat? After sharing their findings with the class, students discussed possible questions or comments they might send to Jane. The computer aide helped them compose letters to Jane on the computer.

Laura finished, "I had the opportunity to share the project with the superintendent of our district on Tuesday when he visited the school. I must say that he was very impressed, as well he should have been! So how on earth am I going to top this? No way. To say it has been a success is a major understatement. I think it has a tremendous number of possibilities . . . far more than my limited schedule can permit." Later, she wrote, "It was a real letdown when I had to go back to my usual 'read 20 minutes, check books out' routine."

Since the initial experiment, several librarians and teachers have borrowed a version of The Box from Jane. Kathy Davis, a teacher in St. Charles, Missouri, has used it several times, creating projects to go along. "This year," she initially wrote (via E-mail) to Jane, "I am not using any textbooks but teaching the curriculum using thematic units. I am teaching seven units about the seven continents. I collect books from each continent to have available in the classroom. Teachers rarely (actually I've not known it to happen) get help from authors, and I think it would really help me with my curriculum." One successful project she created was having each student make a windsock. "We made an Ethiopian flag from large construction paper," Kathy says, "wrote the title and author of *Pulling the Lion's Tail* across the flag, then hung streamers in the colors of the flag. Each streamer had information about the book—something each student thought was important or considered a favorite part. Some even used quotes. We then rolled them to form a cylinder, stapled them together, added string, and hung them from the ceiling. We had them hanging in our room, the hall, and even in the school lobby. We got a lot of compliments."

Schools where Jane has made an in-person visit have also used The Box. Virginia Bohndorf, media specialist at Piper Elementary School East in Kansas City, Kansas, where Jane visited in 1998, wrote, "The box of artifacts you sent ahead was such a help in sharing the stories. The lifestyle is so foreign to most American children; it made Ethiopia seem more real to actually smell *bere bere* and see a fly swish. In reading *Fire on the Mountain*, it helped so much to explain the cold by holding up the *shamma* cloth to demonstrate just how thin it was."

MUSIC

Cathy Signorelli is an author who often focuses on musicians; she's written about them in magazine articles and has a picture book under contract with Harcourt Brace, cowritten with Jane, about Etta Baker, who was an important part of the folk music revival in the United States. Naturally, she often takes tapes to schools with her. When she's talking about the musician Lead Belly she takes samples of the *Last Sessions*. She says, "I love to tell the kids that Lead Belly was already sick with Lou Gehrigs disease by the time they taped his last sessions. His niece, Tiny Robinson, told us that the sessions were done in three parts in the home of Moe Asch. He lived on the sixth floor, and it took three men to carry Lead Belly up those stairs. The first session was a surprise, so Lead Belly, for once, hadn't taken his guitar along—that was very unusual, as he always brought his guitar. But it's my favorite recording of him, because it proves that nothing could stop him from making music. Even without his guitar, he slapped and clapped and tapped, singing his heart out, and it reminds me of the Gray Goose. No matter what you did to it, it wasn't ever going to die." Just to prove that very point, she says, she then uses later recordings by other musicians such as Woody Guthrie, Pete Seeger, Arlo Guthrie, Sonny Terry, Brownie McGhee, and Michael Cooney who went on to record Lead Belly's songs in their own various styles. "I usually cue the tape up to either the "Gray Goose" or to another children's song like "Redbird" or maybe "Irene's Goodnight" and let the kids just get a sample of the music."

When the Etta Baker book comes out, Cathy says, she will use one of Etta's tapes, *One-Dime Blues*, because it has such songs as "Never Let Your Deal Go Down," "One Dime Blues," "Knoxville Rag," and "Dew Drop," most of which are mentioned in the picture book. It also has "Bully of the Town," one of Cathy's favorite Lead Belly pieces. "Between the tapes," Cathy says, "I've told little stories, like how it was Albert Einstein who told Moe Asch to make a recording of Lead Belly, or how Etta let the crowd name the 'Knoxville Rag.' " After the Etta Baker book comes out, Cathy plans to "give kids the chance to listen to the music and come up with their own names for the pieces."

Cathy also notes that Jane's creation of The Box has inspired her to think about how similar things could be done with many books. For instance, she says, it would be great to put together an "Etta Baker Remembers" box. "It would be important to tell kids that the five senses are key to memories, and the box could contain things that she remembered from her pretty life growing up in Appalachia. There would be a sample from a star quilt to see and feel, pictures of the stove, the bathtub, apples for the kids to taste, herbs for them to smell. We could use tapes of their music for them to hear, a set of dominoes and a checkerboard for them to play. A follow-up writing activity could include letting students interview each other or their own relatives about what they remember from growing up."

Author Spotlight: Cathy Signorelli

"Born and raised on the South Side of Chicago, I grew up with a great appreciation for the blues. For several years on Friday nights, my husband and I packed up our two sons and headed to the North Side to hear some of the finest musicians perform at Chicago's Old Town School of Folk Music. One summer, we got tired of the drive and decided to start our own coffeehouse right there, in our own neighborhood. (Who did we think we were, anyway?) We named it 'Irene's Goodnight,' to honor Mr. Huddie Leadbetter, a.k.a. Lead Belly, King of the Twelve String Guitar.

"Much to our surprise, Irene's Goodnight grew to become a hub of family entertainment, making room for hundreds of musicians on its stage, some as young as 3, others as young as 93. In the end, we left it, still kicking, still wailing, still singing along, as we took the longest drive of our lives and finally settled in northern California, where I now sit on the board of Brownie McGhee's Blue's Is Truth Foundation, centered in Oakland.

"Something I love to tell kids is this: The great joy of music is that it's right there inside you. There's no going anywhere without it, no stripping it down, no taking it away. This idea is key to understanding the blues, and Lead Belly's 'Gray Goose,' and Etta Baker's 'One Dime Blues' are perfect examples."

READ AND FEEDS

Other teachers have been exploring ways to use the five senses as well. Myrna Fields, library media specialist at Owen Valley Middle School in Spencer, Indiana, says, "We are constantly working at improving what we do with our author visits, and we're kind of proud of some of the things we do." One of the things they've done, she says, was to take an idea from *Fiction, Food, and Fun* (Libraries Unlimited, 1998) and expand on it to create "Read-and-Feeds," something they have tried both with and without author visits. "What we basically do," she explains, "is create a scene out of the book in a double room in our school. One of our teachers is our game designer. She designs a game that relates somehow to the book. Questions are sometimes based on recall of information in the book, sometimes reactions to something in the book, sometimes pure luck! We try to have food that is mentioned in the book for the kids to eat." About 75 students who have read the book are invited to each Read-and-Feed; the activity is so popular with students that they have random drawings to select participants.

For a specific example, Myrna describes an upcoming Read-and-Feed that will be part of an author visit by Will Hobbs. "We are in the process of creating a scene from his book *Far North*," she explains, "complete with waterfall/river, brush teepee, airplane, stuffed animals (borrowed from a taxidermist), and many other items from the book." Place mats (made by students) are maps of the Nahanni River. Each table will represent a location in the book. "We are eating bannock, 'moose meat' (actually beef jerky) and 'rose-hip tea' (actually Cherry 7up) and playing a game that was loosely based on Candyland." Teacher Rebecca Hayes adds that the Read-and-Feed "is really a celebration of the book. We try to re-create scenes from the book and immerse the students in that scene with games based on the book, food from the book, and treat bags with items mentioned in the book." Author Ben Mikaelsen, one of the author visitors to Owen Valley Middle School, says, "The thing that makes Read-and-Feeds so great is how they bring the story alive to the kids. Now they can play, act, smell, touch, and see all the great things they experienced in the story. The first Read-and-Feed only drew a handful of students. After the first one, they had to limit the numbers!"

Students are well prepared for each visit. "We really promote the author's books heavily," Myrna says. "For Will Hobbs, every student in the school has read *Far North* and most of the staff, too. Even our superintendent has read the book and will come for the Read-and-Feed." The result, she adds, is that the "*tons*" of Will Hobbs books in the library are "always checked out." Meanwhile, a student-operated bookstore in the school sells copies of the author's books to have autographed. "We hope [all our work] makes students feel reading is a worthwhile experience," says Rebecca, "while celebrating the work of an author. Really, we just want them to read more and enjoy reading more. It seems to work."

The school also finds creative ways to let the community know what's going on. "My cohort, Darla Staley, found someone willing to haul a real plane in front of the school on which we will place a Welcome Will Hobbs banner," Myrna says. "We call all local businesses with signs and have them put welcome signs up for our authors. Our local newspaper prints articles before and after the visits."

The result of all this preparation, says Rebecca, is that in their school it is "cool" to have read books. In their overall approach, she notes, the staff tries hard "never to trivialize" what students like to read, and then they build on students' interests. In that vein, they "shoot for authors whose work we know appeals to kids. This has made a real difference." All in all, she notes, "An author visit is a perfect tool for getting kids to read because they feel a real sense of belonging when that author is speaking about a book they have read. In preparation for our current visitor, Will Hobbs, all of our students have read (or had read to them) *Far North*. We have talked about things like setting, characters, and plot. When Will shows them slides of those settings, they will feel as if they've been there and, in turn, read his other works. It never fails."

Ben agrees, calling this school visit one of his very best. "Authors visiting a school are most productive when the reading teachers have prepared the students by having them read one or more of the author's books before their arrival," he says. "I compare it to hands clapping. I am one hand. I can swing as hard as I want, but if the other hand isn't there, the visit is empty. This truly is a joint effort. When the effort is made, my visits have been absolute magic."

Pulitzer Prize–winning historian and former Librarian of Congress, Daniel Boorstin, concludes his article in *Parade* magazine, "By reading, we discover our world, our history and ourselves." The people you have met in these pages are convinced that they know a few of the secrets for getting young people excited about reading and about discovering more of their world, their history, their selves. Whether you connect with bookpeople through a school visit, at a bookstore, in cyberspace, at a library, or through some intriguing prop or other resource isn't terribly important. The important thing is to pick a place to start that seems appealing, important, and doable. Then jump in. The water is more than fine. It's terrific.

REFERENCES

Appelt, Kathi. *Bat Jamboree*. With illustrations by Melissa Sweet. New York: Morrow, 1996.

——. *Just People and Other Poems for Young Readers & Paper/Pen/Poem*. With photographs by Ken Appelt. Houston: Absey and Co., 1997.

Boorstin, Daniel J. "I Cannot Live Without Books." *Parade* (July 12, 1998): 12–13.

Carris, Joan. *Aunt Morbelia and the Screaming Skulls*. With illustrations by Doug Cushman. New York: Pocket Books, 1990.

——. *Beware the Ravens, Aunt Morbelia*. Boston: Little, Brown, 1995.

——. *Just a Little Ham*. With illustrations by Dora Leder. New York: Pocket Books, 1989.

Closter, Kathryn, Karen L. Sipes, and Vickie Thomas. *Fiction, Food, and Fun: The Original Recipe for the Read 'N' Feed Program*. Englewood, CO: Libraries Unlimited, 1998.

Falwell, Cathryn. *Dragon Tooth*. New York: Clarion, 1996.

——. The *Letter Jesters*. New York: Houghton Mifflin, 1994.

——. *Shape Space*. New York: Clarion, 1992.

——. *Word Wizard*. New York: Clarion, 1998.

Hobbs, Will. *Far North*. New York: Morrow, 1996.

Kurtz, Jane. *Fire on the Mountain*. With illustrations by E. B. Lewis. New York: Simon &Schuster, 1994.

——. *Pulling the Lion's Tail*. With illustrations by Floyd Cooper. New York: Simon & Schuster, 1995.

——. *The Storyteller's Beads*. San Diego: Harcourt, 1998.

——. *Trouble*. With illustrations by Durga Bernhard. San Diego: Harcourt, 1997.

Kurtz, Jane and Christopher. *Only a Pigeon*. With illustrations by E. B. Lewis. New York: Simon & Schuster, 1997.

Regan, Dian Curtis. *Dear Dr. Sillybear*. With illustrations by Randy Cecil. New York: Holt, 1998.

——. *Fangs-giving*. New York: Scholastic, 1997.

——. *Home for the Howl-i-days*. New York: Scholastic, 1996.

——. *Monsters and My One True Love*. With illustrations by Melissa Sweet. New York: Holt, 1998.

——. *Monsters in Cyberspace*. With illustrations by Melissa Sweet. New York: Holt, 1997.

——. *Princess Nevermore*. New York: Scholastic, 1995.

Wardlaw, Lee. *101 Ways to Bug Your Parents*. New York: Dial, 1996.

——. *Bow-Wow Birthday*. With illustrations by Arden-Johnson Petrov. Honesdale, PA: Boyds Mills Press, 1998.

——. *Bubblemania: The Chewy History of Bubble Gum*. With illustrations by Sandra Forrest. New York: Aladdin Books, 1997.

——. *Punia and the King of Sharks: A Hawaiian Folktale*. With illustrations by Felipe Davalos. New York: Dial, 1997.

Wood, Audrey. *King Bidgood's in the Bathtub*. With illustrations by Don Wood. San Diego: Harcourt, 1985.

References

Agell, Charlotte. *Dancing Feet*. San Diego: Harcourt, 1994. ISBN: 0152004440

——. *I Swam with a Seal*. San Diego: Harcourt, 1995. ISBN: 015200176X

——. *The Sailor's Book*. Willowdale, Ontario: Firefly, 1991. ISBN: 0920668917

——. *To the Island*. New York: DK Ink, 1998. ISBN: 078942505X

——. *Up the Mountain*. New York: DK Ink, 1999. ISBN: 0789426102

Alexander, David. *The Little Wide Mouth Gecko*. With illustrations by Yoes Rizal. Topeka, KS: Desktop Publishers, 1996. ISBN: 1892455005

Anderson, Lisa. *Proud to Be Me, Peewee Platypus*. Pleasant Ridge, MI: Ridge Enterprises, 1990. ISBN: 0962832308

Angelou, Maya. *Life Doesn't Frighten Me*. With illustrations by Jean-Michel Basquiat. Edited by Sara Jane Boyers. New York: Stewart, Tabori & Chang, 1993. ISBN: 1556702884

Appelt, Kathi. *Bat Jamboree*. With illustrations by Melissa Sweet. New York: Morrow, 1996. ISBN: 0688138829

——. *Just People and Other Poems for Young Readers & Paper/Pen/Poem*. With photographs by Ken Appelt. Houston: Absey and Co., 1997. ISBN: 1888842075

Balan, Bruce. *Buoy, Home at Sea*. With illustrations by Raul Colon. New York: Delacorte, 1988. ISBN: 0385325398

——. *The Cherry Migration*. With illustrations by Dan Lane. San Diego: Green Tiger, 1988. ISBN: 0881380989

——. *In Search of Scum*; *A Picture's Worth*; *The Great NASA Flu*; *Blackout in the Amazon*; *In Pursuit of Picasso*; *When the Chips Are Down*. Cyber.kdz Series. New York: Camelot, 1997–1998.

——. *Pie in the Sky*. With illustrations by Clare Skilbeck. New York: Viking, 1993. ISBN: 0670851507

Balgassi, Haemi. *Peacebound Trains*. With illustrations by Chris Soentpiet. New York: Clarion, 1996. ISBN: 0395720931

——. *Tae's Sonata*. New York: Clarion, 1997. ISBN: 0395843146

Banks, Lynne Reid. *The Indian in the Cupboard*. With illustrations by Brock Cole. Garden City, NY: Doubleday, 1980. ISBN: 0385170602

Barlow, Genevieve. *Latin American Tales: From the Pampas to the Pyramids of Mexico*. With illustrations by William M. Hutchinson. Chicago: Rand McNally, 1966. LCCN: 6610391

Bartoletti, Susan Campbell. *Dancing with Dziadzu*. With illustrations by Annika Nelson. San Diego: Harcourt, 1997. ISBN: 0152006753

——. *Growing Up in Coal Country*. Boston: Houghton Mifflin, 1996. ISBN: 0395778476

——. *Kids on Strike*. Boston: Houghton Mifflin, 1999. ISBN: 0395888921

——. *No Man's Land*. New York: Scholastic, 1999. ISBN: 059038371X

Bates, Katharine Lee. *O Beautiful for Spacious Skies*. With illustrations by Wayne Thiebaud. Edited by Sara Jane Boyers. San Francisco: Chronicle, 1994. ISBN: 0811808327

Berger, Melvin. *Oil Spill! Let's Read-And-Find-Out Science, Stage 2*. With illustrations by Paul Mirocha. New York: HarperCollins, 1994. ISBN: 0060229098

Bernier-Grand, Carmen T. *In the Shade of the Nispero Tree*. New York: Orchard, 1999. ISBN: 0531301540

——. *Juan Bobo: Four Folktales from Puerto Rico*. With illustrations by Ernesto Ramos Nieves. New York: HarperTrophy, 1994. ISBN: 006441857

——. *Poet and Politician of Puerto Rico: Don Luis Muñoz Marin*. New York: Orchard, 1995. ISBN: 0531068870

Billingsley, Franny. *The Folk Keeper*. New York: Atheneum, 1999. ISBN: 0689828764

——. "Searching for a Plot." *Book Links* 6 (July 1997): 13–17.

——. *Well Wished*. New York: Atheneum, 1997. ISBN: 0689812108

Boorstin, Daniel J. "I Cannot Live Without Books." *Parade* (July 12, 1998): 12–13.

Bowie, C. W. *Busy Toes*. With illustrations by Fred Willingham. Dallas: Whispering Coyote, 1998. ISBN: 1879085720

Boyers, Sara Jane. *Teen Power Politics: Make Yourself Heard*. Brookfield, CT: Twenty-First Century, 1999. ISBN: 0761313079

Bradford, Karleen. *Dragonfire*. Toronto, Ontario: HarperCollins Canada, 1998. ISBN: 0006481809

——. *There Will Be Wolves*. New York: Lodestar, 1996. ISBN: 0525675396

Brennan, Linda Crotta. "The Dream Violin" in *The Dream Violin*. Honesdale, PA: Boyds Mills, 1994. ISBN: 0875346235

——. *Flannel Kisses*. With illustrations by Mari Takabayoshi. Boston: Houghton Mifflin, 1997. ISBN: 0395736811

——. *Marshmallow Kisses*. With illustrations by Mari Takabayoshi. Boston: Houghton Mifflin. Forthcoming.

Brown, Susan Taylor. *Did Not, Did So*. With illustrations by Liz McIntosh. Bothell, WA: Wright Group, 1996. ISBN: 0780240685

——. *A Pony Named Midnight*. With illustrations by Linda Sniffen. Boise, ID: Writer's Press, 1998. ISBN: 1885101945

——. *The Very Patient Pony*. With illustrations by Linda Sniffen. Boise, ID: Writer's Press, 1998. ISBN: 1885101953

Burnett, Frances Hodgson. *A Little Princess; Being the Whole Story of Sara Crewe Now Told for the First Time*. With illustrations by Ethel Fanklin Betts. New York: Scribner, 1938. Re-issue, 1974. ISBN: 0684207591

Buzzeo, Toni. "The Finely Tuned Author Visit." *Book Links* 7 (March 1998): 10–15.

Carrick, Carol. *Whaling Days*. With illustrations by David Frampton. New York: Clarion, 1993. ISBN: 0395509483

Carris, Joan. *Aunt Morbelia and the Screaming Skulls*. With illustrations by Doug Cushman. New York: Pocket Books, 1990. ISBN: 0671747843

——. *Beware the Ravens, Aunt Morbelia*. Boston: Little, Brown, 1995. ISBN: 0316129615

——. *Just a Little Ham*. With illustrations by Dora Leder. New York: Pocket Books, 1989. ISBN: 0671747835

Casanova, Mary. *Moose Tracks*. New York: Hyperion, 1995. ISBN: 0786811374

——. *Riot*. New York: Hyperion, 1996. ISBN: 0786812494

——. *Stealing Thunder*. New York: Hyperion, 1999. ISBN: 078680324

——. *Wolf Shadows*. New York: Hyperion, 1998. ISBN: 0786803258

Chaikin, Miriam. *Clouds of Glory : Jewish Legends & Stories About Bible Times*. With illustrations by David Frampton. New York: Clarion, 1998. ISBN: 039574654X

Closter, Kathryn, Karen L. Sipes, and Vickie Thomas. *Fiction, Food, and Fun: The Original Recipe for the Read 'N' Feed Program*. Englewood, CO: Libraries Unlimited, 1998. ISBN: 1563085194

Creeden, Sharon. "The Warmth of a Fire." In *Fair Is Fair: World Folktales of Justice*. Little Rock, AR: August House, 1997. ISBN: 0874834007

Crider, Bill. *A Vampire Named Fred*. Lufkin, TX: Ellen C. Temple Publishing, 1990. ISBN: 0936650117

Curtis, Gavin. *The Bat Boy and His Violin*. New York: Simon & Schuster, 1998. ISBN: 0689800991

Davis, Katie. *I Hate to Go to Bed!* San Diego: Harcourt, 1999. ISBN: 0152019200

——. *Who Hops?* San Diego: Harcourt, 1998. ISBN: 0152018395

Del Negro, Janice. *Lucy Dove*. With illustrations by Leonid Gore. New York: DK Ink, 1998. ISBN: 0789425149

Dionetti, Michelle. *Coal Mine Peaches*. With illustrations by Anita Riggio. New York: Orchard, 1991. ISBN: 0531059480

——. *Painting the Wind*. With illustrations by Kevin Hawkes. Boston: Little Brown, 1996. ISBN: 0316186023

Duey, Kathleen. *Sarah Anne Hartford, Massachusetts, 1651*; *Emma Eileen Grove, Mississippi River, 1865*; *Anisett Lundberg, California Gold Fields, 1851*; *Mary Alice Peale, Philadelphia, 1779*; *Willow Chase, Kansas Territory, 1857*; *Ellen Elizabeth Hawkins, Texas, 1887*; *Alexia Ellery Finsdale, San Francisco, 1905*; *Evie Peach, St. Louis 1857*; *Celou Sudden Shout, Wind River, 1826*; *Summer MacCleary, Virginia Colony, 1749*; *Agnes May Gleason, Walsenburg, Colorado, 1932*; *Amelina Carrett, Thibodaux, Louisiana, 1860*. American Diaries Series. New York: Aladdin, 1996–1999.

——. *Titanic*; *Earthquake, San Francisco, 1906*; *Blizzard, Estes Park, CO, 1887*; *Fire, Chicago 1876*; *Flood, Mayersville, Mississippi, 1927*; *Death Valley, California, 1849*; *Cave-in, Pennsylvania, 1859*; *Trainwreck, Kansas, 1892*; *Hurricane, New England, 1840*. Survival Series. New York: Aladdin, 1998–1999.

Edwards, Frank B. *Mortimer Mooner Stopped Taking a Bath*. With illustrations by John Bianchi. Newburgh, Ontario: Bungalo, 1990. ISBN: 0921285205

Falwell, Cathryn. *Christmas for 10*. New York: Clarion, 1998. ISBN: 0395855810

——. *Dragon Tooth*. New York: Clarion, 1996. ISBN: 0395569168

——. *Feast for 10*. New York: Clarion, 1993. ISBN: 0395620376

——. *The Letter Jesters*. Boston: Houghton Mifflin, 1994. ISBN: 0395668980

——. *Shape Space*. New York: Clarion, 1992. ISBN: 0395613051

——. *Word Wizard*. New York: Clarion, 1998. ISBN: 0395855802

Fleming, Candace. *Women of the Lights*. Illustrated by James Watling. Morton Grove, IL: Whitman, 1995. ISBN: 0807591653

Gardella, Tricia. *Blackberry Booties*. With illustrations by Glo Coalson. New York: Orchard, Forthcoming. ISBN: 0531301842

——. *Casey's New Hat*. With illustrations by Margot Apple. Boston: Houghton Mifflin, 1997. ISBN: 0395720354

——. *Just Like My Dad*. With illustrations by Margot Apple. New York: HarperCollins, 1993. ISBN: 0060219378

——. *Writers in the Kitchen: Children's Book Authors Share Memories of Their Favorite Recipes*. Honesdale, PA: Boyds Mills, 1998. ISBN: 1563977133

Gibbons, Gail. *Beacons of Light: Lighthouses*. New York: Morrow, 1990. ISBN: 0688073794

——. *Sunken Treasure*. New York: Crowell, 1988. ISBN: 0690047363

Gold, Bernice. *My Four Lions*. Illustrated by Joanne Stanbridge. Toronto, ON: Annick Press, 1999. ISBN: 1550376039

Green, Rhonda Gowler. *When a Line Bends . . . A Shape Begins*. With illustrations by James Kaczman. New York: Houghton, 1997. ISBN: 0395786061

Grindley, Sally. *Peter's Place*. With illustrations by Michael Foreman. New York: Harcourt, 1996. ISBN: 0152009167

Guiberson, Brenda Z. *Lighthouses: Watchers at Sea*. New York: Holt, 1995. ISBN: 0805031707

Harlan, Judith. *Girl Talk: Staying Strong, Feeling Good, Sticking Together*. New York: Walker, 1997. ISBN: 0802786405

Hawkes, Kevin. *His Royal Buckliness*. New York: Lothrop, Lee & Shepard, 1992. ISBN: 0688110622

——. *Then the Troll Heard the Squeak*. New York: Lothrop, Lee & Shepard, 1991. ISBN: 068809757X

Hines, Anna Grossnickle. *Miss Emma's Wild Garden*. New York: Greenwillow, 1997. ISBN: 0688146929

Hobbs, Will. *Far North*. New York: Morrow, 1996. ISBN: 0688141927

Hopkinson, Deborah. *A Band of Angels*. With illustrations by Raul Colon. New York: Atheneum, 1999. ISBN: 0689810628

——. *Birdie's Lighthouse*. With illustrations by Kimberly Bulcken Root. New York: Atheneum, 1997. ISBN: 0689810520

——. *Fannie in the Kitchen*. With illustrations by Nancy Carpenter. New York: Atheneum. Forthcoming. ISBN: 068981965X

——. *Maria's Comet*. With illustrations by Deborah Lanino. New York: Atheneum, 1999. ISBN: 0689815018

——. "Shining Light on History." *Book Links* 7 (November 1997): 35–40.

——. *Sweet Clara and the Freedom Quilt*. With illustrations by James Ransome. New York: Knopf, 1993. ISBN: 0679823115

——. *Under the Quilt of Night*. With illustrations by James Ransome. New York: Atheneum. Forthcoming. ISBN: 0689822278

Jackson, Ellen. *Brown Cow, Green Grass, Yellow Mellow Sun*. With illustrations by Victoria Raymond. New York: Hyperion, 1995. ISBN: 0786800100

——. *The Book of Slime*. With illustrations by Jan Davey Ellis. Brookfield, CT: Millbrook, 1997. ISBN: 0761300422

Jacobson, Jennifer Richard. *Moon Sandwich Mom*. With illustrations by Benrei Huang. Morton Grove, IL: Albert Whitman, 1999. ISBN: 0807540714

——. *A Net of Stars*. With illustrations by Greg Shed. New York: Dial, 1998. ISBN: 0803720874

Jacobson, Jennifer, and Dottie Raymer. *The Big Book of Reproducible Graphic Organizers: 50 Great Templates to Help Get More Out of Reading, Writing, Social Studies, & More.* New York: Scholastic Professional Books, 1999. ISBN: 0590378848

Jaffe, Nina. *In the Month of Kislev.* With illustrations by Louise August. New York: Viking, 1992. ISBN: 0670828637

Jones, Dorothy H., and Ruth S. Sargent. *Abbie Burgess: Lighthouse Heroine.* Rockport, ME: Down East, 1976. ISBN: 0892720182

Ketteman, Helen. *Bubba the Cowboy Prince (A Fractured Texas Tale).* With illustrations by James Warhola. New York: Scholastic, 1997. ISBN: 0590255061

——. *Grandma's Cat.* With illustrations by Marsha Lynn Winborn. Boston: Houghton Mifflin, 1996. ISBN: 039573094

——. *Heat Wave.* With illustrations by Scott Goto. New York: Walker, 1998. ISBN: 0802786448

——. *I Remember Papa.* With illustrations by Greg Shed. New York: Dial, 1998. ISBN: 0803718489.

Klein, Tom. *Loon Magic for Kids.* Milwaukee: Gareth Stevens, 1990. ISBN: 0836804023

Knight, Margy Burns. *Talking Walls.* With Illustrations by Anne Sibley O'Brien. Gardiner, ME: Tilbury House, 1992. ISBN: 0884481026

——. *Welcoming Babies.* With Illustrations by Anne Sibley O'Brien. Gardiner, ME: Tilbury House, 1994. ISBN 0884481239

Koller, Jackie French. *The Dragonling*; *A Dragon in the Family*; *Dragon Quest*; *Dragons of Krad*; *Dragon Trouble*; *Dragons and Kings.* The Dragonling Series. New York: Minstrel, 1995–1997.

——. *Impy for Always.* With illustrations by Carol Newsom. Boston: Little Brown, 1989. ISBN: 0316501476

Kurtz, Jane. *Fire on the Mountain.* With illustrations by E. B. Lewis. New York: Simon & Schuster, 1994. ISBN: 0671882686

——. *I'm Sorry, Almira Ann.* New York: Holt, 1999. ISBN: 0805060944

——. *Miro in the Kingdom of the Sun.* With illustrations by David Frampton. Boston: Houghton Mifflin, 1996. ISBN: 0395691818

——. *Pulling the Lion's Tail.* With illustrations by Floyd Cooper. New York: Simon & Schuster, 1995. ISBN: 0689803249

——. *River Friendly, River Wild.* With illustrations by Neil Brennan. New York: Simon & Schuster. Forthcoming. ISBN: 0689820496

——. *The Storyteller's Beads.* New York: Harcourt, 1998. ISBN: 0152010742

——. *Trouble.* With illustrations by Durga Bernhard. New York: Harcourt, 1997. ISBN: 0152002197

Kurtz, Jane and Christopher. *Only a Pigeon.* With illustrations by E. B. Lewis. New York: Simon & Schuster, 1997. ISBN: 0689800770

Lantier-Sampon, Patricia. *The Wonder of Loons.* Milwaukee: Gareth Stevens, 1992. ISBN: 0836808568

Legacy for a Loon. Prod. by Walter and Myrna Berlet, 20 min., Maine Inland Fishes and Wildlife Department, 1982, videocassette.

Levine, Gail Carson. *Ella Enchanted.* New York: HarperCollins, 1997. ISBN: 0060275103

Lewis, Valerie, and Walter Mayes. *Valerie and Walter's Best Books for Children: A Lively, Opinionated Guide.* New York: Avon, 1998. ISBN: 0380794381

Light Spirit: Lighthouses of the Maine Coast. Prod. by Jeff Dobbs, 50 min., Jeff Dobbs Productions, 1997, videocassette.

MacLachlan, Patricia. *Sarah, Plain and Tall.* New York: HarperCollins, 1985. ISBN: 0060241012

Martin, Jacqueline Briggs. *Bizzy Bones and the Lost Quilt.* With illustrations by Stella Qrmai. New York: Lothrop, Lee & Shepard, 1988. ISBN: 0688074073

——. *Bizzy Bones and Moosemouse.* With illustrations by Stella Qrmai. New York: Lothrop, Lee & Shepard, 1986. ISBN: 0688057454

——. *Bizzy Bones and Uncle Ezra.* With illustrations by Stella Qrmai. New York: Lothrop, Lee & Shepard, 1984. ISBN: 0688037828

——. *The Finest Horse in Town.* With illustrations by Susan Gaber. New York: HarperCollins, 1992. ISBN: 0060241519

——. *Good Times on Grandfather Mountain.* With illustrations by Susan Gaber. New York: Harper-Collins, 1992. ISBN: 0531059774

——. *Grandmother Bryant's Pocket.* With illustrations by Petra Mathers. Boston: Houghton Mifflin, 1996. ISBN: 0395689848

——. *Higgins Bend Song and Dance.* With illustrations by Brad Sneed. Boston: Houghton Mifflin, 1997. ISBN: 0395675839

——. *Snowflake Bentley.* With illustrations by Mary Azarian. Boston: Houghton Mifflin, 1998. ISBN: 0395861624

——. *Washing the Willow Tree Loon.* With illustrations by Nancy Carpenter. New York: Simon & Schuster, 1995. ISBN: 0689804156

Matthews, Mary. *Magid Fasts for Ramadan.* With illustrations by E. B. Lewis. New York: Clarion, 1996. ISBN: 0395665892

Mead, Alice. *Junebug.* New York: Farrar, 1995. ISBN: 0374339643

Moore, Robin. *Awakening the Hidden Storyteller*, audiocassette. Boston: Shambhala, 1991. ISBN: 0877736235

——. *The Bread Sister of Sinking Creek.* New York: HarperCollins, 1992. ISBN: 0064403572

——. *Maggie Among The Seneca.* New York: HarperCollins, 1990. ISBN: 0397324561

Morris, Deborah. *Shark Attack*; *Over the Edge*; *Tornado!*; *Runaway Bus!*; *Lightning Strike*; *Firestorm!*; *Adrift in the Atlantic*; *Runaway Hot Air Balloon!*; *Explosion!*; *Glacier Rescue.* Real Kids, Real Adventures Series. New York: Berkley, 1997–1998.

Morris, Deborah, and Garrett Ward Sheldon. *What Would Jesus Do?* Nashville: Broadman & Holman, 1997. ISBN: 080540189X

Nye, Naomi Shahib. *Fuel.* Rochester, NY: BOA Editions, 1998. ISBN: 1880238632

——. *Habibi.* New York: Simon & Schuster, 1997. ISBN: 0689801491

——. *Lullaby Raft.* With illustrations by Vivienne Flesher. New York: Simon & Schuster, 1997. ISBN 0689805217

——. *The Space Between Our Footsteps: Poems & Paintings from the Middle East.* New York: Simon & Schuster, 1998. ISBN: 0689812337

O'Brien, Anne Sibley. *The Princess and the Beggar: A Korean Folktale.* New York: Scholastic, 1993. ISBN: 0590460927

Parent, Michael, and Julien Olivier. *Of Kings and Fools: Stories from the French Tradition in North America.* Little Rock, AR: August House, 1996. ISBN: 0874834813

Pfitsch, Patricia Curties. *Keeper of the Light*. New York: Simon & Schuster, 1997. ISBN: 0689814925

Pringle, Laurence P. *Oil Spills: Damage, Recovery, and Prevention*. A Save-the-Earth Book. New York: Morrow, 1993. ISBN: 0688098614

Quest: Investigating the World We Call Maine. "Episode 301: Oil Spill!" Prod. Kate Arno, 55 min., Maine Public Television, 1997, videocassette.

Rappaport, Doreen. *The New King*. With illustrations by E. B. Lewis. New York: Dial, 1995. ISBN: 0803714602

Regan, Dian Curtis. *Dear Dr. Sillybear*. With illustrations by Randy Cecil. New York: Holt, 1998. ISBN: 0805050655

——. *Fangs-giving*. New York: Scholastic, 1997. ISBN: 0590968211

——. *The Friendship of Milly and Tug*. With illustrations by Jennifer Danza. New York: Holt, 1999. ISBN: 0805059350

——. *Home for the Howl-i-days*. New York: Scholastic, 1996. ISBN: 0590487728

——. *The Kissing Contest*. New York: Scholastic, 1990. ISBN: 0590439111

——. *Liver Cookies*. New York: Scholastic, 1991. ISBN: 0590443372

——. *Monster of the Month Club*. With illustrations by Laura Cornell. New York: Holt, 1994. ISBN: 0805034439

——. *Monsters and My One True Love*. With illustrations by Melissa Sweet. New York: Holt, 1998. ISBN: 0805046763

——. *Monsters in Cyberspace*. With illustrations by Melissa Sweet. New York: Holt, 1997. ISBN: 0805046771

——. *Mystery of the Disappearing Dogs*. Ghost Twins Series. New York: Scholastic, 1995. ISBN: 0590252410

——. *Princess Nevermore*. New York: Scholastic, 1995. ISBN: 0590457586

Roop, Peter and Connie. *Keep the Lights Burning, Abbie*. Illustrated by Peter E. Hanson. Minneapolis: Carolrhoda, 1987. ISBN: 0876142757

Rosenberg, Liz. *Monster Mama*. With illustrations by Stephen Gammell. New York: Philomel, 1993. ISBN: 0399219897

Ruurs, Margriet. *Emma and the Coyote*. With illustrations by Barbara Spurll. Toronto, Ontario: Stoddart, 1999. ISBN: 0773731407

——. *Emma's Eggs*. With illustrations by Barbara Spurll. Toronto, Ontario: Stoddart, 1996. ISBN: 0773729720.

——. *A Mountain Alphabet*. With illustrations by Andrew Kiss. Toronto, Ontario: Tundra, 1996. ISBN: 088776374X

——. *On the Write Track*. Vancouver, British Columbia: Pacific Educational Press, 1993. ISBN: 0888650868

Ryan, Pam Muñoz. *The Flag We Love*. With illustrations by Jerry Polatta. Watertown, MA: Charlesbridge, 1996. ISBN: 0881068454

Sabuda, Robert. *ABC Disney Pop-Up*. New York: Disney Press, 1998. ISBN: 0786831324

Schertle, Alice. *Down the Road*. With illustrations by E. B. Lewis. San Diego: Harcourt, 1995. ISBN: 0152766227

Smith, Cynthia Leitich. *Jingle Dancer*. With illustrations by Cornelius Van Wright and Ying-Hwa Hu. New York: HarperCollins. Forthcoming.

Smith, Roland. *Journey of the Red Wolf.* New York: Viking, 1996. ISBN: 0525651624

——. *Thunder Cave.* New York: Hyperion, 1995. ISBN: 0786800682

Smith, Roland, and Michael J. Schmidt. *In the Forest with Elephants.* San Diego: Harcourt, 1998. ISBN: 0152012893

Stanbridge, Joanne. *The Leftover Kid.* Red Deer, Alberta: Read Deer College Press, 1997. ISBN: 0889951608

Suen, Anastasia. *Air Show.* New York: Holt. Forthcoming.

——. *Baby Born.* With illustrations by Chih-Wei Chang. New York: Lee & Low, 1998. ISBN: 08800006807

——. *Man on the Moon.* With illustrations by Benrei Huang. New York: Viking, 1997. ISBN: 0670873934

——. *Window Music.* With illustrations by Wade Zahares. New York: Viking, 1998. ISBN: 0670872873

Testa, Maria. *Dancing Pink Flamingos and Other Stories.* Minneapolis: Lerner Publications, 1995. ISBN: 0822507382

——. *Nine Candles.* With illustrations by Amanda Schaffer. Minneapolis: Carolrhoda Books, 1996. ISBN: 0876149409

——. *Someplace to Go.* With illustrations by Karen Ritz. Morton Grove, IL: Albert Whitman, 1996. ISBN: 0807575240

——. *Thumbs up, Rico!* With illustrations by Diane Paterson. Morton Grove, IL: Albert Whitman, 1994. ISBN: 0807579068

Tololwa, M. Mollel. *Big Boy.* With illustrations by E. B. Lewis. New York: Clarion, 1995. ISBN: 0395674034

Walton, Rick. *Once There Was a Bull . . . (Frog).* With illustrations by Greg Hally. Salt Lake City, UT: Gibbs Smith, 1995. ISBN: 0879056525

Wardlaw, Lee. *101 Ways to Bug Your Parents.* New York: Dial, 1996. ISBN: 0803719019

——. *Bow-Wow Birthday.* With illustrations by Arden-Johnson Petrov. Honesdale, PA: Boyds Mills Press, 1998. ISBN: 1563974894

——. *Bubblemania: The Chewy History of Bubble Gum.* With illustrations by Sandra Forrest. New York: Aladdin, 1997. ISBN: 0689817193

——. *Me + Math = Headache.* With illustrations by Deborah Stouffer. Santa Barbara, CA: Red Hen Press, 1986. ISBN: 0931093074

——. *Punia and the King of Sharks: A Hawaiian Folktale.* With illustrations by Felipe Davalos. New York: Dial, 1997. ISBN: 0803716826

Washington, Donna. *A Pride of African Tales.* With illustrations by James Ransome. New York: HarperCollins, 1999. ISBN: 0060249323

——. *The Story of Kwanzaa.* With illustrations by Stephen Taylor. New York: HarperCollins, 1996. ISBN: 0064462005

Werlin, Nancy. *Are You Alone on Purpose?* Boston: Houghton Mifflin, 1994. ISBN: 039567350X

——. *The Killer's Cousin.* New York: Delacorte, 1998. ISBN: 0385325606

——. *Locked Inside.* New York: Delacorte. Forthcoming.

Whittington, Mary. "Ahvel." In *Vampires,* edited by Jane Yolen and Martin Greenberg. New York: HarperTrophy, 1991. ISBN: 0064404854

——. "Leaves." In *Bruce Coville's Book of Ghosts II: More Tales to Haunt You*, compiled and edited by Bruce Coville. New York: Scholastic, 1997. ISBN: 0590852949

——. "Somewhere a Puppy Cries." In *The Haunted House*, edited by Jane Yolen and Martin Greenberg. New York: HarperTrophy, 1995. ISBN: 0064406466

Winters, Kay. *Did You See What I Saw? Poems About School*. New York: Viking, 1996. ISBN: 0670871184

——. *How Will the Easter Bunny Know?* With illustrations by Martha Weston. New York: Bantam Doubleday Dell, 1999. ISBN: 0385325967

——. *The Teeny Tiny Ghost*. With illustrations by Lynn Munsinger. New York: HarperCollins, 1997. ISBN: 0060273585

——. *Where Are the Bears?* With illustrations by Brian Lies. New York: Bantam Doubleday Dell, 1998. ISBN: 0385322917

——. *Wolf Watch*. With illustrations by Laura Regan. New York: Simon & Schuster, 1997. ISBN: 0689802188

Wood, Audrey. *Heckedy Peg*. With illustrations by Don Wood. San Diego: Harcourt, 1987. ISBN: 0152336788

——. *King Bidgood's in the Bathtub*. With illustrations by Don Wood. San Diego: Harcourt, 1985. ISBN: 0152427309

Yolen, Jane. *The Devil's Arithmetic*. New York: Viking, 1988. ISBN: 0670810274

——. *The Emperor and the Kite*. With illustrations by Ed Young. New York: Philomel, 1988. ISBN: 0399214992

——. *Owl Moon*. With illustrations by John Schoenherr. New York: Philomel, 1987. ISBN: 0399214577

——. "Rich Man, Poor Man." In *Favorite Folktales from Around the World*, edited by Jane Yolen. New York: Pantheon, 1988. ISBN: 0394751884

——. *The Seeing Stick*. With illustrations by Remy Charlip and Demetra Maraslis. New York: Crowell, 1977. ISBN: 0690004559

——. "Sister Emily's Lightship." In *Starlight*, edited by Patrick Neilsen Hayden. New York: Tor, 1996. ISBN: 0312862148

Yolen, Jane, ed. *Favorite Folktales from Around the World*. New York: Pantheon, 1986. ISBN: 0394543823

Yolen, Jane, and Bruce Coville. *Armageddon Summer*. New York: Harcourt, 1998. ISBN: 0152017674

Suggested Readings

East, Kathy. *Inviting Children's Authors and Illustrators*. New York: Neal Schuman, 1995. ISBN: 1555701825

McElmeel, Sharron L. *ABCs of an Author/Illustrator Visit*. Professional Growth Series. Worthington, OH: Linworth, 1994. ISBN: 0938865331

Melton, David. *How to Capture Live Authors and Bring Them to Your Schools*. Kansas City, MO: Landmark Editions, 1986. ISBN: 0933849036

Bookperson Index

Agell, Charlotte, 36
Alexander, David, 44, 46, 47
Anderson, Lisa P., 17, 38, 79
Appelt, Kathi, 9, 148, 149
Arnosky, Jim, 17
Aylesworth, Jim, 25

Balan, Bruce, 110, 130
Balgassi, Haemi, 38, 39, 104, 118, 119–20,
    124–25
Banks, Lynne Reid, 23
Bartoletti, Susan Campbell, 26–27, 39–40, 79
Baylor, Byrd, 49
Begin-Callanan, Maryjane, 17
Berenstain, Jan, 125
Berenstain, Stan, 125
Bernier-Grand, Carmen T., 78
Billingsley, Franny, 41, 73–74
Boyers, Sara Jane, 52–53
Bradford, Karleen, 114, 116–17, 129–30
Brennan, Linda Crotta, 19
Brown, Susan Taylor, 114, 115–16

Carlson, Nancy, 48
Carris, Joan, 151–52
Casanova, Mary, 14, 19, 25, 32, 35, 41, 66, 71,
    92, 149
Clay, Wil, 149
Cole, Joanna, 143
Crider, Bill, 17–18, 103
Crutcher, Chris, 143, 144
Cumming, Peter, 93
Cushman, Doug, 48, 49

Davis, Katie, 25, 34–35, 80–82
Deegan, Bruce, 143
DeFelice, Cynthia, 17, 59–60
Del Negro, Janice, 43, 47
Dionetti, Michelle, 17, 62
Dueland, Joy, 17
Duey, Kathleen, xii, 20, 95–97, 141, 143, 144

Edwards, Frank B., 51
Ehlert, Lois, 31, 49

Falwell, Cathryn, 18, 23, 25, 27–28, 32, 35, 72,
    79, 149–50
Fox, Mem, 31

Gardella, Tricia, 94–95, 104
Gibbons, Gail, 17, 66, 70
Gill, Shellye, 31

Hancock, Lyn, 22
Harbo, Gary, 33, 91
Harlan, Judith, 126–27
Hawkes, Kevin, 62, 80
Haynes, Max, 49
Hines, Anna Grossnickle, 136, 138
Hobbs, Will, 143, 158–159
Hopkinson, Deborah, 63, 64, 66, 74, 79, 80, 104,
    107, 113, 137–38, 151

Ingraham, Erick, 17
Ippisch, Hanneke, 57

Jackson, Ellen, 39
Jacobson, Jennifer Richard, 15, 40, 77
Jarombek, Kathy, 45–46

Kellogg, Stephen, 49, 60
Ketteman, Helen, 90–91
Koller, Jackie French, 99, 101–2, 104, 111, 124,
    130, 137

Lattimore, Deborah Norse, 149
Levine, Gail Carson, xi, 21
Lewis, E. B., 24–25
Lowry, Lois, 17
Lubar, David, 109

Martin, Jacqueline Briggs, 52, 64–65, 69, 70, 78,
    80, 82, 103, 104, 152
Martin, Rafe, 56
Masiello, Ralph, 49
Mayes, Walter M., 32, 33, 37, 64, 70, 76, 93
McDermott, Gerald, 143
Mead, Alice, 69
Mikaelsen, Ben, 25, 27, 57, 141–42, 158–59
Moore, Robin, 8, 15, 23, 25, 53, 55, 111
Morris, Deborah, 105, 106, 118–19, 123, 124

Nye, Naomi Shahib, 142, 144

O'Brien, Anne Sibley, 80
Old, Wendie C., 99, 109–10
Osborne, Mary Pope, 125

173

Parent, Michael, 44, 46, 47, 53, 54, 55
Park, Barbara, 125
Parnall, Peter, 49
Pfitsch, Patricia Curtis, 16, 66, 69
Pollatta, Jerry, 49
Prelutsky, Jack, 72, 125

Regan, Dian Curtis, 19, 69, 77, 79, 87, 101, 105, 110, 140, 152, 153
Riggio, Anita, 62
Rockman, Connie, 47–48
Ruurs, Margriet, 23, 117–18

Sabuda, Robert, 143
Signorelli, Cathy, 157–58
Smith, Cynthia Leitich, 138–39
Smith, Roland, 13, 26, 33, 39, 64, 66, 104, 105, 123
Soentpiet, Chris, 104
Staley, Darla, 159
Stanbridge, Joanne, xi, 22
Stine, R. L., 127
Suen, Anastasia, 41–43, 72, 74, 77

Terban, Marvin, 27–28
Testa, Maria, 15

Walter the Giant Storyteller. *See* Mayes, Walter M.
Walton, Rick, 114, 115
Wardlaw, Lee, 14–15, 69, 94, 147, 148, 153–55
Warner, Sally, 125
Washington, Donna, 23, 25, 35–26, 45, 47, 76, 77
Wells, Rosemary, 48
Werlin, Nancy, 37, 106, 107
Whittington, Mary, xii, 71–72
Winters, Kay, 1, 103–4
Wolff, Patricia Rae, 92, 93
Wood, Audrey, 152

Yolen, Jane, 66, 102–3, 140
Yoshi, 49

Title Index

Abbie Burgess: Lighthouse Heroine, 66
ABC Disney Pop-Up, 143
Air Show, 42
American Diaries Series, 97
Are You Alone on Purpose?, 106
Armageddon Summer, 102
Aunt Morbelia and the Screaming Skulls, 152
Awakening the Hidden Storyteller
    (audiocassette), 111

Baby Born, 42
Band of Angels, A, 64
Bat Boy and His Violin, The, 24
Bat Jamboree, 148
Beacons of Light: Lighthouses, 66
Beauty, 120
Beware the Ravens, 152
Big Book of Reproducible Graphic Organizers, 40
Big Boy, 24
Birdie's Lighthouse, 64, 66, 79, 80, 138
Bizzy Bones Series, 52, 80
Blackberry Booties, 94
Book of Slime, The, 39
Bow-wow Birthday, 154
Bread Sister of Sinking Creek, The, 110
Brown Cow, Green Grass, Yellow Mellow Sun, 39
Bruce Coville's Book of Ghosts II: More Tales to
    Haunt You, 72
Bubba the Cowboy Prince: A Fractured Texas
    Tale, 90
Bubblemania: The Chewy History of Bubble
    Gum, 94, 153–54
Buoy, Home at Sea, 110
Busy Toes, 109

Casey's New Hat, 94
Cherry Migration, The, 110
Christmas for 10, 35
Clouds of Glory: Jewish Legends & Stories
    About Bible Times, 63
Coal Mine Peaches, 62
Cyber.kdz Series, 110

Dancing Feet, 36
Dancing Pink Flamingos and Other Stories, 15
Dancing with Dziadzu, 27

Dear Dr. Sillybear, 153
Delivery, 42
Devil's Arithmetic, The, 102
Did Not, Did So, 114
Did You See What I Saw? Poems About School,
    103
Down the Road, 24
Dragon Tooth, 35, 149
Dragonfire, 117
Dragonling Series, 101, 111, 137
Dragonling, The, 137

Ella Enchanted, xi, 21
Emma and the Coyote, 118
Emma Eileen Grove, Mississippi River, 1865,
    143
Emma's Eggs, 118
Emperor and the Kite, The, 102

Fair Is Fair: World Folktales of Justice, 65
Fangs-giving, 153
Fannie in the Kitchen, 63, 64
Far North, 158–59
Favorite Folktales from Around the World, 66,
    103
Feast for 10, 35
Fiction, Food, and Fun: The Original Recipe for
    the Read 'N' Feed Program, 158–59
Finest Horse in Town, 70
Fire on the Mountain, 20, 65, 67, 88, 136, 155,
    156, 157
Flag We Love, The, 49
Flannel Kisses, 19
Folk Keeper, The, 74
Four Lions, 22
Friendship of Milly and Tug, The, 101
Fuel, 144

Ghost Twin Series, 79
Girl Talk: Staying Strong, Feeling Good,
    Sticking Together, 126
Good Times on Grandfather Mountain, 70
Grandma's Cat, 90
Grandmother Bryant's Pocket, 52, 82
Growing Up in Coal Country, 26, 27, 39, 79
Growing Up Is a Full-Time Job, 44

Habibi, 144
Haunted House, The, 72
Heat Wave, 90
Heckedy Peg, 73
Higgins Bend Song and Dance, 82
His Royal Buckliness, 62
Home for the Howl-i-days, 153
How Will the Easter Bunny Know?, 103

I Hate to Go to Bed, 34, 80
I Remember Papa, 90
I Swam with a Seal, 36
I'm Sorry, Almira Ann, 26, 108
Impy for Always, 102
In Search of Scum, 110
In the Forest with Elephants, 13
In the Month of Kislev, 66, 67
In the Shade of the Nispero Tree, 78
Indian in the Cupboard, The, 23

Juan Bobo: Four Folktales from Puerto Rico, 78
Jingle Dancer, 138
Juan Bobo: Four Folktales from Puerto Rico, 78
Junebug, 69
Just a Little Ham, 152
Just Like My Dad, 94, 104
Just People and Other Poems for Young Readers & Paper/Pen/Poem, 148

Keep the Lights Burning, Abbie, 66
Keeper of the Light, 16, 66, 69
Kids on Strike, 27
Killer's Cousin, The, 106
King Bidgood's in the Bathtub, 152
Kissing Contest, 69

Latin American Tales: From the Pampas to the Pyramids of Mexico, 83
Leftover Kid, The, xi, 22
Legacy for a Loon (videocassette), 65
Letter Jesters, The, 150
Life Doesn't Frighten Me, 53
Light Spirit: Lighthouses of the Maine Coast (videocassette), 66
Lighthouses: Watchers at Sea, 66
Little Princess, A, 73
Little Wide Mouth Gecko, The, 47
Little Women, 120
Live and Learn: The Exploding Frogs and Other Stories, 45
Liver Cookies, 19
Locked Inside, 107

Loon Magic for Kids, 65
Lucy Dove, 47
Lullaby Raft, 144

Maggie Among the Seneca, 111
Magid Fasts for Ramadan, 24
Man on the Moon, 42, 74, 77
Maria's Comet, 64
Marshmallow Kisses, 19
Me + Math = Headache, 69
Miro in the Kingdom of the Sun, 63, 82, 83, 89–90, 136
Miss Emma's Wild Garden, 138
Monster Mama, 73
Monster of the Month Club, 77, 101
Monster of the Month Series, 69
Monsters and My One True Love, 153
Monsters in Cyberspace, 105, 153
Moon Sandwich Mom, 40
Moose Tracks, 14, 41
Mortimer Mooner Stopped Taking a Bath, 51
Mountain Alphabet, A, 118
My Four Lions, 22

Net of Stars, 40, 77
New King, The, 24
Nine Candles, 15
No Man's Land, 27

O Beautiful for Spacious Skies, 53
Of Kings and Fools: Stories from the French Tradition in North America, 44
Oil Spill!, 65
Oil Spills: Damage, Recovery, and Prevention (A Save-the-Earth Book), 65
On The Write Track, 118
Once There Was a Bull . . . (Frog), 114
101 Ways to Bug Your Parents, 154
Only a Pigeon, 24, 79, 88, 155
Owl Moon, 102

Painting the Wind, 62
Peacebound Trains, 39, 120, 124
Peter's Place, 65
Picture's Worth, A, 110
Pie in the Sky, 110
Poet and Politician of Puerto Rico: Don Luis Muñoz Marin, 78
Pony Named Midnight, A, 116
Pride of African Tales, A, 45
Princess and the Beggar: A Korean Folktale, The, 80

Princess Nevermore, 69, 152
Proud to Be Me, Peewee Platypus, 17, 79
Pulling the Lion's Tail, 20, 88, 136, 155, 156

Quest: Investigating the World We Call Maine
(videocassette), 65

Real Kids, Real Adventures Series, 105, 106
Riot, 14
River Friendly, River Wild, 75

Sailor's Book, The, 36
Sarah, Plain and Tall, 88
Sea Otter Rescue, 13
Seeing Stick, The, 103
Shape Space, 32, 35, 79
Snowflake Bentley, 52, 78, 103
Someplace to Go, 15
*Space Between Our Footsteps: Poems &
Paintings from the Middle East, The*, 144
Story of Kwanzaa, The, 45
Storyteller's Beads, The, 21, 71, 79, 88, 90, 112,
155
Sunken Treasure, 70
Survival Series, 97
Sweet Clara and the Freedom Quilt, 64, 80, 113,
137–38, 151

Tae's Sonata, 39, 120
Talking Walls, 80
Teen Power Politics: Make Yourself Heard, 53
Teeny Tiny Ghost, The, 103

Then the Troll Heard the Squeak, 62
There Will Be Wolves, 114
Thumbs Up, Rico!, 15
Thunder Cave, 13
To the Island, 36
Trouble, 20, 21, 27, 63, 79, 88, 114, 136, 155

Under the Quilt of Night, 64
Up the Mountain, 36

*Valerie and Walter's Best Books for Children: A
Lively, Opinionated Guide*, 70
Vampire Named Fred, A, 103
Vampires, 72
Very Patient Pony, The, 116

Washing the Willow Tree Loon, 64, 65
Welcoming Babies, 80
Well Wished, 41, 73, 74
Whaling Days, 63
What Would Jesus Do?, 105
When a Line Bends, a Shape Begins, 72
Where Are the Bears?, 103
Who Hops?, 34, 80–81
Window Music, 42
Wolf Shadows, 14
Wolf Watch, 103
Women of the Lights, 66
Wonder of Loons, The, 65
Word Wizard, 35, 150
*Writers in the Kitchen: Children's Book Authors
Share Memories of Their Favorite
Recipes*, 94

Subject Index

Abilock, Debbie, 110
Africa, 20, 26, 45, 79, 80, 112, 136, 156
    Botswana, 77
    Egypt, 24, 45
    Eritrea, 21, 79, 136
    Ethiopia, 20, 24, 38, 44, 65, 71, 80, 112, 136, 150, 153, 155, 156, 157
    Kenya, 13, 16
    South Africa, 46, 127
    Tanzania, 24
    Zimbabwe, 24, 80
Agar, Kelly, 81–82
Alabama
    Birmingham, 88–89
Alaska, 31
    Kwigillingok, 113
    Prince William Sound, 13
Alta Vista School (CA), 113
Amazon.com, xii, 104, 141
America Online (AOL)
    Children's Writer's Board, 109
    Parent Soup, 125
Angelou, Maya, 53
AOL. See America Online
Arizona
    Scottsdale, 143
    Tucson, 51
Asia, 127
    Burma, 26
    China, 21, 45, 80
    Hong Kong, 36
    Indonesia, 44, 46, 47
    Indonesia, Jakarta, 46
    Japan, 45, 127, 138
    Korea, 38, 80
    Pakistan, 44, 127
    Thailand, 104
Auclair, Bob, 63, 83
Audience, behavior, 7, 10, 18, 33, 48, 89, 124, 126
Audiovisual materials, 9, 53, 64, 65, 66
Australia, 76, 117, 127
Author's Desk, 142
Authors Mentoring Authors Online: A Writer's Workshop, 113–16
Authors Online, 140
Autographing. See Book sales, signing
Ayers, Susan, 82

Baker, Etta, 157
Basquiat, Jean-Michel, 53
Bates, Katharine Lee, 53
Beeson, Cindy, 142–43
Benke, Lu, 58–59
Bianchi, John, 51
Bibliographies, 61, 64, 67, 117, 128, 129, 136, 138, 139, 140, 143
Blume, Judy, 120
Bohndorf, Virginia, 34, 157
Book sales, 11, 22, 31, 92, 96, 124, 147
    ordering, 11, 58, 143
    signing, 9, 11, 58, 61, 95, 124, 147–49
Boorstin, Daniel J., 13, 159
Boston Public Library, 37
Boston University, 34
Brown, David K., 133
Brown, Jan, 127
Brown, Jane, 79
Bungalo Books, 51
Butch, Serena, 59–60

Caldecott Honor Award, 102
Caldecott Medal, 52, 78, 102
California, 38, 54, 79, 94, 95, 118, 153, 155, 156, 158
    Burbank, 71
    Concord, 116
    Eureka, 95
    Hillsborough, 110
    Hollywood, 71
    Los Gatos, 113
    Oakland, 158
    San Fernando Valley, 71
    San Francisco, 70, 110
    San Jose, 116
    Santa Barbara, 153
    Turlock, 127
Campbell Hall, xii
Canadian Society of Authors, Illustrators, and Performers(CANSCAIP), 16, 134
CANSCAIP. See Canadian Society of Children's Authors, Illustrators, and Performers
Carmel Clay Public Library, 58
Carmel High School (IN), 58
Carnegie Library, 47
Center for the Book, 87
Central Elementary School (VA), 44

Chat rooms, 123, 124–25, 140
Chat rooms, managed sites, 125–27
Chat tours, 12
Children's Book Council, 52, 134
Children's Book Week, 56, 72, 80
Cinderella, xi, 21
Clear Lake Elementary School (WA), 107
Clearwater Public Library (FL), 59
Coffey, Jane, 127, 131
Collaborations, 15, 93, 94, 96
        bookstores and libraries, 95, 151
        bookstores and schools, 95–97
        school and public libraries, 31, 55, 56–60,
            87–88
Colorado, 153
        Colorado Springs, 110
        Fort Collins, 58
        School for the Deaf and Blind, 110
Community High School (ND), 37
Community members, 9, 56, 59
Conant, Audrey, 95
Connecticut, 35
        Hartford, 35
        Monroe, 60
        Stamford, 47
Conner, Janet, 80
Cooney, Michael
Coretta Scott King Honor Award, 24
Cover to Cover, 142–44
Coyne, Jo, 148
Creativity. See Imagination
Critiques, 108, 109, 110, 111, 114, 115, 117, 140
Crome-Guthrie, Lara, 113
Cultural diversity, 38, 44, 47, 76, 78, 79, 110,
        137, 138–39, 155–57
Curriculum areas, 39, 64, 69–83, 136, 141
        art, 5, 9, 14, 20, 62, 63, 67, 69, 80–82, 83,
            130, 137, 138, 156
        drama, 14, 45, 69, 70, 79
        language arts, 5, 32, 40–43, 45–47, 65, 69,
            70, 73–76, 83, 107, 111, 112, 129,
            130, 136, 137, 138, 140, 153–54
        math, 32, 78–79, 83, 130, 137, 154
        movement, 32, 36
        music, 20, 25, 54, 73, 137, 156, 157–58
        science, 13, 14, 39, 42, 64, 65, 74, 77–78,
            83, 138, 154
        social studies, 20, 26, 27, 38, 40, 64, 66,
            79–80, 83, 96, 107, 108–9, 130, 136,
            137, 138, 152, 153–54, 156–57
Curriculum guides, 21, 61, 136, 137, 141, 142,
        143, 152–54
CyberResidency: Imagination Restoration Via
        the Internet, 111

Dalton School, The (NY), xi, 21,106
Davis, Kathy, 156
de Grummond collection, 134
Delmar Elementary School (MD), 113
Dennis Earl Elementary School (CA), 127
Devito, Dana, 81
Diaries, 26, 40, 69, 79, 95, 152
Displays, 3, 9, 14, 55, 61, 130, 144
Doucette Library of Teaching Resources, 133
Downey, Michael, 81
Dutcher Elementary School (CA), 127

Edinger, Monica, xi, xii, 21, 106, 112
Edna Libby School, 79–80
EduCenter. See Talk City
Electronic message boards, 108, 109, 140, 141
Elementary school visits, 19, 34, 35, 40, 45, 46, 49,
        55, 57, 58, 59, 60, 63, 77, 81–82, 138, 156–57
Eureka Author Festival, 95
Europe, 54
        France, 21
            Paris, 54, 62
        Great Britain, 129
        Hungary, 21
        Ireland, Dublin, 15
        Netherlands, 118
        Spain, Barcelona, 74
        Sweden, 36

Fan mail. See Mail
Fanucci, Mary, 26
Feldman, Roxanne Hsu, 134
Ferguson, Catherine, 36
Fields, Myrna, 141–42, 158–59
Financing a visit, 15, 16, 21, 31, 43, 57, 58–59,
        71, 87, 88, 92, 93, 94, 99, 143, 147
        costs, 39, 61, 123, 126, 135
        grants, 56, 151
        honoraria, 7–8, 9, 11, 54, 58, 59, 61, 109,
            111, 133, 135
        travel expenses, 54, 58, 59, 123
Fine, Jana, 59
Florida
        Cape Canaveral, 42
        Clearwater, 59
Folktales, 5, 44–45, 54, 63, 64, 65, 136, 156
Food projects, 19, 63, 69, 77, 158–59
Fort Collins Public Library, 58

Games, 69, 70, 79, 156, 158
George Washington School (NY), 81
Georgia
        Atlanta, 74
        Harlem, 90

Gildart, Joan, 65
Gilmore Foundation, 56
Girl's World Online Clubhouse, A, 126–27
Grand Avenue Elementary School (OK), 127
Guenther, Wayne, 44

Haba, Jim, 142
Hager, Judy, 37
Hanley, Yvonne, 27, 33, 49, 91
Harford County Public Library (MD), 109
Harold, Judy, 151
Hartwood Elementary School (PA), 111
Hayes, Rebecca, 20, 22, 158–59
High school visits, 35, 36–37, 40, 44, 46, 57, 58,
    59, 92
Holzmuller, Karl, 107
Homeschoolers, 58, 77, 117
Houghton Mifflin Education Place, 141
Humboldt County Library (CA), 95
Hurchalla, Carla, 113–15

Illinois
    Chicago, 74, 158
    Normal, 92
Illinois State University, 92
Illustration process, 21, 25, 27, 34, 41, 48–49,
    80, 82
Illustration styles, 34, 49, 62, 63, 72, 79, 80, 149,
    150
Imagination, 15, 23, 35, 47, 53, 55, 71, 72, 78,
    90, 91
Indiana
    Carmel, 58
    Spencer, 141–42, 158
Interactive television, 141–44
Interlibrary loan, 9, 55, 60, 61, 64
International Reading Association (IRA), 74
    Children's Choice List, 115
International Storytelling Colloquium, 54
Internet relay chat, 125
Interviews, 55, 104, 118–20, 134, 139, 140, 141,
    142
Iowa, 52
IRA. *See* International Reading Association
Irene's Goodnight, 158

John F. Kennedy Center for the Performing Arts,
    141
Johnson Space Center, 77
Johnson, Laura, 109
Just for Kids, 141

Kalamazoo County Juvenile Home, 56
Kalamazoo Public Library (MI), 56–57

Kansas, 35, 38, 79
Kansas City, 44, 157
Keene State College Literature Festival, 17
Kellogg Foundation, 56
Kennedy Center Performing Arts Series, 142
Kennedy Space Center, 77
Keppel-Sarawak Public School (Ontario, Canada),
    129–30
Kid Power, 134
Koppleman, Peggy, 48
Kutie Kari Books, 33

Lacey Timberland Library (WA), 57
Leadbetter, Huddie, 157, 158
Lesson plans, 61, 136, 137–38, 139, 140
Library media specialist, role of, 9, 17, 22, 23, 27,
    32, 39, 44, 45, 53, 55, 57, 58, 59, 60, 64–66,
    67, 69, 91, 130, 143–44, 149, 150, 156–57
Lincoln School (ND), 74–75
Listservs, 108, 138
    CHILD_LIT, 21, 107, 112
    KIDLIT, 113
Literacy, 129
Livolsi, Claudia, 60
Longfellow Elementary School (ME), 23, 24, 36,
    60, 63, 64–66, 67, 82, 83, 108
Lucy, Ellen, 80
Lyseth School (ME), 148–49

Madison Junior High School (ME), 130
Magazines, journals and newspapers, 41–42
    American Booksellers Magazine, 39
    Book Links, 10, 73
    Bulletin for the Center of Children's Books,
        39, 43
    Child Magazine, 148
    Crafts 'n' Things, 95
    Cricket, 19
    Family Circle, 105
    Friend, The, 95
    Good Housekeeping, 105
    Grand Forks Herald, 21
    Highlights for Children, 19, 42, 95
    Inklings, 155
    Ladybug, 95
    Leisure Arts, 95
    New York Times Book Review, 39
    Pac-O-Fun, 95
    Parade Magazine, 13, 159
    Ranger Rick, 19
    Reader's Digest, 105, 153
    San Francisco Chronicle, 39
    School Library Journal, 39
    Smithsonian, 39

Mail, 21, 64
    E-mail, xii, 16, 20, 21, 32, 37, 104–20, 123,
        124, 129, 134, 135, 141, 142, 156
    fan mail, xii, 21, 101–6
    postal, 101–4, 105, 123, 124
Maine Association of School Libraries (MASL),
    16, 95
Maine Educational Media Association. *See*
    Maine Association of School Libraries
Maine, 15, 35, 36, 40, 52, 54, 65, 66
    Bangor, 15
    Gorham, 17
    Madison, 130
    Millinocket, 15
    Portland, 15, 23, 36, 60, 65, 83, 108, 148–49
    Sebago Lake, 79
Mandela, Nelson, 46
Manning, Maryann, 93
Manthey, Laura, 63, 113, 156
Martin, Joyce, 17
Maryland
    Baltimore City, 109
    Delmar, 113
    Harford County, 109
MASL. *See* Maine Association of School
    Libraries
Massachusetts
    Boston, 23, 37
    Peabody, 37
    Westfield, 39
    Western, 102
McCain Library and Archives, 134
Mentoring, 113–16, 117
Michigan, 17
    Battle Creek, 56
    Kalamazoo, 56–57
Middle school visits, 36, 40, 46, 57, 59, 92
Middle Tennessee State University, 90
Minnesota, 14, 33, 35, 89
    Fosston, 87
    Grand Marais, 14
    International Falls, 14
Minneapolis, 49
    Sebeka, 20
    Thief River Falls, 92
    Warroad, 71
Missouri, 35
    Kansas City, 34
    St. Charles, 156
Monroe Public Library, 60
Montana,
    Bozeman, 142
    State University, 141

Morken, Mary, 92, 93
Multiple intelligences, 39
Multiple Sclerosis Society, 15
Museums, 60, 63, 139

Nason, Wanda, 79–80
National Geography Week, 80
National Library of Canada, 133
National Library Week, 151
National Storytelling Association, 134
National Storytelling Festival, 54
New Hampshire, 17, 35
    Keene, 17
New Jersey
    Belle Mead, 124
    McKee City, 24
    New Brunswick, 135
New York
    New York City, xi, 21, 32,106
    Public Library
    Schenectady, 59–60
    White Plains, 81
Newbery Honor Award, xi, 16
Nonfiction, 13, 26–27, 39–40, 63, 64. 76, 79, 157–58.
North America
    Canada, 14, 21, 127
    Alberta, Calgary, 133
    British Columbia, Okanagan Valley, 118
    Northwest Territories, 22
    Ontario, Kingston, 22, 51
    Owen Sound, 116, 129–30
    Toronto, 116
    Quebec, Montreal, 22, 36
    Puerto Rico, 21, 78
    Virgin Islands, 21
North Dakota, 14
    Grand Forks, 20, 21–22, 26, 37, 48, 49,
        74–75, 82, 91, 93
    Library Association, 87, 93
    Williston, 87
North Jakarta International School, 46
North Thurston School District (WA), 57
Northland Community Technical College, 92
Northwest Service Cooperative, 92
Northwestern University, 45
Nueva School (CA), 110

O'Keefe, Steve, 125–26
Ohi, Debbie Ridpath, 134
Oklahoma, 87, 153
    Chickasha, 127
    Edmond, 152
Once Upon a Computer, 117

Open Borders: Quebec–U.S. Cultural Exchange Performance Festival, 54
Oregon, 26, 118
    Fresham, 78
    Portland, 16, 78, 88
    Reading Association, 88
    Springfield, 151
    Trail, 26, 108–9
Organizing a visit, 22, 32, 47–48, 87, 91
    contact person, 4, 16, 57, 124
    contacting the bookperson, 3, 10, 16–17, 20, 22, 32, 58, 61, 133–35
    contracts, 61
    gifts for bookpeople, 3, 61, 63, 138
    local transportation and guides, 6, 9, 10, 11, 12, 57, 61
    lodging, 12, 23
    meals, 6, 9, 11, 14, 57, 59, 61, 148
    physical set-up and equipment, 10, 11, 32–33, 48, 54, 61, 89, 144
    scheduling, 4, 6, 7, 9, 10, 11, 44, 54, 57, 59, 61, 149
    selecting a bookperson, 58, 61, 133
    travel arrangements, 23, 56, 89
    volunteers, 16, 69, 75, 82, 91, 97, 149
Owen Valley Middle School (IN), 141–42, 158–59
Owens, Richard, 26

Park, Sherry, 152, 153
Pease, Tom, 87
Pellerin, Laura, 108
Pennsylvania, 26
    Blairsville, 138
    Montgomery County, 111
Philadelphia, 24, 25, 109
Pittsburgh, 47, 111
    Quakertown, 104
Peverada, Mary, 60
Piper Elementary School East (KS), 34, 157
Planet Think: The Interactive Learning Network, xii, 141, 142–44
Plaza Art Circle, 56
Poetry, 41, 72–73, 74–76
Portage County Public Library, 31, 87
Portalupi, JoAnn, 93
Porter, Ann, 74–75
Portland Public Libraries (Oregon), 88
Portland Public Library (Maine), 60
Preparation
    audience development, 33, 44, 53
    storyteller visits, 15, 44, 46, 47–48, 53, 54, 55
    students, 3, 4, 5, 9, 10, 51, 52, 53, 54, 55, 58, 60, 64, 66, 107–8, 124–25, 128, 130, 140, 143–44
Preschool, 34, 35, 36, 48
Presentations
    adult, 56, 59
    family, 56, 58, 59, 111
    public, 56, 58, 59
Prince William Television Network, 142
Principals, 1, 9, 13, 14, 15, 22, 43, 55, 69, 75, 88, 97
Private schools, 56, 57, 58, 59
Promotional materials
    bookpeople, 11, 57, 61
    libraries, 9, 47, 56, 57, 58, 61, 151
    publishers, 61, 126
    schools, 21, 61, 130
Props, 4, 5
    realia, 77, 82, 88, 149–50, 151, 155–56, 157
    slides, 25, 48, 77, 80, 90, 150, 151
    transparencies, 4, 36, 63, 82, 88, 150
Public librarian, role of, xi, 18, 22, 31, 43, 55, 56–60, 64, 66, 67, 87, 126
Public libraries, 9, 14, 18–19, 37, 39, 47, 56–60, 71, 72, 87–88, 129, 147, 151
Publishing process, 25, 34, 80
    rejection letters, 25, 40

Random House Children's Author Chat Series, 125–26
Read Across America, xii, 18–19
Read In Foundation, Inc., 110, 127
Read In!, 127–31
Real-time audio, 124, 126
Real-time video, 123, 124, 126
Realia. See Props, realia
Regional connections, 32, 64, 134
Reluctant readers, 14, 19, 24, 43
Reynolds, W. Ann, 89
Rhode Island, 15, 19
Rhode Island College, 19
Rife, Mary, 56–57
Rizal, Yoes, 47
Rodriguez, Sandra, 81
Rogers, Ginger, 142
Rotary Clubs, 58–59
Rutgers University, 135

Santa Barbara City College, 155
Santa Barbara Public Library, 39
Santa Fe Trail Elementary (KS), 44
SCBWI. See Society of Children's Book Writers and Illustrators

Schenectady County Public Library, 59–60
Scholastic Network, xii, 140
Schutz, Nancy, 57
Self-esteem projects, 24, 76, 77
Seuss, Dr., 120
Sherouse, Linda, 17, 22, 23, 33, 38, 39, 69, 70, 79
Signing. *See* Book sales, signing
Society of Children's Book Writers and Illustrators (SCBWI), 16, 21, 34, 92, 95, 110, 134
South America, 142
    Argentina, 116
    Ecuador, Quito, 143
    Peru, 136
    Venezuela, Puerto La Cruz, 110, 153
Spotlight, Author, 13, 14, 15, 18, 19, 27, 39, 40, 42, 51, 52, 53, 64, 71–72, 74, 78, 90, 94–95, 97, 102–4, 105, 107, 109, 110, 115, 116–17, 118, 127, 139, 144, 148, 151–52, 153, 154, 158
Spotlight, Author/Illustrator, 22, 35, 36, 62,
Spotlight, Illustrator, 24, 34
Spotlight, Storyteller, 45, 54, 70, 111
Springfield Public Library, 151
Stemple, Adam, 103
Stemple, Heidi E. Y., 103
Stemple, Jason, 103
Storytelling, 8, 23, 25, 43–48, 53, 60, 64, 76, 134, 135
Supplemental books, 61, 62–67, 136

Talk City, 125
Teacher, role of, xi, 3, 5, 7, 9, 10, 20, 21, 22, 43, 44, 45, 51, 54, 55, 58, 74, 75, 82, 88, 106, 124, 125, 128, 130, 143–44
Technology fairs, 124
Television programs
    Angel Flight Down, 105
    Audubon, 13
    Barney, 35
    CBS This Morning, 115
    Dancing in the Dark, 105
    Discover the World of Science, 13
    National Geographic, 13
    Reading Rainbow, 35, 115
    Real Kids, Real Adventures, 105
Tennessee.
    Jonesborough, 54
Texas, 42, 153
    Alvin, 18
    Amarillo, 152

    Austin, 89
    College Station, 148
    Garland, 105
    Houston, 125,148
    Rio Grande Valley, 148
    San Antonio, 144
Theme units, 39, 45, 70, 74, 76, 79, 81, 83, 153, 156, 158–59
Thiebaud, Wayne, 53

Underbakke, Clark, 31, 49, 88–89, 93, 149
University of Alabama at Birmingham, 31, 88–89, 93
University of Calgary, 133
University of Connecticut School of Fine Arts, 35
University of Minnesota, 52
University of North Dakota, 27, 93
University of Puerto Rico, 78
University of Rhode Island, 19
University of Southern Maine–Gorham, 17
University of Southern Mississippi, 134
University of Toronto, 116
University of Wisconsin–Stevens Point, 31
Upjohn Foundation, 56
Utah
    Provo, 115

Vaillancourt, Renee, 58
Van Gogh, Vincent, 62
Vandergrift, Kay E., 135
Virginia
    Charlottesville, 54
    Palmyra, 44
Virtual visits, 123–31, 135, 136, 142–44
Vital, Margaret, 130
Vollrath, Elizabeth, 31, 87

Washington, D.C., 141
Washington, xii
    Clear Lake, 107
    Lacey, 57
    Seattle, 90
Walla Walla, 64
Web pages, 21, 61, 92, 104, 108, 114, 115, 117, 124, 126, 128, 133–35, 135–39, 140–41, 142, 143
Wellesley College, 52
Westmount Public Library, 22
Whitman College, 64
Willard Public Library, 56
Willoughby, Dolores, 127

Willson, Karen, 126
Wisconsin, 31, 35, 150
    Stevens Point, 31, 87
Woods Road School (NJ), 124–25
Writing process, 25, 32, 37, 41, 43, 44, 47, 49,
    65, 70–76, 90, 109, 152
    characterization, xi, 19, 37, 41, 73, 91
    five senses, 74–76, 114, 155, 157, 158
    plotting, 37, 40, 73
    revision, 25, 40, 41, 90, 111, 114, 115, 117

Writing with Writers, 140
Writing workshops, 55, 113–16, 117, 140

Yahoo!, 135
Yahooligans, 126
Yale Law School, 15
Young author conferences, 11, 31, 88–93,
    124–25
Zuidema, Kris, 79–80